Latin American Monographs

Second Series

Industrial Development in a Traditional Society

21

Center for Latin American Studies
University of Florida

Industrial Development in a Traditional Society

The Conflict of Entrepreneurship and Modernization in Chile

Henry W. Kirsch

A University of Florida Book

The University Presses of Florida

Gainesville / 1977

Library of Congress Cataloging in Publication Data

Kirsch, Henry W. 1942–
Industrial development in a traditional society.

(Latin American monographs; 2d ser., 21)
"A University of Florida book."
Bibliography: p.
1. Chile—Industries. 2. Chile—Economic conditions. 3. Chile—Social conditions.
I. Title. II. Series: Florida. University, Gainesville. Center for Latin American Studies. Latin American monographs; 2d ser., 21.
HC192.K56 338′.0983 77–8132
ISBN 0–8130–0563–9

A UNIVERSITY OF FLORIDA BOOK
SPONSORED BY THE CENTER FOR LATIN AMERICAN STUDIES

TYPOGRAPHY BY MODERN TYPOGRAPHERS, INCORPORATED
CLEARWATER, FLORIDA

PRINTED BY ROSE PRINTING COMPANY, INCORPORATED
TALLAHASSEE, FLORIDA

Acknowledgments

FOR THE guidance and critical reaction to my work extended me over the years at the University of Florida, I owe a special debt of gratitude to Professors David Bushnell and Lyle McAlister. In addition, Professor Bushnell, as chairman of my supervisory committee, made valuable comments for the improvement of this study.

Carlos Hurtado, Victor Brodersohn, and Gabriel Gasic of the University of Chile contributed their time in helping to pinpoint the key problem areas involved. Mr. Gasic gave especially valuable assistance in the preparation of the foreign sector time series. During the years 1968–70, while I was a faculty member of the University of Chile's Instituto de Economía and Centro de Estudios Socio-Económicos, these centers provided working space and the facilities for initial data processing. I am also personally grateful to Joseph Mullen and Marshall Wolfe of the Economic Commission for Latin America who, through their advice and observations on research techniques and development analysis, motivated me to extend the scope of this study beyond that originally intended. Nevertheless, I bear complete personal responsibility for the statements and interpretation of events in this work.

The funds which made this study possible were provided by the Latin American Teaching Fellowship Program of the Fletcher School of Law and Diplomacy and the Fulbright-Hays Research Fellowship Program.

For Carmen

Preface

INTELLECTUALS, politicians, and policy makers in Chile have long debated over the contribution of that country's manufacturing sector to the pattern of national development. For years Chilean industry has been recognized as being both relatively large and diversified for a country of its size and resource endowment. But analysts have generally concluded that the industrial process has been a failure both in terms of creating a self-sustaining "growth pole" and as an instrument to alleviate mass poverty. To a great extent this disenchantment is the product of a misunderstanding of the role of industry in the development process. Industrialization has been commonly viewed as synonymous with development. The public proponents of import-substituting industrialization in Chile were so impressed by changes in Western Europe and the United States which they attributed fundamentally to the fact of industrial expansion that they equated the term industrialization with economic, social, and even (if only tacitly) political modernization. I believe that disillusionment arose as it became increasingly evident that, instead of industrial growth contributing to a style of development acceptable in terms of human well-being and equity as well as viable from an economic standpoint, the development process was being warped to suit the needs of a certain kind of industrial growth.

This type of industrial growth, in Chile as in many parts of Latin America, has been characterized by a lack of autonomy and ever greater financial, managerial, and technological dependence on the world centers; this has led to an unfavorable relation between the inflow of investment funds and the outflow of profits and royalties. In addition, the structure of manufacturing is essentially monopolistic and oriented inward to the domestic market, particularly to the final customer. National entrepreneurs have insisted on high-yield, short-run investments which maximize present returns with little regard to competitiveness and comparative advantage in world markets and this has been at the cost of sustained future long-term growth. The power exerted by Chilean capitalists in decision-making levels of national politics has won preferential treatment for national industry through the creation of distortions in capital and labor markets under conditions of state protection and subsidies.

Those who initiate an industrial process are usually viewed as a separate group, a bourgeoisie with its own demands upon society, which inevitably brings it into conflict with the existing elites. The emerging "industrial bourgeoisie" is thus supposed to remove a "landlord oligarchy" from its path by promoting agrarian reforms. It has been assigned to perform a modernizing role leading to social transformation. That this did not occur in Chile has been a major cause of frustration. No classic industrial consciousness, entrepreneurial bourgeois spirit, or distinct middle-class culture arose to challenge and displace the dominant value system which was rooted in the rural and mining enclave traditions of nineteenth-century Chile.

Numerous studies have been done in an attempt to explain the failure of Chilean industry to fulfill the developmental role assigned to it. But since most are based on the premise that the process of industrialization in that country is a recent one, analysis is usually limited to the events that followed the Great Depression. The assumption that Chile's industrial experience is a product of the last three decades has also led all but a few authors to attempt only a cross-sectional analysis. Finally, inquiry is confined primarily to macroeconomic questions and evades study of the social and political forces which were at play. Although central to the problem, these aspects have commonly been ignored and never systematically examined.

My position parts from the base that those factors which conditioned Chilean industrialization were already fully active from the late nineteenth century and that the role of industry in the social and economic evolution of Chile was essentially defined before the decade of the twenties had ended. For these reasons I believe that the problem merits historical study over the period from the War of the Pacific to the Great Depression. But in what terms can the performance of industry be explained? I submit that the explanation must be sought in the nature of Chilean society itself because the industrialization process as a component of any style of development is inescapably societal. This approach tries to break down traditional dividing lines among the "economic," the "social," and the "political." It focuses attention instead on the agents involved, the interests and values which govern their actions as well as the opportunities and constraints that confront them.

Without first looking into the global opportunity structure which circumscribed his range of activity, it is impossible to understand why the entrepreneur in Chile did not accomplish his "historic mission." Inevitably, the macroeconomic aspects must be studied to understand what was evolving since the nature of Chilean industry, even the very fact of its existence, was virtually unknown or rejected until World War I and not clearly portrayed by any author from then to the depression. The purpose of the first three chapters is to provide the reader with this necessary information, to show that industrialization existed, and to analyze its failure to provide a "growth pole."

In chapter 1, I examine those events and forces which sufficiently altered the Chilean social and economic order in the last quarter of the nineteenth century as to provide an environment amenable to entrepreneurial activity. The circumstances of industrial movement before and after the War of the Pacific are contrasted in chapters 1 and 2. The main concern of the latter is an examination of industrial activity until the end of World War I, and it demonstrates that a real process of industrialization was indeed underway. The quantitative macroeconomic aspects of the problem are carefully studied to reveal the growth and structure of industry through newly assembled series and new interpretations of data. In this section I have tried to provide the reader with an interesting case study of the possible uses and limitations of advanced tools of economic analysis and computer techniques in the context of historical research. The use of these analytic instruments combined with information from fairly obscure company documents also serves to probe the impact of World War I on the evolution of industry. Finally, since industrialization implies much more than a significant rise in the rhythm of secondary output, recourse is had to a descriptive historical model to review early Chilean industrial expansion from a qualitative as well as a quantitative perspective.

Chapter 3 is a discussion of the failure of industry to provide a "growth pole" for the Chilean economy under the curious circumstances of the success of the industrialists in achieving modern production techniques and high growth rates for their own sector. The interesting questions refer to structure—what was produced and how. In this connection the growth of specific industries, product lines, and firms is studied to reveal how the investment decisions of Chilean capitalists prevented industry from becoming an autonomous self-sustaining productive force capable of stimulating and restructuring the rest of the economy. Sources of industrial credit are also examined to show the close ties which bound together industry and the traditional oligarchy and excluded the proprietors of small- and medium-sized enterprises from this key aspect of the money market.

In the fourth chapter, I test the theory sustained by many authors that Chilean industrialists arose as a discrete group in conflict with the landed oligarchy and representatives of the export enclave which shaped the social, political, and economic tone of the country. Analysis is focused directly upon the social origin of the industrialists, delving into the nature of the elite structure of Chile, its economic activities, and its relation to industry. This is most important because, although I view changes in the productive possibilities of the economy as motivating industrial development, my basic assumption is that the social characteristics, interests, and values of the entrepreneurs themselves are the key factors in defining the course of industrialization and its ability to act as a vehicle of institutional change.

This orientation also underlies chapters 5 through 7. In chapter 5, the failure of industrialists to act as agents of institutional change is examined at one of the crossroads of Chilean national development, the Civil War of 1891. In chapter 6, we view the origin and crystallization of one of the fundamental characteristics of Chilean manufacturing, its uncontrolled concentration of economic power. The early monopolistic pattern of the manufacturing sector served to reinforce the process of dependent industrialization. But, of greater importance, it meant that the inequitable distribution of national income (a correlate of monopoly rents) and future inability of manufacturing to absorb a growing labor force (a consequence in part of the mindless transfer of modern foreign technology to monopolistic firms) would aggravate the mass urban poverty typical of present-day Chile. Finally, in chapter 7, there is a shift in the framework of analysis to the interaction between industry and the state to refute the widely diffused affirmation that industry was at the margin of the state until the period following the collapse of the export sector in 1930. Much before that event, as now, industry and the focus of political power were fused to benefit the interests of a privileged sector of the population.

Contents

KEY TO ABBREVIATIONS

ABCS	Archivo de la Bolsa de Comercio de Santiago
ANMH	Ministerio de Hacienda, Archivo Nacional
ASFF	Archivo de la Sociedad de Fomento Fabril
BSFF	*Boletín de la Sociedad de Fomento Fabril*
CCU	Compañía Cervecerías Unidas
CRAV	Compañía de Refinería de Azúcar de Viña del Mar
ELECMETAL	Compañía Electro Metalúrgica
ESVAL	Compañía Electro Siderúrgica e Industrial de Valdivia
FAMAE	Fábricas y Maestranzas del Ejército
MIOPAN	Ministerio de Industrias y Obras Públicas, Archivo Nacional
SFF	Sociedad de Fomento Fabril

1. Industrial Preconditions

ALTHOUGH the subject has received attention from a number of students of Chilean economic history, the origins of that country's industrialization remain obscure. Periods of expansion and stagnation, output levels and rates of growth, and the structural composition of production, particularly before World War I, are problems which have heretofore eluded systematic research. Yet interpretations of the process and its relation to overall Chilean development are not lacking. They are present in virtually all essays dealing with the social and economic evolution of Chile and, almost invariably, they are heavily conditioned by the ideological commitment of the writer.

Thus, it is possible at the moment to hold any of several positions with respect to the point at which Chile began to experience sustained industrialization and to the essential characteristics of that process. For a long time it had been held that the beginning of Chilean industrialization came during the years following the Great Depression of the thirties.[1] In view of recent findings, however, this

1. A few examples of this interpretation: Aníbal Pinto, *Chile, un caso de desarrollo frustrado*, p. 49; Max Nolff, "Industria manufacturera," pp. 511–17;

hypothesis can be regarded as nothing more than a shibboleth which persists mainly because of the wide popular diffusion of the texts in which it is found. In a carefully executed analysis of long-term growth in Chilean manufacturing since World War I, Oscar Muñoz has provided substantial evidence of considerable industrial activity before 1930.[2] Not possessing sufficient evidence for the period prior to the war, however, Muñoz could not discern the intensity and structure of manufacturing until 1914.

On the other hand, it has been said that the years between 1840 and 1860 witnessed the emergence of a significant manufacturing sector which later lost impetus and stagnated throughout the second half of the nineteenth century.[3] Variations on this theme also refer to industrial beginnings in the first half of that century but emphasize the growth which this sector experienced from 1860.[4]

Most of these positions regarding the initial phase of industrialization in Chile rest almost exclusively upon an analysis of the formulations of governmental economic policy. The conventional approach to the problem area has generally been guided by an attitude assumed by one of the first serious students of Chilean industrial evolution who wrote shortly after World War II: "In examining the growth of the ready-to-wear clothing plants per se or, for that matter, of any of the other industrial enterprises of this period (1860–1900), one must analyze the policies of the Chilean government towards manufacturing."[5]

Those who conclude that no real process of industrialization existed do so primarily because they have found no evidence of an overall, consistent policy of protectionism. But clearly this explanation is inadequate. The vitality of industry cannot be assessed merely by examining changes in the tariff system; careful consideration must be given to those forces operating within the country which determine the productive possibilities of the economy. This is the technique I will use to sustain the proposition that Chilean industrialization got under way as a consistent process during the years

---

Claudio Véliz, "La mesa de tres patas." Although Pinto does not deny the existence of industry before 1930, he places emphasis entirely on its incipient nature, backwardness, and aborted evolution throughout the period. Complete information on references may be found in the Bibliography.

2. Muñoz, *Crecimiento industrial de Chile 1914–1965.*
3. Ricardo Lagos, *La industria en Chile: antecedentes estructurales*, p. 15.
4. Jacinto Vaello, *Estructura y evolución de la economía colonial*, pp. 123–35.
5. Jack Pfeiffer, "The Development of Manufacturing Industry in Chile, 1820–1940," p. 28.

in which that nation was at war with its northern neighbors, 1879–84.

Industrial establishments certainly existed before the War of the Pacific, and some of the firms which were to undergo expansion after the war may be traced back to the 1850s. In this sense, as is so often the case with historical processes, no sharp break is formed. Nevertheless, the available evidence presses for a periodization of Chilean industrial evolution which employs the war years as the first demarcation point. As will be discussed in detail, the period following this event witnessed a set of developments which had great impact upon the economic structure of the country, and it is from the war that manufacturing embarked upon a course markedly different from the path it had followed previously.

Before the conflict, Chilean manufacturing consisted of a small number of isolated factories and an extensive array of artisan shops. One of the major sources of information for this period is the journal *La industria chilena*, of which eighty-five issues were published between September 1875 and November 1877. The image of Chilean industry presented in this periodical is distinctly one in which the phenomenon of industrial enterprise producing goods in an organized, commercialized, and capitalized fashion, responsive to the demand fluctuations of an urban market economy, was rare. Factory owners were active in defending their position in this publication, but artisan interests dominated the scene. A listing of the manufacturing establishments which had been represented in the 1872 Santiago exhibition sponsored by the Sociedad Nacional de Agricultura (SNA) and by producers from Valparaíso and Concepción further confirms this observation.

These data alone, however, do not provide any real insight into the nature of the firms themselves. Most of these were quite small (for example, those engaged in the production of tiles and candles), although several had mechanized their production lines and employed from 50 to 150 workers. Such was the case of the Andwandter Brewery in Valdivia (not included in Table 1), which was founded in 1851. Nevertheless, as will be seen, the real "take-off" of this firm came later during the decade of the 1880s. Until then the brewery had not expanded its production levels at a significant pace for over twenty years.[6] The same is true also for the woolen cloth factory at Bellavista, Tomé, near Concepción. Founded by an American,

6. See pp. 30–31 of this text and Julio Pérez Canto, ed., *La industria nacional, estudios y descripciones de algunas fábricas de Chile,* p. 127.

William Délano, in 1865, the factory passed through a series of owners after Délano left the business in 1878. None was able to turn the factory into a profitable venture or to develop it much in size. It was not until 1904, when the plant was acquired by Carlos Werner, a vigorous entrepreneur who had made a considerable fortune in mining, that the factory underwent real expansion. He completely renovated the mill, imported new machinery, and substantially increased production capacity.[7] A number of the other factories existing in the 1870s experienced this same abortive devel-

TABLE 1
MAJOR MANUFACTURING ESTABLISHMENTS IN THE CITIES OF SANTIAGO, VALPARAÍSO, AND CONCEPIÓN, 1872[a]

Product	Santiago	Valparaíso	Concepión
Flour		a	4
Vermicelli	4	3	
Chocolate		1	
Biscuits		1	
Starch	19		
Animal oils	4	1	
Liquor	2	6	
Beer		9	1
Cigarettes, cigars	1		
Cloth	1		1
Silk goods	1		
Sacks	2	1	
Footwear	1		
Leather	1	a	1
Boat sails		1	
Processed wood		4	
Crockery		1	
Tiles, bricks, firebricks	52	17	1
Horse carriages, wagons	25	3	
Candles, soap	15	9	1
Wax	1		
Perfume	1		
Kerosene		1	

SOURCE: Recaredo Tornero, *Chile ilustrado.*
a. It must be noted that although these are considered major producers, no basis is given in the source for this description, and Tornero does mention other establishments such as four leather-tanning firms, a flour mill, etc., in Valparaíso. He distinguishes these and others, such as shoemakers and tailors, from those listed in the table. That the latter refer solely to factories may be open to question in view of the inclusion of such a large number of tile and brick producers.

7. *Chile en Sevilla*, pp. 253–60; Virgilio Figueroa, *Diccionario histórico y biográfico de Chile*, 4:1088.

opment.[8] Even though a few of the small light industries launched during this period were to mature into consumer goods producers of national importance, they did so under greatly different circumstances than those which provided them only uncertain and interrupted existence prior to 1880.

Before an examination of the empirical evidence which is available for late nineteenth-century industry, it is important to consider the effects of those events and forces which influenced the Chilean social and economic order sufficiently to spawn a consistent system of industrial production. These operated to increase internal markets, provide an urban labor force, and in other ways to afford viable productive possibilities for manufacturing. Contributions to the development of industry came from the War of the Pacific and concurrent fiscal policy, demographic trends, especially an increase in the urbanization rate, and changes in other sectors of the economy, particularly transportation, mining, and agriculture.

The War of the Pacific and Fiscal Policy from 1878

The decisive influence which wars have had on the evolution of industry in Latin America has often been commented on, and that domestic manufacturing was stimulated by the curtailment of imports during the two world wars of the twentieth century is well known. The War of the Pacific had a similar impact upon the Chilean economy, differing from the later conflicts in that, rather than accelerating a cumulative process, it contributed to the initiation of a new economic pattern. It was not the lack of imports which affected industry during the War of the Pacific so much as the substantial increase in demand from the government which had to arm, equip, and maintain its large expeditionary forces over a five-year period.

Francisco Encina impresses upon one the impact which the war effort produced on Chile's industry. In his customary grandiose style, he reports that manufacturing "expanded ten, twenty, and even one hundred times the production of clothing, footwear, leather goods, powder, chemical and pharmaceutical products, bar-

8. Tornero, *Chile ilustrado*, pp. 100, 339–40. Tornero refers to several which gave unsatisfactory results such as the cloth factory at El Salto near Santiago which was founded in 1850 and the bottle factory in Corral which went out of business five years after its opening in 1864.

rels, knapsacks, gun carriages, boilers for ships engines, etc."[9] Foundries and metal-working shops were under tremendous pressure to meet the government's demand for their products. In general, importation had not been severed during the war. Iron imports rose from 3,396 to 8,447 metric tons. Yet certain import lines did decline. In one of its meetings shortly after the end of the war, the executive council of the Sociedad de Fomento Fabril (SFF) referred to the admirable effort of the national factories in producing and repairing machinery since "when the war was declared, the orders for foreign equipment ceased."[10] And only a decade later one of the more meticulous observers of the industrial process reported that the War of the Pacific had a very positive influence upon the national factories and "from this point they underwent considerable development."[11]

Fiscal policy during the war also tended to benefit industry. At the outset of hostilities, Chile was in the midst of an economic depression, which culminated with the passage of a law suspending bank note convertibility and the promulgation of a new import tariff. During the previous years, the nation had suffered the effects of a negative balance of payments, poor agricultural harvests, and increasing budget deficits, which had reached crisis proportions after 1876. To augment fiscal resources with which to meet its increasing debts and to alleviate the balance of payments problems, the administration of Aníbal Pinto went off the gold standard and increased import duties considerably from the levels established in the Tariff of 1872. Many articles previously taxed with a 25 per cent ad valorem duty were placed in a new 35 per cent category, and a 10 per cent surcharge was levied upon all merchandise in both the highest category and the 25 per cent duty level, which was the basic tax for imported goods. Although the 10 per cent surcharge was initially to last only for a period of ten months, it was constantly renewed during the war and only ceased to be applied in 1885.[12] On certain products, such as beer, specific rather than ad valorem duties had to be paid. These were substantially increased in 1878

9. Encina, *Historia de Chile*, p. 94.

10. Consejo Directivo de la Sociedad de Fomento Fabril, "Acta de 15 de mayo de 1885," "Libro de Actas del Consejo Directivo," Archivo de la Sociedad de Fomento Fabril (hereafter referred to as ASFF).

11. Mariano Martínez, *Industrias santiaguinas*, p. 5.

12. Ricardo Anguita, *Leyes promulgadas en Chile desde 1810 hasta 1 de junio de 1913*, vol. 2, passim.

and by all accounts were much more effective in the long run than the ad valorem duty.[13]

Although not caused by the War of the Pacific, the concurrent suspension of convertibility which marked the beginning of Chile's indiscriminate courtship of paper currency also must have affected domestic production. Between the end of the war and the close of the century, the gold value of the peso fell by almost 50 per cent, and this should have benefited domestic industry by increasing the cost of imported manufactured goods.

Demographic Trends

Shifts in the demographic profile of a country affect two key variables upon which industry is based, market size and labor force. Increase in the urban population stimulates both of these, and the possibilities for industrial growth are greatly enhanced. Not only are internal markets for goods formerly supplied by artisan or small shop production expanded, but there is an increase in feasibility of investing capital in goods not previously produced. At the same time an expanding manufacturing sector depends upon the availability of an urban labor force, and whatever the initial causes of urban population growth, it strengthens this process by exerting an attraction to the cities where new job opportunities are being created.

Thus, a set of relationships and feedbacks exist between the growth of cities and that of domestic industry so that urbanization to some extent may be regarded as an indicator of industrial advance. Whether or not industry is present at the outset of urban growth is not essential, since once the urban population begins to expand, manufacturing, in any case, will appear in short order.

As may be seen in Table 2, the rural population grew at consistently lower rates than the urban sector throughout the entire period from 1865 to 1930. But it should also be noted that between 1865 and 1907, the total population of Chile rose at an average annual rate of 1.4 per cent for a total percentage increase of 77.6 per cent. During the same period the proportion of the population

13. This is so because the amount paid on ad valorem taxes depended upon the assessed taxable value of the article, which diminished in relation to its real worth as the result of negligence on the part of the customs service to revise the *Tarifa de Avalúos* in accordance with increasing prices.

living in communities of two thousand inhabitants or more rose from 22 to 38 per cent and maintained an average annual growth rate of 2.7 per cent.

TABLE 2

Distribution and Growth of the Population of Chile According to Rural and Urban Residence, 1865–1930[a]

	Rural Population			Urban Population			Total Population	
Year	Number (000)	Percentage of Total Population	Growth Rate	Number (000)	Percentage of Total Population	Growth Rate	Number (000)	Growth Rate
1865	1,421	78.1		398	21.9		1,819	
1875	1,536	74.0	0.8	540	26.0	3.1	2,076	1.4
1885	1,790	71.4	1.5	717	28.6	2.9	2,507	1.9
1895	1,774	65.8	0.0	922	34.2	2.6	2,696	0.7
1907	2,009	62.2	1.1	1,222	37.8	2.4	3,231	1.5
1920	2,132	57.2	0.5	1,598	42.8	2.1	3,730	1.2
1930	2,219	51.8	0.4	2,068	48.2	2.6	4,287	1.4

Source: Adapted from Carlos Hurtado, *Concentración de población y desarrollo económico—el caso chileno*. Tables 2, 3, 8.

a. Urban population defined in this table as the number of people in centers of 2,000 inhabitants or more.

Equally relevant to the industrial sector was the concentration of people in urban areas located in the Santiago-Valparaíso-Concepción triangle. It was from these key provinces that the industrial labor force was recruited, and the intense urban growth of the period 1865–1920 is shown in Table 3. Of great importance for the rise of industry, however, was the rapid expansion of the largest urban centers, for it was there that Chilean manufacturing was to be concentrated. Cities of 20,000 inhabitants or more, excluding Santiago, grew at rates ranging from 2.8 to 5.9 per cent in the late nineteenth century, while the capital itself sustained an annual growth of 2.6 per cent between 1865 and 1907 (Table 4). In the latter year, over 22 per cent of the nation's population was living in these large urban centers, the cities of Iquique, Antofagasta, Valparaíso, Viña del Mar, Santiago, Talca, Chillán, and Concepción. Suggestive of the impact upon the nation that the expansion of large urban areas had is the fact that, while the total increase of Chile's population from 1865 to 1907 was about 78 per cent, that of these seven cities surpassed 280 per cent.

The impact of the opening of new areas in the country was also

TABLE 3

DISTRIBUTION AND GROWTH OF THE POPULATION OF THE PROVINCES OF VALPARAÍSO, SANTIAGO, AND CONCEPIÓN ACCORDING TO RURAL AND URBAN RESIDENCE, 1865–1920

Year	Rural			Urban			Total		
	Number (000)	Per Cent of Total Province	Growth Rate	Number (000)	Per Cent of Total Province	Growth Rate	Number (000)	Per Cent of Total Country	Growth Rate
Province of Valparaíso									
1865	50	35.0		93	65.0		143	7.9	
1875	43	24.0	−1.5	136	76.0	3.9	179	8.6	2.3
1885	48	23.6	1.1	155	76.4	1.3	203	8.1	1.3
1895	48	21.7	0.0	173	78.3	1.1	221	8.2	0.9
1907	52	18.5	0.7	229	81.5	2.3	281	8.7	2.0
1920	54	16.9	0.3	266	83.1	1.2	320	8.6	1.0
Province of Santiago									
1865	200	58.5		142	41.5		342	18.8	
1875	180	49.2	−1.0	186	50.8	2.7	366	17.6	0.7
1885	102	30.9	−5.8	228	69.1	2.1	330	13.2	−1.1
1895	116	27.9	1.3	300	72.1	2.7	416	15.5	2.3
1907	154	29.8	2.4	363	70.2	1.6	517	16.1	1.8
1920	138	20.1	−0.8	547	79.9	3.2	685	18.4	2.2
Province of Concepión									
1865	107	73.3		39	26.7		146	8.0	
1875	104	68.9	−0.3	47	31.1	1.9	151	7.3	0.3
1885	116	63.7	1.1	66	36.3	3.5	182	7.3	1.9
1895	93	49.5	−2.2	95	50.5	3.7	188	6.7	0.3
1907	100	46.1	0.6	117	53.9	1.8	217	6.7	1.2
1920	105	42.5	0.4	142	57.5	1.5	247	6.6	1.0

SOURCE: Chile, Servicio Nacional de Estadística y Censos, *XII Censo General de Población*, 1952, Table 9, pp. 44–45.

significant, particularly with the incorporation of the northern nitrate provinces after the War of the Pacific. Between 1875 and 1885, the Chilean population of the *Norte Grande* rose from a little over 2,000 to over 90,000.[14] Also significant was the migratory flow from the rural sectors of the Central Region (i.e., the area extending from Aconcagua to Ñuble) to the provinces stretching from Concepción to the south, which was the result of the final pacification of the Araucanians in 1883 and the subsequent colonization of the area. In 1875, the south contained 20.9 per cent of the total popula-

TABLE 4

DISTRIBUTION AND GROWTH OF THE POPULATION OF SANTIAGO AND CITIES OF 20,000 INHABITANTS AND OVER, 1865–1930

	Cities of 20,000 Inhabitants or More, Excluding Santiago			Santiago		
Year	Number (000)	Per Cent of Total Population	Growth Rate	Number (000)	Per Cent of Total Population	Growth Rate
1865	70	3.8		115	6.3	
1875	98	4.7	3.3	150	7.2	2.7
1885	173	6.9	5.9	189	7.5	2.3
1895	229	8.5	2.8	256	9.5	3.1
1907	384	11.9	4.4	333	10.3	2.2
1920	536	14.4	2.6	507	13.6	3.3
1930	692	16.1	2.6	696	16.2	3.2

SOURCE: Adapted from Hurtado, *Concentración,* Tables 5, 6.

tion of the country, whereas in 1907 this figure had risen to 29.0 per cent. Of equal importance was the fact that the proportion of the country's population living in urban areas in the south had risen from 5.0 per cent to 8.0 per cent, and the number of urban centers (between 2,000 and 20,000 inhabitants) in this region had risen, over the decade 1875–85, from nine to sixteen.[15] The impact of these new areas, however, must be understood in connection with the major economic developments of the era: the northern nitrate boom, a broadening of the agricultural base and expansion of coal mining in the south, and the construction of a railroad network linking vital areas of the nation.

14. Hurtado, *Concentración,* Table 2.
15. Ibid., Table 3.

Railroads, Agriculture, and Mining

I believe that it may be safely argued that the developments which characterized these sectors of the Chilean economy, especially after the last quarter of the nineteenth century, not only provided a series of preconditions vital for the existence of industrialization but, in a more positive fashion, made contributions which directly propelled the initiation of that process. The close relationship which exists between the establishment of railroads and the rise of industry has been evident in almost every country which has undergone a meaningful development of its manufacturing sector.

Although the first railroads to be constructed in Chile were built in the 1850s and 1860s, the major effort of laying down the network that would unite the country was made during the period from the 1870s to just before the beginning of World War I. In 1860, there were only three relatively short lines operating in the country: Copiapó to the port of Caldera in the north (81 kilometers), Valparaíso to Quillota (30 kilometers), and south from Santiago to the town of Requinoa, passing through the heart of the rich agricultural provinces of O'Higgins and Colchagua (100 kilometers). But by 1877, the longitudinal line ran as far south as Concepción, a distance of over 500 kilometers, and a decade later, total railroad coverage extended for over 2,000 kilometers.[16] The intensity of this process increased until the outbreak of the First World War, at which time Chile had a network of over 8,000 kilometers (Table 5).

TABLE 5
Extension of Chilean Railroads, 1890–1920
(in kilometers)

Year	State Owned	Privately Owned	Total
1890	1,106	1,641	2,747
1900	2,125	2,229	4,354
1905	2,329	2,449	4,778
1910	2,830	3,114	5,944
1913	5,009	3,061	8,070
1915	5,122	3,094	8,216
1920	4,579	3,632	8,211

Source: Chile, Dirección de Estadística y Censos, *Sinópsis estadística año 1928*, p. 106.

16. Santiago Marín Vicuña, *Los ferrocarriles en Chile*, passim.

Railroads themselves provided a market for the goods and services of heavy industry. The foundries of Santiago, Valparaíso, and Antofagasta first had the task of repairing and servicing imported railroad equipment. Ample evidence also exists to indicate that Chilean heavy industry was a significant supplier of locomotives and cars as early as 1887.[17] Hardie y Cía., owners of the large Valparaíso foundry La Unión, owed a substantial part of their business to this type of work. Established as a small workshop in 1869 by A. C. Bower, a Scottish immigrant, the firm developed slowly until around 1880, when Santiago Hardie became a partner. From then it expanded rapidly until, by 1895, approximately 500 workers were employed in a plant with a fixed capital value of over 860,000 pesos; the installed capacity in trolley cars alone could produce 700 units a year.[18]

Railroads also performed a unique role as catalyst for the different sectors of the Chilean economy. Commissioned by the Chilean government in 1889 to study the feasibility of implanting iron industry in the country, the French engineer Charles Vattier wrote, "Until the present, the major difficulty which mining and manufacturing enterprises encountered was the lack of easy and economical transportation in regions located away from the coast; the roads were few and bad, the railroad line was too far from the different centers of mineral, industrial and agricultural production, the rates were very high on the privately owned railroads and often shipments had to be made by mules. But these conditions are changing with the great new network presently under construction."[19]

The construction of the transverse lines in the north was essential for the nitrate boom of the late nineteenth century. Before the construction of the nitrate lines only those fields close to the coast could be exploited, and the minerals had to be shipped to the ports in mule-drawn wagons. With the extension of the northern railroads, fields much farther inland could be opened.[20] The opening of these interior *salitreras* gave continued vigor to Chilean exports which in turn would have an impact upon manufacturing possibilities. Agriculture also benefited from the growth of railroads since it became easier and more profitable to reach the expanding internal markets.

17. See pp. 32–33 of this text.
18. "Progreso industrial"; "La fábrica de los señores Hardie y Cía."
19. Charles Vattier, *L'Avenir de la Metallurgie du Fer au Chili*, p. 1.
20. For a more detailed discussion of the impact of railroad expansion see Hurtado, *Concentración*, pp. 63–65.

From the last decade of the nineteenth century the government railroad policy was particularly effective in linking together production, distribution, and consumption centers in the Central Valley and the South through the intense activity in laying down lines which, by 1913, united Santiago with Puerto Montt, with numerous branch lines criss-crossing the major agricultural regions.[21]

The evidence which is available to date concerning agriculture generally supports the affirmation that as early as the last quarter of the nineteenth century this sector entered into a period of relative stagnation.[22] However, there is reason to believe that changes occurred in Chilean agriculture when it was faced with the loss of its lucrative export grain market. On one hand there was the increase in cattle raising which, by 1906, accounted for approximately 1.6 million head of cattle in central Chile alone.[23] This figure does not include the sheep and cattle ranches which were being formed in Magallanes. In fact, these were enormous capitalistic enterprises which not only provided raw materials for industry in the form of wool and hides but engaged in numerous manufacturing activities also. Enterprises such as the huge Sociedad Explotadora de Tierra del Fuego, founded in 1893 and linked to the wide range of holdings which formed the Edwards family empire and the prominent English trading house of Duncan Fox, were totally integrated production centers. Its products were wool, canned, chilled and frozen meat, grease and oils, sheep skins, and tanned hides. It also possessed a factory for the production of cans. But perhaps this was not so complete an example of vertical and horizontal integration as the case of the Sociedad Ganadera "Gente Grande," formed in 1883, which owned a lumber-processing plant as well as its own shipyards.[24]

There are indications of other shifts which occurred in Chilean agriculture following the War of the Pacific which, if they do not describe a vigorous trend, certainly demonstrate that this sector was not entirely stagnant. The combined forces of an accelerated process of urbanization, the opening of the southern frontier region,

21. Between 1893 and 1907, the tonnage shipped on the state railroads rose from 1,960,000 to 3,500,000 tons, and the number of passengers carried increased from 4,678,000 to 10,910,000 (ibid., Table 19).

22. Arnold Bauer, "Expansión económica en una sociedad tradicional: Chile central en el siglo XIX," pp. 158–61, 214–20.

23. Ibid., p. 218.

24. Alberto Márquez, *Libro internacional sudamericano: sección comercial chilena*, 2:793.

and the extension of the railroad lines provoked a positive, if not entirely adequate, response on the part of agriculture. This reaction was oriented towards satisfying the increasing demand of the internal, primarily urban, market. From 1860 to 1908, wheat production in the southern part of Chile, comprised of the province of Concepción, the adjoining frontier area, and the lake region, rose from 131,000 tons to 2,203,000 tons, an average annual growth rate of 6 per cent.[25] This wheat supplied the flour milling industry, which underwent technological innovations after 1890.[26] On the other hand, in the Central Valley, agrarian interests responded to the more diversified demand of the growing urban market by an increase in the production of fruits, vegetables, and wine.[27] These changes had cumulative effects on industry. Backward linkages developed as the demand for such inputs as new steam-powered roller mills and wine-processing equipment increased. Forward effects were also experienced with the appearance of sizeable food-processing and canning plants near Santiago and Valparaíso.[28]

A direct stimulus to industry was also forthcoming from the addition of the northern nitrate mines to Chile after the War of the Pacific. Although the mining enterprises (particularly the largest firms) imported the vast majority of their capital goods, a substantial market for producer durables, which were not always profitable to import, was created for Chilean heavy industry. Most of the foundries of Santiago and Valparaíso and all of them in the northern cities of Iquique and Antofagasta depended upon mining for a great portion of their business. The foundries produced narrow gauge locomotives, built hand- and mule-drawn railways, caldrons, overhead cable ore transports, and mineshaft ventilators.[29] Equipment for the refining of other minerals was produced as well. Furnaces, purifiers, and converters for copper and amalgamators for gold all formed part of the Chilean heavy industry product line. An indication that this work was executed with some degree of proficiency is the fact that the largest foundries, such as Balfour Lyon y Cía., exported as much as 25 per cent of their output to Bolivia, Perú, and Argentina, while up to 60 per cent of the total

25. Hurtado, *Concentración*, Table 16.
26. See pp. 38–39 of this text.
27. Hurtado, *Concentración*, pp. 72–73, Tables 16, 17.
28. Luis Galdames, *Geografía económica de Chile*, p. 190.
29. Pérez Canto, *La industria nacional*, pp. 1–16; "Progreso industrial"; "Fundición y fábrica de Orchard Hnos."

production of others, like Lever Murphy y Cía., was shipped from Valparaíso to the north and south of Chile.[30]

Manufacturing depended in a much broader sense on the development of mining. Nitrate exports produced the foreign exchange essential for the importation of raw materials and capital goods upon which Chilean industry relied so heavily. Although adequate data do not exist for the period 1880–1914, it is possible to project further on the basis of evidence from the decade of the 1920s which relates trends in manufacturing to foreign trade. Industrial production levels then closely followed the import-export cycles. As exports grew, so did industry. This was the result of the multiplier effect which expanded exports had upon the national economy. The increased buying power consequent upon the larger national income intensified both imports and demand for the products of domestic industry. Two industrial cycles occurred in the decade 1920–30, which correspond exactly to the foreign trade cycles of that period to the point that an almost perfect fit exists between the curve of industrial production and the values of total exports and imports.[31]

As per capita income levels rose, Engel's law was confirmed and demand for industrial goods climbed.[32] It is reasonable to assume that the same stimulus to manufacturing provided by the operation of the economic forces just described for the 1920s was at work to vitalize industry during the export boom following the War of the Pacific.[33]

Import Structure, 1880–1920

One of the best sources of empirical data available with which to substantiate the foregoing conclusions is the time series of Chile's imports broken down according to their sector destination. Close examination of the import data, moreover, provides insight into the

30. Pérez Canto, *La industria nacional*, pp. 6, 13.
31. Muñoz, *Crecimiento*, p. 44, Figs. 1, 2.
32. It is also important to remember that the large mining operations themselves represented urban concentrations. At the microeconomic level the dependency of individual enterprises upon mining developments is evidenced by the 1921 annual report of the major glass producer which stated, "the shut down of operations in the majority of the salitreras has proportionately diminished the consumption of beer in the north and forced the Compañía Cervecerías Unidas to stop their order of bottles which, in turn, has obliged us to close the Rancagua factory; and we will soon close the San Diego plant."
33. For the growth and structure of Chilean exports, 1870–1930, see Table A-1.

nature of industrialization and relates that process directly to important aspects of Chilean economic history in the early twentieth century.

With the exception of the period 1895–99 (which may be explained by the economic depression of 1897–98), Chilean imports of raw materials and capital goods destined for industry rose consistently between 1880 and 1919 (Table 6). As a percentage of total imports, raw materials ranged between 42 and 48 per cent throughout these years, while the machinery, tools, and equipment imported for industry rose from 2.8 to 5.4 per cent of the total imports from the end of the War of the Pacific to the outbreak of World War I. Since these figures do not include fuels, a category which could not be broken down according to its destination, industrial inputs are even underestimated. Thus, the growth rates of these imports confirm my hypothesis that significant developments in industry were occurring from the end of the nineteenth century.

TABLE 6
RAW MATERIAL AND INDUSTRIAL CAPITAL GOODS IMPORTS, CHILE 1880–1919

	Raw Material[a]			Industrial Capital Goods[b]		
Period	Value[c] (000)	(1910–14= 100)	Percentage of Total Imports	Value[c] (000)	(1910–14= 100)	Percentage of Total Imports
1880–84	46,927	37	48.5	2,668	17	2.8
1885–89	49,831	40	47.0	4,209	26	3.9
1890–94	64,061	51	45.8	6,906	43	4.9
1895–99	58,265	46	45.9	3,708	23	2.9
1900–1904	67,964	54	48.2	6,527	41	4.7
1905–9	102,946	82	42.9	15,313	95	6.4
1910–14	126,220	100	41.9	16,064	100	5.4
1915–19	142,709	113	46.6	10,761	67	3.6

SOURCE: Calculated on the basis of data in Chile, Oficina Central de Estadística, *Anuario de comercio exterior*, 1880–1920.
a. Includes all goods except fuel not destined for direct consumption but which are processed by Chilean factories to produce the finished product.
b. Only capital goods for the manufacturing sector are included.
c. These are average values per year expressed in pesos of 18d.

Oscar Muñoz has demonstrated that during the decade 1920–30 industrial output was not correlated in any way with a reduction of imports.[34] In the period before 1914 this phenomenon is almost

34. Muñoz, *Crecimiento*, p. 44.

certainly to be found also.[35] Aside from the fact that the income effects produced by the nitrate export boom were probably of such magnitude as to create higher demand for both imported and nationally produced goods, the very nature of Chilean industry was such that it depended heavily upon imports. Not only did machinery come from abroad, but, as has already been seen, imports supplied manufacturing with a large portion of all other inputs. These included not only raw materials in the narrow sense but also many intermediate goods such as unrefined granulated sugar, textiles, iron, paper, and chemicals which were processed by Chilean industry to turn out the finished product for final consumption.

It was not unusual for a Chilean factory's contribution to the transformation process to be little more than a screwing together or weaving and dyeing of a semifinished item. It was just this characteristic of early Chilean manufacturing which motivated men like the powerful congressman of the Liberal Party, Luis Aldunate, to seek to undo the protectionism afforded industry by the Tariff of 1897.[36] This dependence upon imports was recognized by the industrialists themselves, and it was generally accepted that in the first decade of the twentieth century 75 per cent of Chilean industry relied heavily upon the acquisition of foreign materials.[37] Thus it may be concluded that contrary to common expectation industry did not develop in conflict with the dominant foreign trade sector which had initiated a crucial stage of Chile's economic growth, but existed rather as a complement to the basic economic activity of the country.[38]

A unique insight into the behavior of industry during the critical moments of general economic crisis is also afforded by the import data. Following 1900, nitrate exports flourished, and in 1905, the country experienced a balance of trade more favorable than in any

35. See pp. 24, 44–45, and 46 of this text for an indication of the relation between imports and the intensity of the early industrialization process.

36. *El Ferrocarril*, December 16, 1906, p. 4.

37. "Estadística comercial." In 1907, Pedro Luis González, the editor of the *Boletín*, gave the following list of industries which used imported materials exclusively: clothing, hemp sandals, woolen textile factories (there were no spinning mills in Chile so the wool was first exported to be made into thread), knitwear, foundries and metal-working factories, book-binding, publishing, and chemical plants; other industries which depended to a great degree upon imported materials were beer, candle-making, sweets, flour-milling, footwear, and construction materials (*BSFF* 24 [January 1907]: 3–5).

38. This does not imply, of course, that particular industries were not in competition with imported consumer goods.

other year prior to World War I.[39] Interest rates on bank loans fell, and the dividends earned on mortgage loans were lower than in any year since 1888.[40] Chile's economic profile depicted unparalleled firmness. Each year the Chilean peso was quoted at higher rates of exchange, and prices on the London market for Chilean nitrate, copper, and wheat advanced steadily.[41] Even events on the international political front were propitious. The territorial dispute with Argentina which had carried the two countries to the brink of war in 1898 had been placed under English arbitration. This resulted in the signing of a treaty in May 1902 which brought assurance of peace between Chile and Argentina.

TABLE 7
INVESTMENT IN NEW CHILEAN CORPORATIONS, 1900–1907

Year	Subscribed Capital in New Corporations (millions of pesos of 18d.)
1900	27
1901	23
1902	12
1903	20
1904	74
1905	342
1906	208
1907	66

SOURCE: Zegers, *Estudios*, p. 7.

In the midst of this exuberant scene, investors feverishly sought out new ventures for their capital. Bank loans increased by 50 per cent in 1905, and stock exchange activity was spurred by the issue of over 70 million pesos in paper money between 1904 and 1906.[42] The amount of corporate stock issues far surpassed anything previously witnessed in Chile. Capital invested in new corporations rose from 20 million pesos in 1903 to 342 million in 1905 (Table 7).

There were indications, however, that most of this financial structure was built on a very weak base. Of the 770 million pesos of capital subscribed in the corporations formed between 1900 and 1907, only 125 million was actually paid in.[43] In 1905, Pedro Luis

39. See Tables A-1, A-2.
40. Frank Fetter, *Monetary Inflation in Chile*, p. 121.
41. Julio Zegers, *Estudios económicos, 1907–1908*, pp. 170–76.
42. Ibid., p. 191.
43. Roberto Espinoza, *Cuestiones financieras de Chile*, p. 310.

González, spokesman for the Sociedad de Fomento Fabril, warned of the dangers of the wildly speculative situation: "Unquestionably there is a great deal of sham in the unusual stock activity of the new corporations; many unscrupulous people subscribe hundreds of shares not with the intention of paying in the nominal capital represented by those shares but for the purpose of selling them as soon as their price rises and before having paid even a portion of the subscribed capital; stocks are acquired in much the same way as lottery tickets."[44] González foresaw an economic crisis approaching as a result of this abuse. Then, in 1906, the bubble burst. The signs of strain were evident as many of these shell companies collapsed, credit tightened, and bank reserves fell drastically. Chile entered a depression which was undoubtedly aggravated, but not caused by, the world-wide economic crisis of 1907.[45]

A great deal of the blame for this occurrence has been placed on those urban interests who were intent upon industrializing the country.[46] This interpretation, however, does not appear adequate. Industrialists were making significantly productive investments throughout this period. The data for imports during the years 1905–9 indicate substantial sums of money being spent on capital goods and raw materials. Spending of this nature, aimed at expanding production, actually increased greatly over the levels reached in the period 1900–1904 and continued on this consistent upward swing until World War I. Such is not the behavior of capitalists whose goal is mere speculation. The manufacturing sector was little affected by the wave of bankruptcies of 1906–7. Indeed, many of the most prominent industrial firms came into being or took corporate form during the first years of the twentieth century. Examples are such solid enterprises as the Compañía Molinos y Fideos Carozzi (1907), Compañía Cervecerías Unidas (1902), Imprenta y Litografía Universo (1906), Sociedad Fábrica Nacional de Vidrios (1904), Compañía de Cemento El Melón (1906), Compañía Industrial (1901), and Fábrica Nacional de Envases y Enlozados (1906).

There is no doubt that speculation existed on a wide scale, but relatively little of it was to be found in Chilean industry. On the contrary, much of this financial gambling may be traced to such undertakings as the numerous land development ventures of the extreme south formed at this time. Corporate entities of this type

44. Pedro Luis González, "Las nuevas empresas industriales."
45. Espinoza, *Cuestiones*, p. 336; Zegers, *Estudios*, p. 258.
46. Frederick Pike, *Chile and the United States 1880–1962*, p. 102.

were established for over 20 million pesos in 1904 and for over 90 million in 1905.[47]

In summary, the era beginning with the War of the Pacific may be looked upon in many respects as a "watershed" in the periodization of Chilean economic history. It heralded a new expansion in the economic forces of that country which influenced other changes of a social and demographic nature. In addition to the characteristics noted, the period following the war also marked the appearance of other important aspects of market economy and capitalistic organization. The Santiago Stock Exchange was founded in 1893 and that of Valparaíso was formally incorporated in 1898. All of the changes—urbanization, population movements to the north and south, developments in transportation, agriculture, mining, and foreign commerce—operated to provide the preconditions for the implantation of a meaningful industrialization process in Chile.

47. Zegers, *Estudios*, p. 31.

2. Industrial Response: Rate, Structure, and Spread

In response to the auspicious set of conditions for its development following the War of the Pacific, Chilean manufacturing progressed considerably. The number of industrial establishments grew rapidly, new product lines were opened, capital investments were greater, the amount of labor absorbed by manufacturing increased significantly, and output was qualitatively distinct from the preceding decades. Unfortunately, adequate and reliable statistical data do not exist upon which time series may be based whose coverage would encompass all of these aspects (see Appendix 2). Fragmentary data, however, are available, to permit a reconstruction of the process until the end of the century.

Industrial Growth to the End of the Nineteenth Century

In 1883, for the first time since its appearance in 1876, mention of the existence of manufacturing is made in the *Sinopsis estadística*. This annual publication prepared by the government does not go into great detail, but does refer specifically to large-scale industrial production in such lines as flour, sugar, metallic and mechanical products, and cloth and clothing.[1] The Sociedad de Fomento Fabril affirmed that, although in 1867 a total of 463 establishments were registered in the tax rolls of Valparaíso and 570 in 1895, "in the former year very few establishments could be regarded as true factories; most were only small shops quite different from the splendid factories which exist today."[2]

An appreciation of industrial expansion is also given in the national exhibitions. According to one of the most prominent members of the SFF, "the National Exhibition of 1884 was a real surprise not only for the public but also for the industrialists themselves who had not realized the development of many of our budding industries. In the exhibits of 1869 and 1875, the industrialists had not been represented but they entered with confidence in that of 1884 because they were conscious of their own strength."[3]

Still, the task of determining in statistically acceptable and quantitatively precise terms the growth of Chilean industry during the decade from 1875 to 1884 (milestones provided only by the national exhibitions held prior to and following the War of the Pacific) is most difficult. Comparable materials from earlier exhibits are missing; no published reports, written records, or other detailed sources exist other than the catalogues which merely enumerate the objects exhibited without information concerning their origin—organized factory, small workshop, or individual artisan. Nevertheless, sufficient source material is available to permit an appraisal of the process underway.

During this period (1875–84), the number of factories producing articles for popular consumption increased substantially and the variety of their output became more diverse. Reporting on the opportunities for European immigrants in Chile on a commission for the Chilean government, Louis Dorte, a French businessman of long residence in the country, listed 3,561 factories and small artisan shops in 1883. If we exclude those specific products most likely produced in small shops by artisans such as shoemakers, tailors, blacksmiths, bakers, etc., and correct on the basis of other con-

1. Chile, Oficina Central de Estadística, *Sinopsis estadística y geográfica de Chile en 1883*, p. 32. This does not imply that large-scale flour milling did not exist prior to the 1870s. Indeed, with the wheat export boom of the 1850s, this industry developed much before the rest.

2. Sociedad de Fomento Fabril, *Boletín de la estadística industrial, Valparaíso*, p. 89.

3. Pedro Luis González, *La Sociedad de Fomento Fabril, su labor durante veinticinco años*, p. 12.

temporary figures for industries such as flour mills, the list is reduced to a little over 2,100, a more likely appraisal of the number of factories at that time.[4] From the documents of the 1884 exhibition, we learn that during this decade for the first time the Chilean industrial roll listed the existence of a factory at Valparaíso producing machine-made cigarettes, an acid factory at Quilpué which produced sulfuric, nitric, and chlorhidric acids, essential for other industries, a bottle factory at Lota, and a fruit and vegetable canning factory.[5]

But according to the observers of the 1884 exhibition, Chilean industrial progress was not to be characterized so much by the appearance of new industry, but by much improved production techniques in sectors which had existed prior to 1875. Their judgment in this respect was "it has been observed that during the last ten years the production systems have been improved and expanded in such fashion that without exaggeration it may be said that industry has only been established in Chile in this period of time."[6] Among those areas singled out for the progress achieved were food, beverages, tobacco, furniture, upholstery, leather-tanning, footwear, barrel-making, edible and industrial oils, paper, and metallurgical processes. On the other hand, little progress was apparent in the textile, clothing, soap, candle, and glazed pottery industries.[7]

The industrial census conducted by the SFF in 1895 gives an approximate measure of the rate by which manufacturing grew in Chile. Due to reporting errors and coverage limitations, the overall trend represented is more important to observe than the absolute figures at any given date. Of the total number of establishments listed in that year, 76 per cent were founded after 1880 and 41.9 per cent during the five years following 1890 (Table 8). This indicates an annual growth rate of 5.9 per cent in the 25-year period from 1870 to 1895.[8] The manufacturing plant of the Santiago-Valparaíso area which accounted for approximately 60 per cent of the factories and shops listed exhibited an identical pattern of expansion.

4. Louis Dorte, *El porvenir en Chile de los emigrantes europeos*, pp. 252–53.
5. "La exposición nacional I."
6. Ibid., p. 430.
7. Ibid., pp. 423–25; Dorte, *El porvenir*, pp. 268–80.
8. Roughly the same trend is reported in the 1895 industrial exposition. Of 164 participating establishments which replied to the question, 11 per cent were founded before 1875, 16.5 per cent in 1876–88, and 72.6 per cent in 1889–94 (*BSFF* 12 [1895], passim).

A Forecast Equation for Aggregate Chilean Industrial Production, 1880–1913

Inasmuch as the only data apparently comparable are those which appear after 1914, I attempted to reconstruct the trend of Chilean aggregate industrial output from 1880 to 1913. In the effort to produce an economically meaningful, statistically defensible, and reasonably accurate method for uncovering the quantitative industrial pattern during this period, I used the least-squares multiple regression technique. This selection was influenced by several factors. First, it is relatively simple and not overly expensive to employ, and it seemed particularly applicable to the only data available which might be chosen as independent variables. Essentially this

TABLE 8

Founding Dates of Factories Listed in 1895 Industrial Census[a]

	Chile		Santiago and Valparaíso	
	Number	Percentage	Number	Percentage
Before 1870	241	9.8	136	9.3
1870–79	336	13.7	188	12.8
1880–89	846	34.6	546	37.2
1890–95	1,026	41.9	596	40.7
Total	2,449	100.0	1,466	100.0

Source: Sociedad de Fomento Fabril, *Boletín de la estadística industrial.*
a. Small shops were included although artisan work, such as shoemaking and carpentry, was not. Excluded from this table are seven gas and electric companies which were reported in the census, the total geographical coverage of which was from Petorca to Ancud.

was a problem of matching statistical techniques to the available data. Finally, it afforded an opportunity to test the relevance of somewhat sophisticated tools of economic analysis and computer techniques in the context of historical research.

The first of the major problems to be overcome in this exercise was that of identifying the independent variables which might be used in conjunction with total industrial output and for which time series were available for the period. The only contenders with a meaningful economic relation to industry for which data existed were the foreign trade series broken down according to total exports and those imports which were directly related to industrial production, i.e., raw and intermediate goods and capital goods. The close association discovered between the foreign trade sector and domestic manufacturing before the Great Depression, as discussed, made it quite plausible to assume that industrial output might be expressed as a function of one or a combination of these variables. Needless to say, however, other forces were operating upon the different sectors of Chilean industry: natural demographic increase, changes in the spatial distribution of the population, expanding infrastructure facilities, protectionist policies by the state, etc. In order to account for these factors which would otherwise be contained in an unexplained residual, a time trend variable was included to remove the effect on the dependent variable, industrial output, of net, monotonically operating changes in these other unspecified variables. In addition, a dummy variable representing the presence or lack of significant legislation in the tariff system in a given year was also utilized.

The basic hypothesis to be tested is that for the period from the War of the Pacific to 1930, changes in Chilean industrial output vary directly with fluctuations in total exports, the importation of raw and intermediate materials (inputs to domestic manufacturing), and the immediate effects of protectionist measures. To test this hypothesis seven sets of independent variables were employed and four potentially acceptable linear functions, yielding twenty-eight equations, each of which has a meaningful economic content for forecasting the growth in manufacturing output during the period. The four functions are specified and discussed in Appendix 2 and the seven sets of independent variables are listed in Table A-10. As indicated there, of the twenty-eight equations, all but two were eliminated out of hand by the rigorous statistical screening criteria established. Only these could thus be considered as viable instruments with which to forecast Chilean industrial output in the period under study. Since one of these equations produced results in which 60 per cent of the explanatory power of the coefficient of determination (R^2) came from the time trend variable, a surrogate device, I decided that the utility of that equation was diminished too much to proceed any further with it.

The following conclusions were drawn from the results of the regression analysis. First, the rates of change in Chilean industrial output were significantly related to the rates of change in foreign trade and the immediate effects of protectionist tariff legislation as expressed in the working hypothesis. Second, since changes in total exports are greatly reflected in the fluctuations of raw and intermediate materials imports, the latter variable is best used alone with the dummy variable of tariff legislation. This approach which subsumes the export variable in that of imports produces statistically sounder and more probable results. The forecast pattern of industrial growth, 1880–1913, is given in Table 9 together with the observed trend for 1914–30.

It is obvious that at a 95 per cent confidence level the range of

TABLE 9
CHILEAN INDUSTRIAL PRODUCTION, 1880–1930[a]
(index 1918=100)

	Industrial Output		
Year	Low	Most Probable and Observed[b]	High
1880	36	50	70
1885	39	55	77
1890	47	67	96
1895	47	71	101
1900	48	71	97
1905	52	75	108
1910	64	94	137
1912	64	94	137
1913	64	94	138
1914		68	
1915		75	
1916		86	
1917		94	
1918		100	
1919		101	
1920		96	
1921		98	
1922		98	
1923		107	
1924		116	
1925		115	
1926		111	
1927		107	
1928		113	
1929		114	
1930		144	

SOURCE: 1880–1913, Appendix 2; 1914–30, calculated on the basis of Muñoz, *Crecimiento*, Table II-2, col. C.

a. The figures under "low" and "high" for 1880–1913 were derived by applying the standard error of the forecast to the "most probable" trend line values for each year, operating at the 95 per cent confidence level.

b. From 1914 on, the figures are based on actual observed data.

acceptable values is extremely broad; in fact, its width is too great to be considered useful. Nevertheless, the most likely trend line yields results which are both economically and statistically acceptable. It indicates rising levels of industrial activity for most of the period with some occasional stagnation. From 1880 to 1910, an average annual rate of growth of 2.1 per cent is the most probable. Certain decades experienced more robust growth, for example, 1880–90, when the growth rates might be considered to be on the order of 3.0 per cent. The decade 1900–1910 evidenced a respectable growth pattern of 2.9 per cent; on the other hand, the period between 1890 and 1900 appears to have been one of stagnation.[9]

I do not contend that the figures given in Table 9 represent the actual index values for Chilean manufacturing production, 1880–1913. Rather, under the assumptions of the least-squares technique, results were produced which have sufficiently high economic and statistical significance to be considered the most probable long-run trend of domestic production after the War of the Pacific and are more defensible than any other time series known to me. Notwithstanding, as discussed in Appendix 2, under the circumstances of the paucity of pertinent data, it must be concluded that the least-squares technique has certain limitations in this case and no great accuracy can be expected, nor is claimed, in forecasting absolute levels of output at a given date.

Although this conclusion is negative in nature, in general the exercise was fruitful. Valid results which fill a gap in the knowledge of the long-term evolution of Chilean industry prior to the outbreak of World War I have been produced, and a case study of the possible uses and limitations of advanced tools of quantitative economic analysis in historical research has been offered. The results of the exercise clearly indicate that among the major factors which condi-

9. Although the production levels of 1897 were not forecast, the tariff promulgated in that year was protectionist in nature, and the documents of the period refer to its beneficial influence on numerous product lines. Since tariff legislation was only included as a dummy variable (in other words, promulgation or no promulgation of a tariff), the intensity of a tariff's effects on production levels in later years could not be evaluated. The only manner of doing this for 1900 was to include the existence of the protectionist tariff in the computer program for that year. This yielded an index of 79 for an annual growth rate during the five-year period 1895–1900 of 2.1 per cent, but this procedure would distort the later levels which also benefited to some degree from the law. For the impact of the 1897 tariff see Sociedad de Fomento Fabril, "Memoria, 1900," *BSFF* 18 (February 1902): 36; "Estadística industrial del país I"; "Efectos de la ley de impuestos del 23 de diciembre de 1897; el progreso de la industria nacional."

tioned early Chilean industrial development were the foreign sector (exports and imports) and to a lesser extent protectionist action by the government. The degree to which each of these variables influenced the growth of domestic manufacturing is also made apparent by the regression analysis. A need remains, nonetheless, to buttress these findings by other types of evidence, some of a more qualitative kind, in order to discern more completely the nature of this early period of industrialization.

Chilean Industrial Development and the Gerschenkron Model

In this section the framework of analysis is shifted somewhat with the implementation of another instrument with which to assess the intensity of the process underway before World War I and to probe into the sectoral aspects of Chilean industrial development. The basis for this approach is the body of research conducted by Alexander Gerschenkron into the economic growth of France, Germany, Russia, Italy, and Bulgaria, all countries which started to industrialize in a setting of relative economic backwardness. When taken together, Gerschenkron's work forms a descriptive historical model explaining the process of European economic development and offering a set of conditions deemed essential for increases in the rate of secondary output to be considered as defining a process of industrialization in the qualitative as well as in the quantitative sense.[10]

In summary form these propositions call for the existence of four conditions: the simultaneous nature of development along many lines of industrial activity; the borrowing of foreign and more advanced technologies; the creation of an urban labor force, "a stable, reliable and disciplined group that has cut the umbilical cord connecting it with the land and has become suitable for utilization in factories"; and the existence of a state of tension created by the awareness of the disparity between "the actual state of economic activities in the country and the existing obstacles to industrial

10. Alexander Gerschenkron, *Economic Backwardness in Historical Perspective, A Book of Essays*, pp. 5–10. These factors which Gerschenkron believes form an essential background for industrialization should not be confused with his summary of the relationship between the degree of economic backwardness and the subsequent variation which industrial development may take in a given country. For the latter see ibid., pp. 353–54.

development on the one hand, and the great promise inherent in such a development on the other."

In chapter 1 we examined the first of these factors and concluded that sufficient preconditions existed in the economic expansion following the War of the Pacific so that the movement "along a broad front" required in Gerschenkron's framework for industrialization to take hold was indeed to be found in Chile.

Developments in mining, transportation, agriculture, commerce, and demographic changes galvanized the domestic industrial effort and helped to accelerate production in a variety of consumer and producer goods industries. The shift in the orientation of agriculture toward the internal market coincided with the rise of meat-processing industries, some of which contained completely integrated production systems. In the Central Valley, food-processing industries were founded which reflected this change in the nature of Chilean agriculture. The first of these appeared in 1882.[11] By 1910, Luis Galdames referred to the advances which had been made in the processing of fruit and vegetables. He reported the existence of thirty factories processing a wide range of products with most of these plants operating in Rancagua, Valparaíso, and Santiago and mentioned that over 75 per cent of the raw and intermediate inputs to these industries was of national origin.[12] Representative of the larger of these plants was the Fábrica Nacional de Conservas Alimenticias founded in 1906 by the agriculturist Juan Nicolás Rubio on his estate El Estanque, near Rancagua. The factory developed very rapidly, especially after 1907 (while Chile was in the midst of a serious depression), and had a capital investment of 3 million pesos, a respectable sum for any firm at the time. Its annual production was 2 million cans which were distributed throughout Chile and exported to countries to the north with a small amount even being sold in Europe. It employed twenty technicians and "white-collar" workers, and at harvest time the factory alone absorbed over a thousand workers. A completely integrated firm, it was equipped with a wide variety of food-processing machines driven by electric, steam, and gasoline engines and produced its own packaging materials, tin cans as well as wooden boxes. Housing was provided for

11. Tadeo Laso, *Catálogo de la exposición permanente y museo industrial de la Sociedad de Fomento Fabril*, p. xix.
12. Galdames, *Geografía*, p. 190.

all employees, and the firm maintained a primary school with day and evening courses for its manual laborers.[13]

Printing was another sector which made significant advances during this era. Furnished with the most modern equipment, including linotype machines, much of it only recently imported from Europe and the United States, the printing enterprise Litografía e Imprenta Gillet Hnos. was printing stamps for the Bolivian government before 1900. What was to become the largest of the Chilean publishing houses and exercise a monopoly over most areas of the publishing business of that country (except newspapers), even before World War I, the Imprenta Universo, appeared in 1895. Another enterprise, the Imprenta Litografía y Encuadernación Barcelona, which was founded on the base of the Imprenta Católica in 1891 by the Spanish immigrant Ignacio Balcells with a modest capital investment of 15,000 pesos, expanded so rapidly that seven years later its capital had increased ten times to 150,000 pesos. It employed 142 workers and in 1897 produced 270,000 pesos worth of printed material for the Santiago and Valparaíso markets.[14] This industry represents one of the sectors which depended to a great degree on the export-import cycles since most of its capital equipment and all of the paper, type, printer's ink, cloth for binding, and other primary materials had to be imported at this stage of development. Only binding leather, glue, and small amounts of cardboard could be obtained locally.

Although the resource endowment of Chile was relatively limited and lacked the appropriate technology to work certain untapped natural resources, such as iron deposits, the development of certain industries should have been impeded, but this was not the case.[15] Increasing demand by the populace for a wide variety of consumer products, the peculiarities of the bulk-weight-to-cost ratio in shipping goods from abroad, and the marginal profitability of producing certain finished items, especially under early protectionist measures which favored specific industries representing the vested interests

13. *Chile industrial y comercial* (November 1909), pp. 31–32; Alberto Prado Martínez, *Anuario Prado Martínez, Chile, 1902*, p. 42; Adolfo Ortúzar, *Chile of Today: Its Commerce, Its Production and Its Resources*, p. 385; Sociedad de Fomento Fabril, *Exhibición de productos industriales, informe de los jurados, 1904*, p. 4. The latter gives examples of other notable food-processing firms.

14. "La litografía y la imprenta Gillet"; "La imprenta y encuadernación Barcelona."

15. Chilean coal producers, for example, delayed long before implanting a suitable coking method. Consequently, enterprises which required coke had to import it.

of the oligarchy, resulted in the evolution of an industrial profile that by 1914 was both widely diversified and technically advanced.[16]

A number of firms were producing on a relatively large scale and some of these enjoyed a significant export market to neighboring countries. The report of the SFF committee, which was responsible for the 1904 industrial exposition, reported notable advances in a number of product lines: food and beverages in general, clothing, woolen cloth, cotton prints and knitwear, leather products, footwear, wood products and furniture, printing and paper goods, chemical products, nonmetallic minerals, and the wide variety of goods produced by foundries, machine shops, and metal-working establishments. This was accomplished in spite of formidable obstacles such as insufficient skilled labor, the lack of competent technical personnel, consumer preferences which showed a marked disdain for all national products, and a lack of domestic capital.[17] Protectionist tariffs, state production and export subsidies, the favoring of those national producers with government contracts, and the establishment of industrial credit institutions were recommended—all themes which would be constantly present throughout the period until the demands were eventually met.

Examples of the increased rhythm of production in consumer and producer goods are given in Table 10. Once again a pattern emerges in which the output levels registered for the period following the War of the Pacific are qualitatively distinct from previous ones. This is clearly evident in the case of the beer industry. The production of the Anwandter Brewery in Valdivia, the oldest and one of the principal breweries of the country, was substantially higher in the period 1881–92 than before, and other breweries with installed capacities similar to that of Anwandter were founded only during that decade. The situation for another basic consumer item, refined

16. Based upon a classification established by Hollis Chenery in which countries are grouped according to the diversification of their natural resources, Muñoz stresses that the long-run tendency of manufacturing in Chile was to produce "a more diversified industrial structure than is common in the international economy" or which might be justified, given the fact that the natural resource endowment was limited or, in any event, more concentrated than in the international setting. Although he refers to the failure to create external markets for industrial goods, the apparent relationship of the contradiction seems to be that export markets were not sought primarily. Rather the main goal was to produce as diversified an industrial structure as possible with which to satisfy a domestic market closed off from external competition through protectionist measures (Muñoz, *Crecimiento*, pp. 67, 133).

17. Laso, *Catálogo*, pp. x–xlv.

TABLE 10

Chilean Production of Locomotives, Bridges, Refined Sugar, Beer, and Sulfuric Acid before World War I

Locomotives[a]		Bridges[b]		Refined Sugar[c]		Beer[d]		Sulfuric Acid[e]	
Year	No.	Year	No.	Year	Kilograms (000)	Year	Liters (000)	Year	Kilograms (000)
1886	4	1889–		1873–		1854	90	1903	1,744
1887	6	96	10	75	4,600	1864	120	1904	1,730
1888	12			1876	1,334	1875	1,500	1905	1,518
1893	12			1894	11,891	1878	1,473	1906	1,664
1898	10			1895	13,175	1881	2,508	1907	1,672
1899				1896	13,273	1882	3,200	1908	797
1908	38			1897	14,293	1883	3,804	1909	1,415
1909	18			1898	16,470	1892	8,000	1910	1,646
1910	18			1899	18,968				
1911	18			1900	20,479				
1912	18			1901	21,096				
1913	18			1902	24,440				
1914	18			1903	24,285				

Sources: The sources for this table are numerous and varied. They serve to give the reader an idea of the complexity of reconstructing the structural trends of Chilean industry prior to World War I.

Locomotives: Sociedad de Fomento Fabril, *Boletín*, 1887–1914; Chile, Ministerio de Industrias y Obras Públicas, *Boletín*, 1888–1900; *Chile industrial y commercial* (Valparaíso), May 15, June 1, 1911.

Bridges: Congreso Nacional, Cámara de Diputados, *Boletín de las sesiones extraordinarias*, December 12, 1896.

Refined sugar: Laso, *Catálogo de la exposición permanente y museo industrial de la Sociedad de Fomento Fabril*, pp. 16–17; Compañía de Refinería de Azúcar de Viña del Mar, *50 años*, pp. 6, 16.

Beer: Sociedad de Fomento Fabril, "La exposición nacional," in *Boletín*, 1884, p. 433; Julio Pérez Canto, *La industria nacional: estudios y descripciones de algunas fábricas de Chile*, p. 127.

Sulfuric acid: report of Dirección General de Contabilidad to Sr. Ramon Beylia, Inspector Ministerio de Industria, May 12, 1905, and Decrees of Ministerio de Industria for payment of sulfuric acid subsidy 1905–8 in MIOPAN, vol. 1,357; Jorge Hormann, *Chile industrial y económico 1897–1917.*

a. With the exception of 1886, when locomotives were produced by a state foundry, this represents the production of private firms in which all major parts except wheels were produced in Chile.

b. These include the most important bridges produced by private Chilean firms and not imported in sections for assembly. They are Maule, 480 meters in length; Lircay, 15 meters; Ñuble, 505 meters; Perquilauquen, 175 meters; Laja, 50 meters; Bío-Bío, 505 meters; Río Choapa in Pintacura; and in the city of Santiago over the Río Mapocho: Mackenna, Purísima, and 21 de Mayo.

c. This column represents the production of the Refinería de Azúcar de Viña del Mar, the major sugar refinery of the country. The only other refinery of importance was located in Penco and in 1894 produced 4,444,000 kilograms of sugar and from 1898 to 1901 averaged about 10,500 kilograms per year.

d. This includes only the production of the Anwandter Brewery in Valdivia, the oldest and one of the principal breweries. Others with a production capacity similar to that of Anwandter were the Limache Brewery, founded in 1883, and the Gubler and Cousiño Brewery, established in 1886.

e. This refers to the production of the Sociedad Chilena de Fundiciones, the only producer of sulfuric acid which sold this chemical to other industries.

sugar, is much the same. An interesting trend is provided by the production of railroad locomotives. The first Chilean-made locomotive was produced in 1886, by the state-owned foundry in Santiago. From then on, all domestically produced locomotives were made by private firms. In spite of the relatively small number produced yearly, the fact that even on a competitive basis (domestic producers could not exceed by 10 per cent the price quoted by foreign producers) locomotives could be almost entirely manufactured by Chilean foundries shows that a technically advanced heavy goods industry existed before World War I.[18] This is also indicated by the production of bridges, which were made by the same firms as the locomotives and not imported in sections for later assembly. The commercial production of sulfuric acid is also of some importance, as this was a key ingredient for use in numerous other industries, food and beverages, for example, as well as heavy industry.

Sufficient data are available for 1910 so that we can examine the capital-output ratios for eleven sectors of Chilean industry composed of thirty-seven selected product lines in which factory rather than artisan or small shop production was measured.[19] This ratio helps us to assess the relative productivity of capital. From the data presented in Tables 11 and A-4, I conclude that a fairly well diversified Chilean industrial structure, with varied and relatively advanced technologies for the period, had evolved by 1910. The spread of the capital-output ratios is wide, ranging from a low of 0.36 in the case of synthetic fertilizer to 7.17 for cement (Table A-4). The reason for the exceptionally high value of cement was that it represented the heavy capital investments of the recently formed (1906) Portland cement factory. El Melón could not be expected to have

18. The subsequent fate of the heavy goods industry up to 1930 is dealt with in pp. 51–58 and 146–51. For comparative purposes, perhaps it is well to consider that, in the first decade of the twentieth century, one of the major United States producers, Baldwin Locomotive Works, was reported to have an annual output of 1,000 engines while North British and Borsig, two principal British enterprises who exported to Chile along with Baldwin, each turned out approximately 400 locomotives annually (*El Ferrocarril*, February 26, 1908, p. 1).

19. The problem in the 1910 statistics discussed in Appendix 2 does not substantially affect this analysis since the data were used only for specific product lines in which small shop production was of little importance or where corrections could be applied, e.g., in the case of flour mills only those listed as "industrial mills" were included. Data for entire sectors were not used. The results accounted for 73 per cent of total industrial capital, 76 per cent of fixed capital, and 56 per cent of gross value added. Certain industries such as printing were totally excluded since it was impossible to separate factory from small shop production.

an output corresponding to its full capacity, a level it quickly reached, however, in 1911.[20]

The wide variations noted between ratios I and II may be explained by the very liquid condition of many firms which held a considerable part of their capital in the form of raw materials, semifinished goods, and inventory. This technique of holding a large reserve of capital in such fashion was often used as a protection

TABLE 11

CAPITAL-OUTPUT RATIOS FOR CHILEAN INDUSTRY, 1910–40

	1910		1914–16		1938–40	
Industry	I[a]	II[b]	I	II	I	II
Food products	2.40	1.11	2.07	0.98	2.31	0.81
Beverages	2.67	1.44	3.32	2.29	2.21	0.69
Tobacco products	1.76	0.87	0.67	0.43	0.95	0.31
Textiles	3.61	1.66	2.34	1.09	2.78	1.31
Clothing, footwear	1.79	0.53	1.51	0.42	1.89	0.44[c]
Leather products	2.93	1.07	2.87	1.02	2.39	0.41[d]
Wood products, furniture	1.92	0.74	2.57	1.31	2.33	0.73
Paper	2.88	1.60	1.95	1.21	2.39	1.50
Chemical products	2.08	1.02	2.19	1.10	1.78	0.56
Nonmetallic mineral products	4.26	3.11	2.68	2.08	2.48	1.22
Metallic products	2.20	1.22	2.18	1.33	2.25	1.03
Total	2.34	1.05	2.05	1.03	2.20	0.84

SOURCE: For 1910, Table A-4; for three-year averages 1914–16, 1938–40, Muñoz, *Crecimiento*, Table V-I.

a. The ratio of total capital to gross value added.

b. The ratio of fixed capital to gross value added.

c. Footwear excluded.

d. Footwear included.

against the fluctuations in exchange rate of the peso and in foreign trade which might mean sudden ruptures in the supply of imported materials used in domestic industry.[21]

In order to place these data in a dynamic context so that comparisons may be made with later periods, Table 11 was prepared. In it the 1910 data are standardized in eleven sectors in accord with Muñoz' presentation from which the 1914–16 and 1938–40 ratios

20. Compañía Cemento El Melón, *Memoria, 1911*, and *Chile industrial y comercial* (October 1909), pp. 9–11.

21. This is the reason given for the failure of the interruption of primary material imports during the early part of World War I to affect the production of the largest match factory in Chile. See Compañía Chilena de Fósforos, *Memoria, 1917*.

are taken. The ratios indicate an advanced state of Chilean industry by 1910 in relation to the situation in 1938–40, and hint at a long-run process up to World War II in which industry was characterized by a nonintensive use of capital probably accompanied by considerable labor force absorption. The five-year period 1910–15 shows the beginning of a slight decline in the relation of total capital to output, probably reflecting the problems which Chilean industry was subjected to with the curtailment of imports in the early part of World War I. Of course, the downward trend covers the entire period 1910 to 1938–40 in which the level decreased 0.6 per cent annually. Although this might be interpreted as a sign of greater capital productivity, the movement is too slight to make a firm judgment. Rather it would seem that the levels attained in 1910 were on a par with those registered by 1940.

Many varieties of industries and technologies were being applied and their interrelations can be highlighted with some concrete examples. Until 1892, Chilean cement production was technically backward since only natural cement was made and this was unsuitable for many construction applications. All artificial or Portland cement had to be imported. In that year, however, a variety of cement which was intermediate between natural and true Portland began to be produced by the recently formed Compañía de Cementos Naturales y Portland de la Calera.[22] This advance was far surpassed in 1904 by the Fábrica Nacional de Cemento de la Cruz established two years before which introduced real Portland cement in Chile. The change to Portland cement production represented a vast expansion of that firm's operations and won it the distinction of being the first Portland cement mill in South America. The increase in its capital investment was 57 per cent of its former total assets and the investment in machinery alone (all of which was imported) was 23 per cent.[23] In 1906, this firm became the Compañía Cemento El Melón which eventually emerged as the largest cement producer in Latin America and the fifth largest in the world. Carlos Barroilhet, a Valparaíso engineer, who was responsible for organizing the technical aspects of the enterprise, had gone to Europe to study the technology utilized there and acquire machinery from F. L. Smith & Co., a Danish firm which supplied cement factories throughout

22. Pérez Canto, *La industria nacional*, pp. 25–28.
23. Fábrica Nacional de Cementos de la Cruz, *Tercera memoria correspondiente al 2° semestre de 1903.*

the world.[24] Moreover, the different industrial sectors did not function in isolation from each other and even in this early period the existence of a quasicomplete economic system was evident as linkages among the various segments of manufacturing began to appear. Founded in 1894, the Valparaíso metalworking firm of Momus Breynat y Cía. produced not only 6,000 pieces of household ironware goods per day but exerted most of its effort in supplying industry and commerce with containers. In 1905, this firm became the Fábrica Nacional de Envases y Enlozados with an initial capital of 1 million pesos. Business developed so well that in 1909, it purchased a glazed-ironware factory, La Esmaltadora Chilena in Santiago, and then greatly expanded its entire product line for both industry and the home.[25]

A firmer basis for interindustry linkages was also evolving in a number of areas. The sugar industry provides a good example. As the industry began to expand in the 1890s, most of the raw sugar was imported from Perú on the Chilean shipping line, the Compañía Sud-Americana de Vapores. Most of the fuel came from the southern coal mines near Concepción, and great quantities of heavy-grade paper for sacks as well as wood and nails for boxes were forthcoming from Chilean enterprises. Examples of forward linkages were also present. As by-products, the refineries produced a variety of goods including alcohol, acids, sweets, and even shoe polish. For these products which often served as inputs for other industries, bottles and tins were required from domestic firms.[26] In 1904, an impressive list was compiled of firms which depended upon the supply of domestically refined sugar for their production. It included thirty-six factories located throughout Chile from Iquique

24. "Estatutos de la Compañía de Cemento El Melón," *Diario Oficial*, August 14, 1906, p. 2,857, and Compañía Cemento El Melón, *Memorias*, various years, but especially those for 1925 and 1967. The latter contains a short history of the firm. Also see United States, Department of Commerce, *Investment in Chile*, p. 155.

25. See Fábrica Nacional de Envases y Enlozados, *Memoria, Balance y Estatutos*. This firm formed the base for two of the most important metalworking enterprises of Chile, FEMSA and the Fábrica de Envases, which dominated their respective markets. A similar case is that of MADEMSA, another of Chile's most important consumer durable producers. Its origin may be traced to 1890 although the real "take-off" period came in 1914–24. See Memoranda of the Santiago Stock Exchange on FENSA dated September 30, 1963 and on MADEMSA dated November 14, 1956 in "Estudio sobre sociedades anónimas con motivo de los setenta años de la bolsa de comercio" (manuscript), vol. 4, ABCS.

26. Jorge Hormann, "Las refinerías de azúcar."

to Valdivia, employing a total of 1,462 manual laborers.[27] Thus, in one fashion or another, by the beginning of the century the sugar industry was closely related to a host of others: "oil, footwear, paper and cardboard, beer, cigarettes, chocolate, soft drinks, food processing, galvanized iron, biscuits, knitwear, soap, liquor, furniture, straw hats, and candle manufacturing."[28]

The beer industry also gave impetus to other product areas: glassware, boxes, bottle caps, caldrons, and other metallic products, to name a few. Some of the factories which made these articles depended almost entirely on the beer industry. The paper factories of Puente Alto and Talca supplied their output almost exclusively to other factories. Backward effects were spurred by the wine producers who relied on the production of the local foundry Raab, Bellet y Cía. for 90 per cent of all the machines used by them from the beginning of the century.[29]

Most characteristic of the industrialization process in underdeveloped economies is that it evolves in accord with production systems which are already known. Technology, machines, and other inputs are all imported directly from the industrialized countries. Albert Hirschman comments, in contrasting the meaning of industrialization for advanced and less developed nations, "This fact is so well known and seemingly inevitable, that it has not received all the attention it merits. It is the fundamental reason why the process of import-substituting industrialization is much more uniform, provokes much less disorganization but at the same time is less intensive in apprenticeship, than was the industrialization of Europe, North America and Japan."[30] Without entering into detail regarding the relative merits and inconveniences of such a process, he does indicate that the industrialization process of Latin America at the beginning only consisted of imitating and importing proven techniques which gave known results. Although the advanced countries

27. Report of the SFF to Ernesto Hubner, Minister of Hacienda, November 2, 1904, Archivo Nacional, Ministerio de Hacienda (hereafter referred to as ANMH), vol. 3,593. At this time the two largest sugar refineries, Viña del Mar and Penco, were also sizeable employers, engaging 1,522 manual laborers between them.

28. Hormann, "Las refinerías."

29. Angel Vicuña Pérez, *Proteccionismo aplicado a la industria chilena*, p. 24; Jorge Hormann, "Efectos de la ley de impuestos de 23 de diciembre de 1897"; Pedro Luis González, ed., *El esfuerzo nacional, estudios de política industrial*, p. 191.

30. Hirschman, "The Political Economy of Import-Substituting Industrialization in Latin America," p. 7.

also began their industrialization primarily on the base of light consumer goods, they were already producing their own capital equipment, if only in an artisan fashion, and, more important, were experimenting to find techniques adequate for their needs. Latin America, in general, did not.

From the late nineteenth century, Chile has evidenced this characteristic in a number of industries. Its manufacturers traveled frequently to Europe and the United States anxious to learn modern techniques, to discover new products which might be amenable to the emerging middle-class market, to find out what machinery was available, and to import required inputs including technicians and in certain cases even skilled workers. The *Boletín* of the SFF is filled with countless examples of this phenomenon and a substantial portion of each issue was dedicated to informing its readers of the latest techniques and equipment to be found in Europe and the United States. Of the 1,052 patent rights for industry registered from 1840 to 1899, over 43 per cent correspond only to the years 1890–99.[31] These were not processes developed by Chileans but were rather brought over by men who intended to use them in their own factories or, as agents for foreign firms, simply wished to have the exclusive representation of a technique or machine in Chile and at a later date lease or sell their rights to others who actually wanted to employ the process specified in the Chilean patent.

The flour-milling industry, one of the most important of the country, especially benefited from imported technology at the end of the last century. Until then, the Chilean mills had not changed their techniques since the middle of the nineteenth century, in spite of the fact that considerable advances had been made in the industrialized nations. Under the impulse of the SFF, however, which organized an exhibition of the latest techniques and machines in 1890 with imported materials, the milling industry underwent considerable technological revamping. A period of transformation then began as the old stone mills previously used gave way to improved purifiers and the roller process of milling flour which employed a mechanized metal cylinder system often run by electric power. A major advantage of the new roller mills rested in their capacity to grind properly the hard winter wheat which produced superior flour. Almost all of the new milling equipment was brought over from Europe and installed by such major European-based trading

31. Chile, Oficina Central de Estadística, *Anuario estadístico, 1909,* 3:506–7.

houses as D. Corbeaux y Cía., A. Goubet, Gunther y Cía., and Breyman y Hubner. By 1904, over 35 roller mills were operating in Chile and the trend was for the other 115 mills of sufficient size to transform their operation as soon as possible.[32]

The rapid development of the beer industry during the decade following 1880 has been linked by contemporary observers to the transplantation of the latest European technology to the Chilean breweries. Application of the findings of Louis Pasteur and the importation of equipment for new production systems improved the quality of Chilean beer, making it more competitive with imports and increasing domestic productive capacity. One of the principal breweries, that of Gubler and Cousiño, established in 1886, applied all the latest techniques with an initial investment of 3 million pesos, with the rest of the major Chilean producers soon following their lead. The result was that imported beer was soon supplanted by Chilean brews, although it must be admitted that higher duty levels for beer after 1878, while not prohibitive, certainly gave the Chilean producers an edge over the imported product in price.[33]

Examples of imported technology in other industries may be found in the Talca match factory of Oehninger, Fernández y Cía. Established in 1902, it was the largest match producer and from the outset employed the production techniques of the Swedish match consortium, Svenska Tändsticks Aktiebolaget.[34] The Sociedad "Fundición de Chile," the principal producer of locomotives and bridges, employed technicians contracted directly in England from whom it also imported all of its raw materials with the exception of fuel. The first blast furnace for the production of steel in Chile was installed by this firm (successors to Lever Murphy y Cía., 1903), which also had the distinction of constructing Locomotive No. 126, the "José Manuel Balmaceda" in 1887, a 22-ton engine, reported to be the first produced by a private enterprise in South America.[35] To meet its contractual obligations with the government

32. Sociedad de Fomento Fabril, *BSFF* 7 (1890), passim; SFF, *Memoria que la Sociedad de Fomento Fabril presenta sobre el concurso de molinería*; Laso, *Catálogo*, p. xxiii; González, *La sociedad*, p. 13.

33. In 1887, with a productive capacity of 5 million liters, the Gubler and Cousiño brewery produced 1.5 million liters of beer; eight years later in 1895, they were producing 9 million liters and had increased their installed capacity to 15 million liters. For contemporary accounts see Pérez Canto, *La industria*, p. 35, and Martínez, *Industrias*, p. 186.

34. *Chile industrial y comercial* 3 (May 15, 1911):17.

35. *BSFF* 22 (November 1905):44–48; Sociedad de Maestranzas y Galvanización, *Album de Caleta Abarca*, p. iii.

for locomotives and bridges, it entered into association with the internationally known French metallurgical firm Schneider y Cía. of Creusot which extended technical assistance to the Chilean firm. In Antofagasta, the foundry of Orchard Hnos. supplied the medium-sized nitrate *oficinas* with a considerable amount of their equipment. A major advance was made by this enterprise in 1911 when their steel-producing section began to operate with a Bessemer steel converter recently acquired from England. The furnace was not particularly large but could forge steel pieces up to three tons in weight.

The textile industry was yet another which relied heavily upon borrowed technology, foreign technicians, imported machines, and raw materials. Until the 1920s, its development was not exceptional and a detailed breakdown of its products reveals that a good portion of them were final consumption items, such as ponchos, blankets, shawls, and knitwear rather than intermediate products to be used in the clothing industry. In 1910, of the fifteen textile factories existent in the country, only one, that of Brusadelli y Fumagalli y Cía., had its own spindles to produce yarn. Moreover, this enterprise was one of the small producers. Thus, Chile found itself in the strange position of exporting wool but importing woolen yarn. The phenomenon may be explained by the identity of the major investors in the textile industry and by certain characteristics on the supply side which made it more profitable to import semifinished goods rather than to make large capital investments for a completely integrated production process. For the most part the major investors in this industry were the merchants and trading houses of Valparaíso. Knowledge of market conditions, foreign contacts, and easy access to credit assisted in establishing an industry in which quicker return with fewer risks could be had from putting the finishing touches on imported materials than by investing in spinning machinery under circumstances in which, at the very least, bulk cotton and certain grades of wool not produced in Chile would have have had to be imported in any event.[36]

In connection with Gerschenkron's third condition, that of a structured urban labor force suitable for factory work, there is sufficient

36. Sociedad de Fomento Fabril, "Monografía sobre la industria textil"; Pedro Luis González, *Chile industrial, 1920*, pp. 24, 104; "Fábricas de tejidos de algodón." Oscar Muñoz believes that the relative underdevelopment of the textile industry was related to the low costs of importing intermediate materials, a situation which did not stimulate investment for the production of yarn (*Crecimiento*, pp. 56, 62).

evidence to demonstrate the existence of an industrial proletariat by World War I. Industrial employment was significant; Luis Galdames reported that this sector absorbed over 75,000 workers in 1909. On the other hand, Ballesteros and Davis estimate that 17.6 per cent of the labor force was engaged in industry and construction by 1907.[37] In 1909, the Gran Federación Obrera was founded as, throughout the country, labor organized itself according to the branch of industrial activity to which it pertained. Under the leadership of Luis Emilio Recabarren, the Gran Federación soon became the nationwide Federación Obrera de Chile (founded in 1916). It was also Recabarren who founded the Socialist Labor Party in 1912 in his determination to transform organized labor into an effective instrument for political action.

The final component of the background to industrialization is that of the state of tension created by the awareness of the incongruence between the actual exploitation of economic forces and the potential that could be extracted from them through industrialization. Identification of this condition in Chile prior to World War I may be had by way of certain publications of the era, the organization of and participation in industrial exhibitions both in Chile and abroad, and the founding of the Sociedad de Fomento Fabril and its activities from 1883.

Several good accounts of the deep concern which existed due to Chile's failure to enter more intensely into manufacturing may be found at the beginning of the 1880s. The first of these was prepared by an important figure in Chilean bureaucracy, Ramón Espech, who was appointed director of the state-owned military clothing factory near Santiago in 1880. Three years later, his work, *La industria fabril en Chile*, was published. It had been commissioned by the government of President Domingo Santa María, who wished to "stimulate industrial activity and develop a group consciousness among manufacturers" and to call the attention of the public to the composition of "imports and exports, the relation of consumption and primary and industrial production in order to determine the approximate proportion which manufacturing contributes to the public wealth of the nation."[38]

Another study done at the request of the Chilean government was by Louis Dorte in 1884. At the same time that he exhorted

37. Galdames, *Geografía*, p. 206; Ballesteros and Davis, "Growth," p. 176.

38. Letter from Pedro Lucio Cuadra, Minister of Hacienda, to the President of the Sociedad Nacional de Agricultura, published in *BSFF* 1 (January 1884):5.

European entrepreneurs, technicians, and skilled workers to establish themselves in Chile, Dorte identified the stumbling blocks to industrial development which must be overcome. Among these, aside from the insufficient numbers of experienced workers, he pointed to the need for a closer integration of the entire economy, between primary sectors and manufacturing, and the necessity of protectionist measures by the state. Finally, the classic essay by Francisco Encina, first published in 1911, must be considered as one of the most important examples of publications which lashed out at public opinion in an attempt to stimulate those changes in the Chilean value system and educational structure which would lead to greater industrial activity in the country.[39]

Perhaps the clearest indication that significant segments of Chilean society believed that the economic future of Chile ought to be increasingly linked to industrial activities was the founding of the Sociedad de Fomento Fabril in 1883. From its beginning the SFF was a multifunctional association: in part pressure group, regulator of internal industrial conflicts, technical service organization, and social club. It represented the institutionalization of Chile's industrial sector into a cohesive nucleus that was large enough to effectively maintain industrial objectives before public opinion and to serve as a direct link with the government.

In the 1870s, prior to the establishment of the SFF, there were several movements, especially after 1876, to organize those people engaged in manufacturing. But these were not of the same intensity as that which stimulated the founding of the SFF. Earlier associations were marked by vacillations and interruptions. Although a handful of industrialists were present in the founding of such organizations as the Sociedad Industrial de Santiago or that of Valparaíso in 1877, these groupings were overwhelmingly dominated by artisan interests.[40]

From the outset the SFF was closely linked to the state through whose initiative it was convoked and from which it received an annual subsidy. This was not unusual, since both the other two economic interest group organizations in existence, those for agriculture and mining, also enjoyed such assistance. But by 1889, the

39. Dorte, *El porvenir*; Encina, *Nuestra inferioridad económica.*

40. See *La industria chilena*, Santiago, 1–85 (September 11, 1875–November 17, 1877). The image of Chilean industry given by this periodical is clearly one in which industrial activity in the sense of factory enterprise was an isolated phenomenon quite distinct from the situation to be found a decade later.

SFF was receiving state funds which surpassed those of either the Sociedad Nacional de Agricultura (SNA) or the Sociedad Nacional de Minería (SNM).[41]

The first issue of the SFF's monthly *Boletín* began with an avid exhortation for the more intensive industrialization of the country.[42] Among other attributes, by its charter, the association was authorized to establish and maintain technical schools, to organize industrial exhibitions, to prepare statistical surveys of the nation's industrial plant, to promote and supervise selected immigration to Chile, to give technical assistance and advice to the government on patent registrations, to sponsor publications designed to promote industry's objectives to the public, to act as intermediary between individual industrialists and the national congress and all governmental agencies (this included the authority to formulate petitions before congress as well as the executive branch for decrees and legislation), and to prepare those reports which the government might request on issues related to the development of industry.

Documents of the period emanating from the press, congress, the SFF, and the reports of its executive council meetings indicate that the organization did indeed prove to be an aggressive force for the promotion of manufacturing interests in this early period of Chilean industrialization.[43] The SFF became a primary instrument of industrialists especially in the difficult decade 1900–1910, when there was widespread discontent over the rising cost of living and a growing antiprotectionist sentiment among the masses. It opened an industrial immigration office which was efficient in subsidizing the movement of European entrepreneurs and skilled labor to the country until the First World War. By 1908, the SFF was operat-

41. Chile, Ministerio de Industrias y Obras Públicas, *Boletín* 3 (June 1889): 197, 213. In that year the SFF received a total of 26,500 pesos from the government, the SNA 33,560 pesos, and the SNM 19,100 pesos.

42. The title of the article was "Chile puede y debe ser industrial."

43. The SFF's journal for 1884 and the following years is filled with numerous examples of the association's gestures before congress, the ministries, and various state agencies in behalf of industrial interests, both individual and collective. In 1884, the society had 305 members, of whom a third were in local councils in other cities. The editorial of *El Heraldo*, Valparaíso, August 23, 1892, summarized all of the obstacles which the SFF would have to overcome in order to increase industrial activity. Among the most important were the lack of skilled labor, the need to import capital equipment and raw material which was subjected to import duty, and insufficient tariff protection. See also Sociedad de Fomento Fabril, *Informe sobre el impuesto de internación y proyecto de reforma del mismo*. This is the first project for the complete revision of the tariff submitted to congress by the SFF.

ing industrial schools in Santiago, Valparaíso, La Serena, Talca, Chillán, Concepción, and Valdivia, with substantial funding by the government. By 1909, these institutions were training over 900 students, of whom half were registered at the technical school in Santiago.[44]

Finally, numerous industrial exhibitions were held. At the first of these organized in 1884 in cooperation with the agricultural and mining associations, the qualitative difference from the past in the attitude among industrialists was reported by one committee: "In the exhibition of 1869 there were but one or two timid national manufacturers; in that of 1875 they were explicitly invited but refused to enter in competition with foreign products. In the present one, our industrialists are present with vigor; it appears that they are now conscious of their strength and truly, they do have a variety of products of good quality to show."[45]

Following this, the national industrial exhibits were held in 1885, 1890, 1894 and 1904, and Chile participated in a series of international exhibitions in Liverpool (1886), Paris (1889), Brussels (1896), Guatemala (1897), Buffalo (1901), and Quito (1909). In Buffalo, "Chile took third place on the prize list, the two higher places having gone to the United States and Mexico."[46]

In summary, it may be concluded that during the period 1880–1914, judged by the criteria of rate of growth, product diversification, systematic linkages with its own sector, integration to the rest of the economy, and technological advance, Chilean industry experienced a considerable expansion and progress. The common belief that a real process of industrialization did not exist before the outbreak of World War I may be considered nothing more than an unsubstantiated myth. This development, however, manifested a high degree of dependence upon the fluctuations of the foreign sector. Indeed, a form of "bottleneck" theory may be reasonably sustained in which the evolution of Chilean industry was largely a function of the export trade and the capacity to import primary materials and technology. As will be seen, this characteristic of

44. Letter from Enrique Budge, president of the SFF, to Manuel Espinoza, Minister of Industry and Public Works, May 13, 1909; "Visita a las escuelas de la Sociedad de Fomento Fabril," June–August 1906; Ministerio de Industrias y Obras Públicas "Decreto N° 380," February 24, 1908; all in Ministerio de Industrias y Obras Públicas, Archivo Nacional (hereafter referred to as MIOPAN), vol. 1,356.

45. "El fallo de los jurados."

46. González, *La sociedad*, p. 15.

external dependence was projected beyond the purely economic sphere and was evident in the social dimensions of Chilean industrialization—in the identity and behavior of its industrial elite.

The Challenge of the War Years

The dependence on the foreign sector meant that a decisive moment arrived for Chilean industry with the outbreak of World War I. On one hand, interruption in the importation of consumer goods left a vacuum in supply which domestic factories were challenged to fill. At the same time national industry was threatened by the curtailment of raw material and capital goods imports. Without such inputs production would eventually falter.

It is common for authors to view the war years as the point at which to depict a new era in Chilean industrialization, but the real significance of World War I is not that clear. Ricardo Lagos, who relied heavily on the Ballesteros and Davis time series, concluded that it was impossible to evaluate the impact of the First World War on Chilean industry by means of statistics, since, lacking data for 1913–15, the figures given for all these years are the same as for 1916. For Oscar Muñoz, on the other hand, the years 1914–18 may be considered a completely independent and quite unique stage in themselves.[47] His series led him to conclude that as a result of the curtailment of competitive imports during the war years, domestic groups were driven to fill the vacuum of consumer demand. Consequently, output underwent a vigorous expansion as the economy engaged in its first massive process of import substitution.

Muñoz' series of industrial output substantiates these remarks which receive additional support from contemporary spokesmen of industry. A closer examination of the available data and other ancillary material, however, calls for more moderate enthusiasm with respect to the significance of the war to domestic manufacturing. In this connection, I call attention again to Table 9 with due regard to the qualifications which must be applied in the use of the data. The figures from 1914 to 1918 based upon Muñoz' study indicate, and he stresses, that production levels jumped by an average annual rate of growth of 9 per cent. This is truly an exceptionally high rate of expansion and contrasts sharply with the period after the war. In the year following the war, to the peak of 1924–25, the growth

47. Lagos, *La industria*, p. 32; Muñoz, *Crecimiento*, p. 40.

rate averaged approximately 3 per cent per year. Yet the most probable trend indicated in Table 9 would suggest first a slump and then, only in 1917, a return to prewar production levels.

Although Muñoz' observations are technically correct, they are drawn somewhat out of context. I explain in Appendix 2 how changes in the preparation of the 1914 statistics distorted that year's reporting. The Chilean Bureau of Statistics itself admitted to sizeable omissions that year.[48] In addition, Chilean foreign trade, both exports and imports, dropped sharply in 1914–15 as a result of the rupture in international commerce caused by the outbreak of the war. From 1912–13 to 1914–15, total exports declined by 25 per cent and total imports by 35 per cent. Of great importance, however, was the fall in raw and intermediate material imports which declined by 41 per cent during the same period (Tables A-1, A-2). This event is treated casually by Muñoz who assigns little significance to the shortage of imported primary materials and capital goods for domestic industry.

We have already seen, however, that constrictions in the capacity to import implied a significant bottleneck for Chile's industrial output. This is also mentioned by the firms themselves in their annual reports to the stockholders as a key element in low production levels or difficulties in maintaining output during 1914–16.[49] Pedro Luis González, secretary of the SFF, summarized the effects of the early part of the war: paralysis of foreign trade, acute maritime shipping shortages, suspension of activities in the nitrate fields and other mining areas, contraction of industrial and agricultural activities, the virtual closing of bank lines of credit, a rapid fall in stock prices, and a rise in the price of food products, all of which lead "to general misery in the lives of all workers."[50]

This should not be construed to mean that the suspension of imported consumer goods was not beneficial to domestic output. By 1916, exports had risen substantially and the importation of materials for input into Chilean industry met their prewar levels in

48. See p. 173.

49. See Fábrica Nacional de Envases y Enlozados, *Memorias*, 1914–16; Compañía Chilena de Fósforos, *Memorias*, 1917–18. The Compañía de Refinería de Azúcar passed through a monetary crisis in which the management considered closing down the factory for lack of foreign exchange with which to import crude sugar (Compañía de Refinería de Azúcar de Viña del Mar, *50 años*, p. 24). The glass factory did close during 1915 due to the foreign sector crisis and its annual reports indicate that beer production was very low in 1914–15 (Sociedad Fábrica Nacional de Vidrios, *Memorias*, 1914–15).

50. "Nuestra situación económica."

1916–17. At the same time the importation of many finished goods lagged behind; some of them were not renewed until the end of the war. This was especially true of such products as refined sugar (shipped primarily from the German port of Hamburg), oils which came from Spain and Italy, and cement.

Thus, Cemento El Melón received a great stimulus from World War I as it increased production to meet the huge orders coming from the large-scale construction of port facilities in San Antonio and Valparaíso as well as from the copper mines El Teniente and Chuquicamata.[51] Compañía Industrial, the firm which held the monopoly of vegetable oil production for industrial use, expanded its output by 70 per cent from 1915 to 1917 to meet the national market needs.[52] The Compañía Refinería de Azúcar de Viña del Mar was another example of a firm which in the later war years was able to profit from the suspension of consumer goods imports. Not only did it meet domestic consumer demand; it also exported considerable quantities of refined sugar to Argentina.[53] The Compañía Chilena de Tejidos, principal manufacturer of cotton knitwear, was able to increase its production from a total of 2.5 million pesos in 1915 to over 2 million pesos in the first semester of 1916, with even brighter prospects for the second half of the year.[54] A final example is provided by the Fábrica Nacional de Envases which was hurt initially by the war. Its situation improved during 1916, as sales increased. This favorable trend continued throughout the period until 1919, especially in the increased production of glazed ironware products for the home, to the extent that the enterprise had to expand its plant and capital equipment in order to keep pace with the flood of orders.[55]

In summary, I believe that, taken as a whole, the years of World War I were a test of Chilean industry. Not only was domestic manufacturing able to overcome the crisis of the initial years in which production levels fell, but it was even able to increase output, in the later years regaining the levels of prewar years and then surpassing them. This performance was in response to the requirements

51. R. Benavides, ed., *Anuario general de Chile, 1919*, p. x.

52. "La reforma del arancel aduanero," p. 81.

53. Compañía de Refinería de Azúcar de Viña del Mar, *Memorias*, 1915–18; *50 años*, p. 24.

54. Letter from G. Corradi, President of G. Corradi y Cía. (later known as Compañía Chilena de Tejidos), to the SFF, August 25, 1916, published in *BSFF* 33 (July 1916):585–86.

55. Fábrica Nacional de Envases y Enlozados, *Memorias*, 1915–19.

of internal demand. It was an important moment during which Chilean industry proved itself capable of large-scale import substitution and demonstrated maturity in its ability to meet the market pressures exerted upon it. Nevertheless, industry's rate of growth should be viewed in a wider perspective, with what went before and that which was to come. Within this framework, the period 1914–18 may not be considered as a completely independent and unique stage in Chile's industrialization process. An interpretation more in keeping with all available evidence indicates that it was rather a period in which previous industrial development was put to a strenuous test, which was passed, and enjoyed favorable, if not entirely spectacular, growth.

3. Industrial Growth and the Failure To Provide a "Growth Pole"

AFTER the war, the Chilean economy experienced a sustained period of economic crisis. Exports declined in 1919 by more than half of what they had been the year before. Previous levels were regained in 1920, and Chilean economic experts such as Daniel Martner, Minister of Hacienda, believed that the crisis had ended.[1] Developments proved them to be mistaken; that very year saw the beginning of a worldwide economic depression which was to last well into 1922. Chilean industrial production was affected by these years of economic decline. Total output stagnated between 1918 and 1919, fell during 1920–22, and only showed a strong comeback in 1923, to reach a peak in the economic boom of 1924–25. The following year Chile was beset by another recession. Only after 1927 did industrial activity rise following the final export surge of the decade.[2] This cycle of industrial expansion ended with the beginning of the Great Depression and, in timing, lagged just behind the 1930 fall in the export market. Nevertheless, the overall trend of

1. Daniel Martner, *Estudio de política comercial chilena e historia económica nacional*, 2:655.
2. Sociedad de Fomento Fabril, "Memorias," 1926–30, *BSFF* 24–28 (1927–31).

industry for the decade beginning in 1920 was quite acceptable; aggregate average growth rates of 4.3 per cent annually were registered in the interim 1920–21 to 1929–30.

Table 12 shows the structure of industrial production in 1917 and 1927 by type of product. In both years the overwhelming bulk of the manufacturing plant was engaged in the production of basic items of daily consumption. Food, beverages, tobacco, clothing, and footwear accounted for 72.9 per cent of the total production in 1917

TABLE 12

SECTORAL DISTRIBUTION OF INDUSTRIAL PRODUCTION 1917 AND 1927

	1917		1927	
Sector	Value[a]	Percentage	Value[a]	Percentage
Food	7,192	44.3	8,420	43.6
Beverages	846	5.2	901	4.7
Tobacco	777	4.8	896	4.6
Textiles	760	4.7	1,221	6.3
Clothing, footwear	3,035	18.7	3,302	17.1
Wood, wood products	1,065	6.5	1,044	5.4
Paper, printing	476	2.9	450	2.3
Leather, rubber products	783	4.8	819	4.3
Chemical products	389	2.4	528	2.7
Nonmetallic mineral products, construction materials	302	1.9	257	1.3
Metallic products	625	3.8	1,491	7.7
Total	16,250	100.0	19,329	100.0

SOURCE: Calculated from Muñoz, *Crecimiento*, Table II-2.2.
a. Expressed in thousands of 1950 escudos.

and 69.9 per cent in 1927. The next largest sectors in 1917 were wood and wood products and leather and rubber products (principally the latter).

In both years the great differences between the textile and clothing industries are of interest. Even if footwear were excluded, the clothing industry would continue to be much larger. This disparity reflects the high degree of dependence of the clothing sector on imported textiles. The low level of development of the domestic textile industry is even more evident when it is recalled that a good portion of the products turned out by the firms in this sector were more properly finished items, even apparel, rather than intermediate goods.[3] In all likelihood this situation lasted so long because of the success of industrialists in both sectors in importing their raw and intermediate materials without having to make larger capital investments in spinning mills and infrastructure which would probably have incurred much longer gestation periods for capital return.

As a whole, however, the textile sector was not stagnant if viewed merely from the perspective of the growth rate of production and not its composition or impact on other areas of the economy. During the ten-year period 1917–27, textiles averaged a 4.9 per cent annual rate of growth which must be considered very satisfactory. (The rate of growth for total industrial production was only 1.8 per cent for the same period.)

A notable change occurred in the metal industry. From 1917 to 1927 its average growth rate was 9.1 per cent per year, and its share in aggregate industrial output doubled from 3.8 per cent in 1917 to 7.7 per cent in 1927, making it the fastest growing sector in all industry. But once again what was produced rather than how much is the interesting question. A breakdown of this sector reveals that it was mainly producing consumer durables rather than capital goods. Over 50 per cent of the production in 1928 can be identified as pertaining to the former category. The other half represents the production of foundries, some metal-working establishments, and shipyards, in whose total production were also to be found a wide variety of products which could not really be considered producer goods.[4]

In many ways more could have been expected from this sector. The local foundries and metal-working plants had proved their worth in the War of the Pacific in a variety of articles they produced for government, industry, and other sectors of the economy. Given sufficient demand from both public and private clients and stimulated by some initial protection, the development of a healthy capital goods sector able to produce many instruments of production for small- and medium-sized mining concerns, construction, agriculture, transport and even for manufacturing itself would not have been an exaggerated goal.

More important, it would not have been unreasonable to expect

3. See p. 40. The sources in the footnote make this quite clear. The letter of G. Corradi to the SFF of August 25, 1916, cited before, shows that almost the entire production of the Compañía Chilena de Tejidos (then G. Corradi y Cía.) was composed of such knitwear as socks, stockings, and underwear.

4. Chile, Oficina Central de Estadística, *Censo de la industria manufacturera y del comercio de 1928*, pp. 56–58.

that basic industry would have been able to evolve in such fashion as to generate a self-sustaining process of expansion with high levels of productivity and modernization in accord with the needs of domestic conditions which would have helped to transform other sectors of the economy. After all, this is what industry was expected to do and is at the heart of the traditional structuralist argument for lessening poverty and eradicating underdevelopment through industrialization.[5]

Nevertheless, this did not occur. Industry as a whole, and heavy industry in particular, were "inward oriented" to the domestic market; the function which overcame all others was to provision the final consumer. The vast majority of industrialists, producers of light consumer goods, opposed protection to basic industry, feeling that it would increase their production costs and provide them with goods whose worth was unproven. The firms which attempted to turn out producer equipment had to operate on a made-to-order basis to meet the specialized and generally sporadic orders which they received. Only for a short time between 1910 and World War I did orders come more consistently to the handful of producers in heavy industry who were not thinking only in terms of supplying the requirements of consumer durables demanded by the expanding urban middle-class market.

The heavy industry sector failed to have a significant impact upon the rest of industry or the economy as a whole. Despite high rates of growth, its development did not provide sufficient stimulus with which to increase and retool the overall productive structure. In great part this was due to the government policies toward heavy industry which, in turn, were conditioned by the particular characteristics of the formation of Chile's economic elite, especially with respect to such matters as the type of industry in which they engaged and their attitude toward the problems of acceptable risk and gestation periods of capital. These issues will be dealt with in greater detail later on. For the moment it is sufficient to look at several aspects of the long-run development of Chilean heavy industry.

The high rates of growth attained in this sector were noted. But

5. A vast body of literature exists which, expecting the industrialization of Latin America to provide the same framework for progress as it did in the developed nations, envisions industry as the key to development in the region. See, for example, Carlos Keller, *La eterna crisis chilena*, pp. 90–103; Naciones Unidas, Comisión Económica para América Latina, *América Latina, el pensamiento de la CEPAL.*

only in these terms may the metallurgical industry be considered to have been dynamic. Throughout the entire period from World War I to the beginning of the decade of the sixties, productivity gains were meager, below that of the average for manufacturing as a whole and even lower than the so-called traditional industries such as food and beverages.[6] This sector did not undergo sufficient changes to become modern and very capital intensive. At the end of the nineteenth century, the heavy equipment industry started to produce machinery for mining, but the venture aborted. As mining activities became more complex due to the exploitation of low-grade ores by large foreign companies, domestic industry could not keep pace with the need for more advanced equipment.[7] On the other hand, small- and medium-sized mining declined rapidly from around 1910 to World War II, in great part due to a lack of technological innovations—developments which could have come from domestic industry.[8] Similarly, domestic industry did little to contribute to a transformation of agricultural production methods or to increase mechanization beyond the plows and threshing machines which were turned out by a couple of local producers.

From the first proposals to establish an iron industry in Chile in the 1890s to the final implantation in 1926 of the government-controlled steel mill, the Compañía Electro-Siderúrgica e Industrial, all efforts to establish basic industry of the type that would be modernizing as well as modern were based on the actions of foreign firms or the state.[9] The case history of the Compañía

6. Muñoz, *Crecimiento*, pp. 61–62.

7. The bulk of this production, however, apparently came from only a handful of foundries: Lever Murphy, Balfour Lyon, Hardie y Cía., Strickler and Kupfer's Fundición Libertad, that of Tomas Stillman, the Fundición Orchard Hnos., Raab Rochette, and the Klein brothers' foundry. These account for the greatest part of heavy industrial production. For a short time during World War I, the Fundición "Las Rosas" of Raab Bellet y Cía. produced articles which had always been imported, such as converters for refining copper, cement mixers, and machines for the tanning industry. But this did not last far beyond the end of the war. See Martinez, *Industrias*, p. 11; Benavides, *Anuario*, p. 189; Pérez Canto, *La industria*, p. 13; "Progreso industrial"; "Fundición Libertad de Strickler y Küpfer."

8. González, *El esfuerzo*, pp. 109, 114–15; M. Carmagnani, *Sviluppo Industriale e Sottosviluppo Economico*, pp. 72–85. On the decline of small- and medium-sized copper mining, see Clark Reynolds, "Development Problems of an Export Economy: The Case of Chile and Copper," in Markos Mamalakis and Clark Reynolds, *Essays on the Chilean Economy*, pp. 214–27.

9. Consejo Ejecutivo de la Sociedad de Fomento Fabril, Acta de 13 de noviembre de 1891, "Libro de actas," ASFF; Carlos Sánchez Hurtado, *Evolución histórica de la industria siderúrgica chilena e ibero-americana*, pp. 121–22; "Ley

Electro-Metalúrgica (ELECMETAL), is quite representative of the course taken by those firms in heavy industry which might have provided—but in fact did not provide—a basic industrial structure in Chile capable of sustaining a truly autochthonous process of technological development and self-sustained capability to transform other industries and areas of the economy.

The enterprise was founded in 1917 by a small group of private investors with a modest capital commitment of 750,000 pesos.[10] Formation of this enterprise had been motivated by the curtailment of steel imports during the war. Its board of directors was composed of both native Chileans and European immigrants, all of enormous wealth which had been earned in successful ventures in commerce, mining, agriculture, banking, and industry. The stated object of the firm was to manufacture finished steel products and machinery for industry, mining, construction, and transport. Remy Cordoen, a French engineer, originally conceived the possibility of such an undertaking in Chile and, after forming a corporation with a group of friends, went to the United States to learn the technical aspects of the electric steel furnaces used there.

The enterprise was an immediate success. By 1919, the company's annual report informed its shareholders of its ability to compete quite favorably with foreign products in the Chilean market. Three years later, the plant facilities were expanded and the capital investment was increased to 1.5 million pesos. This process of expansion was continued without interruption until the Great Depression, the firm showing solid financial gains year after year. By 1926, over 250 tons of steel were produced monthly, some individual pieces weighing up to five tons. From the outset, this enterprise was a very profitable venture. It had received large orders not only from the Chilean state railroads and the domestic mining industry, but was able to compete successfully in the international market, filling sizeable orders from Bolivian and Peruvian mining firms and the Peruvian state railroads. Indeed, the short gestation period required for production to begin and profits to be made in ELECMETAL

4110," *Diario Oficial*, December 12, 1926, pp. 3,574–76. This law determines the initial state control of the Valdivia steel mill. With respect to the efforts of the state and foreign firms, see below, pp. 146–51.

10. Sources for the history of ELECMETAL are Compañía Electro Metalúrgica S.A., *Estatutos*; *Memorias*, 1919–29; Juan Bennett, "La fundición de acero en el país"; memorandum from ELECMETAL to the Santiago Stock Exchange dated September 1963, Bolsa de Comercio de Santiago, "Estudios," vol. 4, ABCS.

at first seem astounding, especially in view of the common image of the primary steel industry as one in which return on capital alone is often a long-term affair.

But ELECMETAL's management had skillfully avoided this problem. It was able to do so by concentrating the firm's production on filling the orders of only simple, uncomplicated products for a relatively small number of customers. A few spare parts, grinding bars, steel bars, and light shapes were the extent of the product line for mining and the Chilean state railroads. The latter was an important and assured customer since, as the 1920s advanced, governmental policy required that all public sector orders be placed with Chilean firms whenever possible, at the same time limiting variety of railroad equipment to the immediate production capacity of ELECMETAL's imported equipment. Simple products for the nitrate fields and copper mining operations could be supplied with the same ease. The company did not exploit its own iron mines, nor did it attempt to expand into other markets or to develop new product lines. Rather, its owners were satisfied to corner a relatively narrow market and exert a monopoly therein. No innovation which might affect the techniques applied in industry or in other sectors was ever to come from ELECMETAL. All of its major technological needs and capital goods were imported with no substantial modifications introduced. For the immediate goals of its investors which rested essentially on quick profits and low risk, ELECMETAL was a success; for the part of the Chilean economy which was in need of modernizing, as well as its already modern industry, the achievements of enterprises such as ELECMETAL are dubious.

In the area of electric power installations, related machinery, and equipment, Chilean entrepreneurs were not to be found at all. This sector was completely controlled from outside the country. In 1907, Siemens-Schuckert Ltd. (Chile), subsidiary of the world's largest producers of electrical machines and equipment, was founded in Santiago with offices in Valparaíso, Concepción, and Antofagasta. By 1913, approximately 80 per cent of all the electric power installations in Chile came from this multinational organization, and the remainder was also produced by firms of foreign origin. Siemens imported all the component parts and maintained only an assembly operation in Chile. It supplied the nitrate fields, the copper mines, and all public power installations.[11]

11. Approximately 80,000 persons were reportedly employed by the Siemens

To return to a point made earlier, the development of Chilean industry was almost totally dependent upon foreign technology. Production techniques were copied, machines and primary materials were imported, and, since the industrial process is a progressive one in developed countries, Chile committed itself to follow their lead in the future without ever really considering the possibility of alternative techniques, adaptation, or innovation. The failure to search for alternatives or to seek ways of adapting foreign techniques to domestic conditions exacts a price not evident for many years, when the reliance on determined suppliers of technology and production systems has become institutionalized. As the progress of industrial techniques in the more advanced countries responds to the changing conditions of their own factor markets with a tendency to relatively scarce, costly labor and inexpensive capital, industry in underdeveloped countries follows the same patterns crystalized long before by entrepreneurial habits and governmental policy decisions vigorously supported by special interest groups seeking to maintain their established production systems and captive internal markets.[12] In the long run, change becomes costly for producers and so their industries behave in conformity with the imported technological matrix rather than in response to the capital-scarce, labor-surplus economy which characterizes their country. This implies costly capital subsidies which burden the nation with an industrial sector incapable of absorbing a rapidly growing labor force and a product mix oriented to only a privileged sector of the population. Chile's problem was not really that of depending on the accumulated expertise and ongoing dynamism of European and American industry but rather its failure to accommodate this package of knowledge to its own needs, to master this dependence and make it a tool of its own development.

Serious concern over this aspect of Chilean industrialization was expressed by such highly regarded essayists as Tancredo Pinochet Le-Brun and Carlos Keller. In 1931, Keller wrote: "The very same spirit of the conquistador which predominates in Chilean capitalism explains why we will never dominate modern technology. Needless to say, this was not created in this continent. We have

---

group in 244 offices, agencies, and factories throughout the world. This was almost equal the number of workers in all of Chilean manufacturing including artisan operations (Salvador Soto Rojas, *Crónicas chilenas*, pp. 214–16).

12. It should be noted that in recent years Chilean as well as Latin American industry in general has often been criticized on these counts.

adopted it through simple imitation, without sharing in its spirit, applying only the results of procedures invented in other nations. Among us there is no precision, no desire to innovate and improve. In all this there is much improvisation, dull headedness and neglect. After all, it is so simple to apply modern technology in an imitative fashion. No overwhelming obstacles exist to impede us from utilizing it, acquiring machines, tools and patent rights as well as contracting foreign technicians as in reality we have done. The imitative manner which fundamentally characterized our being explains the great contrasts of superimposed economic systems: concrete highways alongside almost impassable trails, huge mining enterprises and small operations, etc."[13]

The mentality of Chilean investors and industrialists was such that, while seeking out those investments which would bring high rates of return in a short period, they avoided those ventures with prolonged gestation periods.[14] The reason for this must be sought in the traditional value system which governed the motives of the Chilean oligarchy. No real industrial consciousness emerged nor did an entrepreneurial bourgeois spirit develop, because the dominant value system remained that of the traditional rural society which continued to mold the Chilean elite.[15] As we shall see, landownership prevailed in the Chilean hierarchy of values well into the twentieth century and even the national money market was based upon the institutions of a rural society. Earnings from the urban or mining sectors were diverted to a traditional countryside through the purchase of rural property, and fortunes were directed to the construction of imposing mansions and other forms of conspicuous consumption instead of being channeled toward the creation of an industrial "growth pole." Thus, for investment, light consumer goods or nondevelopmental heavy industry were preferred to other areas which involved more risk and no significant gains in the short run. In such fashion, country estates could be acquired, town houses built, trips to Europe made, and in general

13. Pinochet Le-Brun, *La conquista de Chile en el siglo XX*; Keller, *La eterna crisis*, p. 106.

14. Keller, *La eterna crisis*, pp. 113–14.

15. Arnold Bauer has given us exceptional insight into the importance of the rural sector in setting the social tone of Chile until at least the 1920s in his recent study, *Chilean Rural Society from the Spanish Conquest to 1930*. The most recent portrayal by a Chilean of the dominance of the aristocratic tradition is provided by Julio Heise González, *Historia de Chile, el período parlamentario 1861–1925*, pp. 162–72.

the life style maintained which has branded the oligarchy as the *clase derrochadora* ("squandering class"). Nor was capital ever so scarce as might be believed. The fabled Chilean "economic imperialism" in Bolivia is indicative of that. In 1920, Santiago Machiavello wrote that Chilean capital invested in the high-yield tin mines of Bolivia was then worth $100 million. Apart from Bolivian mining, he added that substantial sums of Chilean capital were also invested in Argentine cattle raising.[16]

Industrial Credit in a Traditional Society

Knowledge of the operation of the money market is of some importance since its characteristics affect the course of industrial growth, determine the identity of the entrepreneurs, and condition the relationship between industry and other sectors of the economy. Industrialists generally have several alternatives from which to choose in order to finance their ventures. New partners may be taken on or, if the firm is a corporation, additional stock may be issued to obtain increased capital. The increment in funds achieved by such measures, however, diminishes the ownership and weakens the control of the enterprise which the former owners enjoyed. In addition, this course of action is not useful for solving the many instances when short-term credit is quickly needed. The availability of credit is obviously essential for the progress of any enterprise.

In Chile many aspects of modern capitalistic organization had made their appearance before the end of the nineteenth century. Commercial and mortgage banking institutions were numerous, stock exchanges listed in Santiago and Valparaíso, and the commercial houses provided credit for the firms whose products they distributed, thereby extending to industry the position of banker that they had traditionally occupied with respect to Chilean agriculture.[17] From 1869 to 1903, banking capital expanded at an an-

16. Macchiavello also referred to an article in *El Mercurio*, Santiago, December 1, 1918, which quotes Kenneth Braden as stating that the copper-mining industry was not the type of business for Chileans. Braden reasoned that although at the beginning they had acquired shares in the El Teniente and Potrerillos operations, the Chileans rid themselves of the stock when the dividends were not soon forthcoming, to search for investments in which return on capital would not take several years. See Santiago Macchiavello Varas, *El problema de la industria del cobre y sus proyecciones económicas y sociales*, pp. 106–10.

17. For the importance of the merchants of Santiago and Valparaíso as primary sources of credit to agriculture, see Bauer, "Expansión," pp. 188–91.

nual rate of 3.5 per cent.[18] Nevertheless, money was not readily available for industrial ventures. In a country where capital was at a premium and credit was commonly used to enhance the life style of the individual rather than being put to productive use, the mere appearance of modern capitalistic institutions did not mean that in fact a fluid, developed capital market existed.[19] This resulted from the elitist nature of the money market, which limited access to the very few and which had shortcomings of an institutional nature reflected by a certain backwardness of the capitalistic structure in Chile. The institutional failings stemmed from the nature of the society in which the money market developed. Given the fact that banks, corporations, and a complete body of commercial legislation existed after mid-nineteenth century, and the fact of close contact between Chile and the centers of Western capitalism, the somewhat primitive nature of the organized credit system is curious unless we recall that it arose in a traditional rural society, in which land was valued over machines which were subject to depreciation and, in any case, were not as liquid as rural property in case of default.

The money market was in fact based essentially on institutions such as the Caja de Crédito Hipotecario established after mid-nineteenth century to meet the credit needs of landowners, and in a rural society land offered one of the best guarantees for loans. Thus entrepreneurs were compelled to seek financing in a system in which credit could not be obtained from a bank other than in the form of a mortgage.[20] Instruments commonplace elsewhere—discount operations, secured loans, and lines of credit in their different varieties—simply did not exist. Furthermore, most of the mortgage loans could usually be obtained only from such institutions as the Caja de Crédito Hipotecario or private mortgage banks since for the most part commercial banks did not maintain large mortgage operations.

The principal difficulty with mortgage operations was that the

18. Hurtado, *Concentración*, p. 75.

19. Bauer provides both a concise summary of the abundant literature on the squandering nature of the oligarchy and fresh evidence of the unproductive uses to which credit granted to landowners was commonly put (*Chilean Rural Society*, chap. 4). A particularly vivid account of the oligarchy's life style after the War of the Pacific is to be found in Heise, *Historia*, pp. 164 ff.

20. Consejo Directivo de la Sociedad de Fomento Fabril, Acta de 13 de septiembre de 1889, "Libro de Actas," ASFF; Santiago Macchiavello Varas, *Política económica nacional*, 1:135; Laso, *Catálogo*, p. x.

loans could not be secured by equipment, machinery, or inventory. Only real estate was acceptable collateral. This severely limited the number of people who could have access to credit. The proprietors of small- and medium-sized industries generally could not have recourse to this credit mechanism since the value of the land and buildings of their factories was usually insufficient or already mortgaged.[21] Thus, unless the industrialist also had landholdings or mining interests which could be mortgaged, he could not qualify for this important source of credit. Only those who had accumulated such tangible forms of wealth could obtain substantial credit or could themselves provide the necessary funding directly to an industrial enterprise. The latter practice was not at all uncommon but occurred almost only when the creditor participated directly in the ownership of the firms.[22]

In the United States, insurance companies were primary sources of credit for corporations. But in Chile the large insurance companies such as La Chilena, La Pacífica, and La Estrella, which all combined with others in 1905 to form the vast insurance complex La Chilena Consolidada, did not invest in industry or lend funds but rather chose to place their capital in commercial and mortgage bank bonds.[23]

The situation did not change substantially until the very end of the 1920s when certain institutional adjustments were made. One of the most important of these was the law of 1929 which institutionalized and regulated the practice of debenture issues on the part of corporations and limited liability companies.[24] Until this time every time that a firm wished to float this type of bond issue, congressional legislation was required, a time-consuming and cumbersome affair. From then on, however, bond issues became a normal part of the credit structure and were placed under the general supervision of the state.[25] Yet, this basic component of capitalistic organization arrived very late in Chile.

The passage of this law also reflects upon the legislative process

21. Examples of this are numerous in the "Registro de hipotecas de Valparaíso" published in *La Revista Comercial*, 1921–27.

22. Statements of Luis Matte Larraín in Consejo Directivo de la Sociedad de Fomento Fabril, Acta de 4 de septiembre de 1925, "Libro de Actas," ASFF.

23. See the annual reports of these insurance companies in ANMH, vols. 2,839, 3,331, 4,227.

24. Guillermo Gandarillas, *Recopilación de leyes y reglamentos sobre fomento de las industrias minera, agrícola y fabril*, pp. 226–35.

25. "Emisión de obligaciones industriales o debentures."

of the time which was often criticized for its unwieldy, langorous pace. One of the major bottlenecks in the overall institutional structure of the country was congress. A bill in behalf of the normalization of debenture operations was submitted to the senate in 1912, but was pigeonholed. In 1927, the SFF presented another bill to congress, but almost two years passed before this legislation was enacted.[26]

Another event which served to provide more flexible credit to industrialists was the founding of the Instituto de Crédito Industrial in 1928. The SFF had long urged the creation of a special financial institution to attend to the needs of industry and lobbied congress for action in this connection.[27] Congressional action was delayed for years. But finally the law was passed quickly through congress in response to pressure applied by the administration of Carlos Ibáñez who gave preferential treatment to industry.[28]

This state financial institution opened in 1928, but its operations were greatly expanded the following year consequent upon modifications in its statutes which permitted a wider variety of credit facilities. These included direct loans at the low interest rate of 7 per cent repayable over a period of up to five years, the guarantee of the institute for certain private credit operations of industry and all bond issues open to the public, direct discount operations of commercial paper and service as an intermediary and sponsor of documents discounted abroad. In addition, in the case of mortgage loans, the Institute of Industrial Credit would accept a wide variety of collateral from industrialists, including machinery and plant equipment, raw materials, semifinished products, and inventory. Of particular interest was the provision in the institute's statutes which required it to provide at least 10 per cent of its total capital and reserves to small industries whose capital did not exceed 5,000 pesos.

The availability of capital to small entrepreneurs was severely cut in 1935 when this requirement was changed to 5 per cent of total equity and the maximum capital for a factory to be consid-

26. "Debentures."

27. Consejo Directivo de la Sociedad de Fomento Fabril, Acta de 13 de septiembre de 1899, "Libro de Actas," ASFF; "Acta de la 39ª junta general de socios en 10 de enero de 1923."

28. Ibáñez also required the Central Bank to lower its rates for discount operation to 6.5 per cent in 1928. Central Bank discount operations for industry had also begun in this period. See Presidencia de la República (Carlos Ibáñez), *Mensaje Presidencial*, May 21, 1927, p. 22, May 21, 1928, p. 12.

ered a small enterprise was raised to 10,000 pesos.[29] Another modification in 1929 made foreign-owned firms which had operated a minimum of five years in Chile eligible for the institute's credit.[30] Moreover, it is questionable if the credit facilities of the institute were ever made available to a much larger number of persons than those who had access to ready credit previously. The 20 million pesos of capital with which the institute worked in its first years was insufficient, given the great pressures on the money market.[31] Furthermore, although its board of directors nominally represented the state agencies which funded the institute, they were either important shareholders or on the boards of a number of the largest industrial enterprises. And it is reasonable to assume that these firms were interested in becoming beneficiaries of the generous credit afforded by the institute. In any event, given the late date at which it began operation, the institute could not have had more than a marginal effect upon the small entrepreneur before the depression years set in.

Another aspect of the credit situation in Chile, characteristically one in which large quantities of money circulated among the very few, was the relation between industry and import-export firms. Throughout the entire period covered by this study, the two were closely associated. Part of this interaction was the recourse which industry often had to the commercial houses for credit. Indeed this was one of the largest sources of credit for industry and there are innumerable cases of merchants acting as bankers for industry.

Julio Bernstein, the founder of the Compañía de Refinería de Azúcar de Viña del Mar, one of the largest enterprises in Chile, received sizeable loans in the late nineteenth century from the American importing houses Alsop y Cía. and Kendall y Cía. of Valparaíso.[32] The Sociedad Industrial de los Andes owned by Martínez, Velasco y Cía. had constant recourse to this merchant firm for loans which in the decade 1920–30 rose to 38 per cent of the industry's total assets.[33] In 1922, W. R. Grace and Company held

29. The original statutes of the Instituto de Crédito Industrial and all of the subsequent modifications to these are to be found in Gandarillas, *Legislación*, pp. 217–25. Also see José Valdivieso, *El Instituto de Crédito Industrial y su labor desarrollada en beneficio de la economía nacional*, p. 24.

30. Instituto de Crédito Industrial, *Memoria*, 1929, p. 6.

31. Ibid., p. 20.

32. Compañía de Refinería de Azúcar de Viña del Mar, *50 años*, p. 6.

33. In 1922 the industry owed 18.2 per cent of its total assets to Martínez, Velasco y Cía., 37.5 per cent in 1925, and 2.3 per cent in 1932 (Sociedad Industrial de los Andes, *Memorias*, 1922, 1925, 1932).

a mortgage on its textile factory, Caupolicán, for the sum of 80,000 pounds sterling.[34] And when the Compañía Manufacturera de Papeles, the country's largest paper producer, was reorganized in 1920, its predecessor, Ebbinghaus, Haensel y Cía. had a sizeable loan outstanding with the English trading house Duncan Fox y Cía.[35] These are but a few of the more important cases in which merchant houses functioned as sources of credit for industry. This role was occasionally assumed as a result of the merchant's position as distributor of the domestic manufacturer's product, but most often it came about due to the direct participation of the importer in the ownership of the industry.

34. "Registro de hipotecas de Valparaíso," *La Revista Comercial,* October 7, 1922, p. 49628.

35. This was for over 91,550 pesos which was 10 per cent of the paper company's paid-in capital. See "Estatutos de la Compañía Manufacturera de Papeles y Cartones y decreto N°589 que los aprueba y la declara legalmente instalada," *Diario Oficial.*

4. The Social Matrix of Industry: Obstacle to Development

TRADITIONALLY, those who initiate an industrial process are viewed as a separate group, a bourgeoisie arising to form a new elite which, in making its own demands upon society, inevitably comes into conflict with the other economic elites which are dominant. Indeed, a basic premise often found in studies of industrial entrepreneurship is that of the inherent conflict between the established economic elite and the emerging industrial bourgeoisie, which, in its supposedly modernizing role, exhibits a potential for social transformation. The central concern of this chapter is an examination of these questions through identification of the industrial elite, its interests, and the nature of its relationship with the dominant sectors of the nation.

The body of literature which contends that industrialization failed as an instrument of global development and that, in any event, manufacturing was missing from Chilean national life prior to World War I and even the Depression does not depend merely on the macroeconomic aspects of the question but to a large degree rests its case on propositions concerning the structure and interaction of social groups. These deal with the nature of the different groups which are hypothesized to have composed the economic elite and whose economic interests were by nature in conflict with domestic manufacturing. Three separate elite groups are usually isolated: the agriculturalists, the miners, and the importers (bankers are usually included in the last group). Since all were involved in foreign trade—the exportation of raw materials and the importation of all their capital goods as well as consumer goods—their self-interests were "absolutely incompatible with the kind of governmental policy necessary for the industrialization of the country."[1]

Claudio Véliz provides the most representative argument and, perhaps, the one which has received widest diffusion. He contends that until the Great Depression the Chilean economy was dominated by three pressure groups.[2] (1) The mining exporters of the north, who were free traders not out of doctrinaire conviction but because of common sense, exported copper, silver, and nitrate in return for pounds sterling or dollars. With this money they purchased machinery, mining equipment or consumer goods of very good quality and at very low prices from abroad. (2) The agricultural exporters of the south, who were also decidedly free traders, exported their wheat and flour to Europe, California, and Australia. They dressed their *huasos* with ponchos made from English flannel and consumed only imported goods in their own daily lives. (3) The great importing houses of Valparaíso and Santiago were also free traders. Is it possible to conceive of an importing firm defending high import duties to defend a national industry? These, then, were the economic elites which dominated the Chilean economy—the "three-legged table" of Chilean national life.

The question of whether or not a protectionist policy was followed will be discussed in a later chapter. The existence of a process of industrialization rooted in the late nineteenth century has already been demonstrated. The nature of the different groups composing the economic elite remains to be examined, however. This is of some importance for a number of reasons. After all, if industry did exist, who were the entrepreneurs? What did they do before entering industry? What were the sources of venture capital and subsequent financing? In summary, what social groups did the industrialists come from and what interests and values did they defend?

1. Véliz, "La mesa," p. 232. Essentially the same point is sustained by Lagos, *La industria*, pp. 40–41, and Nolff, "Industria," pp. 161 ff.
2. Paraphrased from Véliz, "La mesa," pp. 233–34.

Industry and the Chilean Elite Structure

The first issue which stands out in this problem area is that which refers to the validity of defining the Chilean national oligarchy in terms of three discrete component groups. The available evidence indicates that the common picture of oligarchic elements aligned according to separate economic interests is nothing more than a long-lived shibboleth.[3] It is based more on impressions culled from writers such as Alejandro Venegas, Roberto Espinoza, Frank Fetter, Hernán Ramírez Necochea, and Marcelo Segall, and overlooks the classic interpretation of Alberto Edwards who, in the political sphere at least, projects the image of the *fronda aristocrática*, a homogeneous oligarchy bound together by common interests, blood ties, and life style.

Ownership of *fundos* was not a primary source of wealth. In many cases land was a side investment and most often the means whereby to display the accumulated riches of a powerful group of urban businessmen.[4] Their capital was accumulated from mining, railroad, commercial, and banking ventures, as shown by the histories of such families as Edwards, Cousiño, Bunster, Carvallo, Lyon, Subercaseaux, Brown, Ossa, Eastman, Santa María, Tocornal and others.[5] Earnings subsequently were used to purchase fundos illustrating the importance of landownership in the Chilean value system. It is not uncommon to find individuals identified with the "mining oligarchy" simply because they had mining interests or with the "landed oligarchy" on the base of their estates. But this is misleading and meaningless, since a more detailed examination of the holdings of these people often reveals strong involvement in a number of activities.

A case in point is provided by Ricardo Lyon Pérez (1863–1928). Heir to an immense fortune based on import-export ventures, Lyon has been identified with the agricultural elite as "a wealthy and well-known *hacendado*."[6] Virgilio Figueroa, however, refers to him

3. Arnold Bauer, "Chilean Rural Society in the Nineteenth Century," pp. 181–214; Pike, *Chile*, pp. 121, 353.

4. Bauer, "Chilean Rural Society," p. 210.

5. See V. Figueroa, *Diccionario*; Zegers, *Estudios*; Guillermo de la Cuadra Gormaz, *Familias chilenas*; Enrique Amador Fuenzalida, *Galería contemporánea de hombres notables de Chile, 1850–1901*; Octavio Astorquiza, *Lota: antecedentes históricos con una monografía de la Compañía Carbonífera e Industrial de Lota.*

6. James O. Morris, *Elites, Intellectuals and Consensus: A Study of the Social Question and the Industrial Relations System in Chile*, p. 202.

as "the culminating figure of his family line, dynamic, with a sixth sense for business dealings and a keen eye for the value of land, a breeder of fine English thoroughbreds, industrialist, miner and landowner."[7] With a feel for the direction of Santiago's future urban expansion, Lyon's major landholdings were the fundos of Providencia and Las Condes. And he used these not to cultivate cash crops, but to raise his purebreds, awaiting the time in the early twentieth century when he could parcel the land and reap a vast fortune from the sale of these choice sites.[8] Aside from this business, Lyon was very active in finance, mining, and industry. Among other concerns he was a principal figure in the Compañía de Seguros La Chilena Consolidada, Compañía de Seguros La Mundial, Compañía de Lota y Coronel (coal mining), Compañía de Tejidos "El Salto," the Sociedad Fábrica Nacional de Vidrios, and the Sociedad Agrícola de Ñuble y Rupanco.[9]

So common were the multiple ventures of the oligarchy and so numerous the interconnections that it becomes impossible to speak meaningfully of a separate merchant, agricultural, or mining elite. For the most part the elite were involved in all these ventures, but always were imbued with the traditional values of an aristocratic, rural society. A survey of the major industrial enterprises in Chile before the Great Depression reveals the same pattern of interwoven interests.[10]

In the publishing industry, the Edwards family, whose business dealings touched every aspect of Chilean economic life, acquired *El Mercurio* of Valparaíso in 1880. Agustín Edwards MacClure, who had studied modern newspaper methods under James Gordon Bennett of the *New York Herald*, started the Santiago edition of *El Mercurio* in 1900. Two years later he founded the midmorning *Ultimas Noticias* of Santiago, and in 1906 *El Mercurio* of Antofagasta. Other papers completed the *El Mercurio* chain in later years. In 1902, he imported presses, machinery, and photo-engraving equipment. With these he established the publishing house Zig-Zag, which turned out numerous magazines and books.

7. V. Figueroa, *Diccionario*, 4:137.

8. A complete description of Ricardo Lyon's *quinta* "Los Leones" and its surroundings, which contains a number of most interesting photographs, including one of the land being sold in lots, is to be found in Márquez, *Libro*, 1:889–93.

9. See Bolsa de Comercio de Santiago, *La riqueza mobiliaria de Chile*.

10. The following analysis is based upon stockholder lists and a variety of sources too numerous to include in footnotes. I draw heavily in this section on the summary analysis of the stockholder data and sketches of the evolution of ownership and control of forty-two major enterprises given in Appendix 3.

The technical expertise of certain immigrants was another essential ingredient that blended with the industrial efforts of the oligarchs. Augusto Gubler, a Swiss who had managed a brewery in his homeland before coming to Chile, founded an enterprise in 1883, with Carlos Cousiño, one of the wealthiest men in the country. Cousiño formed the pinnacle of an investment group whose holdings included the coal mines of Lota, banks, insurance companies, railroads, a hydroelectric power plant (the first in Chile, installed near Lota in 1897), a small fleet of cargo ships, vineyards, and landed estates. Cousiño contributed the capital and business skill, and Gubler provided the technical know-how. By 1900, Cousiño was the sole proprietor of the firm, and in 1902, the brewery was consolidated with the Fábrica Nacional de Cerveza de Limache. The latter was another case in which a foreign technician had begun an operation with recourse to capital provided by the oligarchy. At the same time of the fusion, the Limache brewery was under the control of the Edwards family. The outcome of the consolidation was the Compañía Cervecerías Unidas. It underwent considerable expansion prior to World War I under the direction of Cousiño and later through the efforts of the Edwards' personal representatives.

These cases are illustrative of a process which was common in the period 1880–1900, especially for those firms which were to become dominant in their particular industries. An immigrant, skilled in an industry either in a purely technical capacity or as entrepreneur, initiated an operation on a relatively small scale. Within several years or certainly during the decade 1900–1910, when many important incorporations occurred, controlling interest in the firm had been acquired by members of the Chilean economic elite. Examples of this are the cases of the Cervecería Andrés Ebner, the Compañía de Refinería de Azúcar de Viña del Mar, and the Compañía Cristalerías de Chile, all of which passed to the control of either the Cousiño or the Edwards interests.

The years 1920–26, however, appear to have been of even more significance for the encroachment of the top echelon of the oligarchy, as represented by the Edwards group, into industry. Before this period they were involved, as pointed out, in several very important ventures.[11] But in the 1920s they diversified their hold-

11. The Edwards family had also founded a very important earthenware factory in 1887, but it was destroyed in the Civil War of 1891 by troops loyal to President José Manuel Balmaceda.

ings considerably. In addition to publishing, sugar refining, and beer production, they entered the areas of tobacco, glass, and textile manufacturing. The mechanisms employed to achieve control of firms are interesting inasmuch as they clearly depict the extensive interrelations among the Chilean oligarchy, foreign interests, and domestic manufacturing.

Occasionally, controlling interest in a corporation was obtained through the direct purchase of stock by members of the Edwards family. This occurred in the case of the Sociedad Nacional de Paños de Tomé, sometime before 1932. In other instances, another firm already controlled by the Edwards was utilized in a pyramiding maneuver. Such was true of the Compañía Cervecerías Unidas, in which, by 1926, only 27 per cent of the stock and two directorates were in the hands of the Edwards group. In turn, the beer company held one-fifth of the total stock in the Compañía Cristalerías de Chile and had representation on the board of directors. The Edwards family and their bank held only about 5 per cent of the Cristalerías stock directly. But since Cervecerías Unidas exercised an almost monopsonistic position with respect to the glass company, in addition to its powerful block of voting stock, through it the Edwards had de facto control of the affairs of Cristalerías.[12]

Most often, however, the Edwards operated in tandem with a British bank, the Banco Anglo Sud-Americano. In 1920, this bank, which had branch offices in Chile, had purchased 60 per cent of the stock of the Banco A. Edwards y Cía., but the usual sort of subsidiary relationship did not follow. On the contrary, in 1922, this majority holding was reduced to a strong minority position as the Edwards bank underwent a huge capital expansion to which virtually all of the Chilean oligarchy subscribed. In any case, the Edwards were the single most important shareholders (with 28 per cent of the total voting stock), followed by the Banco Anglo Sud-Americano, which had 24 per cent.[13] The unusual aspect of the affair was that during the time that this was occurring, Agustín Edwards had become a director of the Anglo Sud-Americano Bank itself.[14] The Chilean and British banks were in an affiliate position

12. The existence of this situation, in fact, was publicly denounced by the president of the glass company, Juan Tocornal, who, in a power struggle for control of the firm, was beaten by the Compañía Cervecerías Unidas. See Juan Tocornal, *Exposición leída por el presidente de la Sociedad Fábrica Nacional de Vidrios en la Junta General del 6 de septiembre de 1921.*

13. Banco de A. Edwards y Cía., *Memorias*, 1920–23, ABCS.

14. David Joslin, *A Century of Banking in Latin America*, pp. 260–61.

to one another rather than the Chilean bank being a subsidiary.

The symbiotic nature of the relationship was reflected in the investment maneuvering of both banks. The Anglo Bank made a number of important investments in Chilean industry during the decade 1920–30. In all instances where the Edwards increased their participation so as to control a firm, they did so by acquiring a portion of the stock held by the Anglo Bank. The sequence was rapid, with the Anglo Bank entering first and shortly thereafter the Edwards. Furthermore, in most of these cases, the Edwards utilized the funds of the Fundación Santa María, which was administered exclusively by Agustín Edwards.[15] Thus, by 1930, the Edwards–Anglo bank combine controlled the Compañía de Refinería de Azúcar de Viña del Mar, the Compañía Cervecerías Unidas, the Compañía Chilena de Tabacos, the Fábrica Nacional de Paños de Tomé, and the Imprenta y Litografía Universo. This, then, was not a simple case of classic external domination in a Latin American country, but rather a working relationship in which the national dominant element entered into free and equal association with the foreign one. It is particularly interesting to note that this combined block was a longstanding one which may be traced into the 1960s.[16]

Industrial entrepreneurship was also evident in another of the foremost members of the Chilean oligarchy, Carlos Cousiño.[17] Before his beer venture with Gubler in 1883, when he was only twenty-three years of age, he had embarked upon another industrial pursuit which was not as successful in the long run. In 1881, he founded the first glass factory in Chile. It produced only glass bottles and closed down in 1902, apparently never having attained any sizeable production. As mentioned, the beer venture resulted in the formation of the Compañía Cervecerías Unidas in 1902, in which Cousiño was to be in league with the Edwards group. Cousiño also owned the Cervecería Andrés Ebner, which was absorbed by the Cervecerías Unidas in 1916.

In addition, his close relationship with the Edwards was evident

15. This foundation had its origin in the vast fortune left by Federico Santa María (somewhat over 58 million pesos). He was one of Chile's biggest capitalists, a speculator in the international sugar market and one of the principal clients and shareholders of the Anglo Bank.

16. Maurice Zeitlin et al., "'New Princes' for Old? The Large Corporation and the Capitalist Class in Chile," p. 106.

17. The material for this profile of Carlos Cousiño comes from Octavio Astorquiza and Oscar Galleguillos, *Cien años de Lota*, pp. 73–83, and Astorquiza, *Lota*, pp. 87–93.

in the Compañía Cristalerías de Chile, over which he exercised controlling minority interest two years after closing down his own glass factory. This control was later shared with the Edwards in the 1920s, and no rivalry was ever apparent, even in the dispute of 1921 between Juan Tocornal, president of the glass company, and the Edwards-controlled Cervecerías Unidas, which led to the withdrawal of Tocornal from Cristalerías.[18] Cousiño interests were important in both corporations and supported the Edwards' position.

Carlos Cousiño had an insatiable appetite for new business ventures and the expansion of his holdings. He founded the first natural cement factory in Chile at La Calera and, in 1883, established an asphalt factory which supplied the city of Santiago with most of its paving material. It is well known that the original base for the Cousiño fortune was the coal mine at Lota, the most important of the country; it underwent expensive modernization and expansion under his direction.[19] In 1897, the year he took over full management of the company, Cousiño installed the first hydroelectric plant in Chile, several miles from Lota. It not only provided power for the mining operations, but also generated electricity for the city of Lota. He considerably increased the small fleet of coal transport ships, and his freighters covered the coastline of Chile, bringing fuel to the rest of the country. Suggestive of the expansion of the corporation was the change of its name in 1921 from Compañía de Lota y Coronel to the Compañía Minera e Industrial de Chile.

Cousiño's dynamism lasted to the end of his life. In 1928, three years before his death, he announced the opening of a lumber mill which would process and distribute wood to the public. The raw material came from a vast forest reserve which he had had planted years before. He also laid down plans for the founding of another glass factory and a new thermoelectric power plant in Lota (the first one had been installed in 1908). The results of his efforts are evident in the evolution of production and employment figures in Table 13. In great part due to the expansion of Lota's output by the 1920s, domestic production met all national demand for coal, and metallurgical coke was being produced.

Despite his tremendous drive, Carlos Cousiño was not primarily

18. Tocornal, *Exposición.*

19. Copper mines owned by the Cousiño family in Los Maitenes and Las Condes also benefited from Carlos Cousiño's interest in modernization, through his new converter system to concentrate the mineral more efficiently.

responsible for all of the enterprise which radiated from the hub of wealth in Lota. He was seldom on the management board of the industries controlled by himself and his family. Instead, these duties were delegated to relatives such as Arturo Cousiño Lyon, in the case of wine-making, or to close associates such as Guillermo Purcell, Ricardo Lyon, H. L. Wessel, or Guillermo Condon, all of whom were directors of Lota for many years while they managed the Cousiño-controlled manufacturing enterprises.

TABLE 13
EVOLUTION OF PRODUCTION AND EMPLOYMENT OF COMPAÑIA MINERA E INDUSTRIAL DE CHILE, 1852–1929

Year	Coal Production (thousands of tons)	Workers: In Mines	Workers: In Other Sections	Workers: Total
1852	8	75	50	125
1862	35	140	200	340
1872	131	616	353	969
1882	252	1,222	680	1,902
1892	263	1,310	900	2,210
1901	352	1,806	1,210	3,016
1912	337	1,559	1,402	2,961
1921	727	5,848	3,100	8,948
1924	899	5,254	3,396	8,650
1929	857	4,198	2,912	7,110

SOURCE: Astorquiza, *Lota*, pp. 132–33.

In like fashion, Cemento El Melón, reported to be the first producer of Portland cement in South America, had its origin in the capital accumulated by the oligarchy in other areas of the economy. It was founded in 1906, and later became the largest cement mill in Latin America and the fifth largest in the world.[20] From the outset, the principal figures in the enterprise were Alfredo Cox, Juan Brown, and his cousin, Rafael Ariztía Lyon, all at the summit of Chile's social-economic elite, with business pursuits in all sectors of national economic life.

An analysis of the directorates of the enterprises whose stock was traded in the Santiago Stock Exchange further confirms this pattern of interwoven interests between manufacturing and the oligarchy. An examination of 207 directors in 1922, presented in Table 14, reveals that 73 per cent were, in that year, directors of corpora-

20. United States Department of Commerce, *Investment*, p. 155.

tions in the areas of finance, mining, construction, and public services. Many were involved in agriculture and in trading houses as well. Of all those identified (151), 77 per cent were important figures in at least two areas outside of industry. Only 23 per cent could not be found to be involved in more than one other economic sector, and 11 per cent could be identified only as major landowners.

TABLE 14
INTERSECTORAL LINKS OF THE DIRECTORS OF MAJOR CHILEAN MANUFACTURING CORPORATIONS, 1922

	Number	Percentage
Unidentified	56	27.0[a]
Identified with one or more of the following sectors:	151	73.0[a]
Finance	69	45.7
Mining	51	33.8
Agriculture	58	38.4
Transportation, public services, construction	36	23.8
Urban real estate	4	2.7
Commerce	26	17.2
Congressional deputy, senator, or minister of state	36	17.4[a]

SOURCES: Bolsa de Comercio de Santiago, *La riqueza*; V. Figueroa, *Diccionario*; *Diccionario personal de Chile*; *Diccionario biográfico de Chile*; Benavides, *Anuario General de Chile, 1919–1924*; Eric Davies, "A History of Duncan, Fox & Co."; Robert Jaffray and George Duval, *Revista del centenario del negocio fundado por Augustus Hemenway de Boston en 1825 y conducido actualmente por Wessel Duval & Co.*; *History and Description of Casa Grace in the Republic of Chile, 1881–1953*; Sociedad Nacional de Agricultura, *Boletín*, 1910–25.
a. This is the percentage of the total number of individuals investigated, i.e., 207.

There is reason to believe that this analysis is conservative since among those who were not linked directly to other economic sectors were men such as Rafael Edwards Sutil, director of the state railroad, whose branch of the Edwards family was very active in commerce and agriculture. There were also members of congress, such as Augusto Vicuña Subercaseaux, prominent figure of the Liberal Party who was unquestionably of the oligarchy, but about whose economic activities, regrettably, little is known. Moreover, the percentage of intersectoral links would be considerably higher if the individual's investments rather than his position as an active principal in an industry, bank, trading house, etc., were the criteria employed. This type of analysis, however, would involve time and resources beyond those at my disposal.

A considerable concentration of power was present in industry itself, evidenced by the incidence of interlocking directorates among the forty largest entities in the manufacturing sector. In 1922, a total of 244 directorates were held by 207 men. While most of these sat on a single board, 31 were on two or more boards. Sixty-seven directorates were held by multiple directors.[21] From all available information, it may be concluded that this convergence of wealth and power would be more intense if nonincorporated enterprises were included. Taking into consideration the high degree of intersectoral links, it would certainly be higher if finance, mining, and public utility companies were added.

The extensive interrelations of Chilean industrial leaders are quite consistent with the generic nature of the oligarchy. Individuals were chosen for directorate positions for a number of reasons. Investment in the company and capacity in the industry were important factors, but quite often the underlying reasons were to be found in the person's connections to major financial institutions and commercial houses, contacts which were essential to the firm. Thus, in 1926, Guillermo Edwards was a director of the Compañía Nacional de Tejidos "El Salto" even though the participation of the Edwards group was less than 1 per cent of total stock. The firm's June balance sheet for that year, however, showed over 10 per cent of the total liabilities to be outstanding in favor of the Banco A. Edwards y Cía.[22] Another factor which may have been influential in Edwards' position on the board of directors was the minority control exercised by the Cousiño family over Tejidos "El Salto" and the fact that Ricardo Lyon, representative of the Cousiños, was president of the firm.[23]

As discussed, it was not uncommon for the two groups to be found strongly represented in a single firm without any cleavage apparent between them. Indeed, the situation bears some semblance to the unseparable nature of the Morgan and Rockefeller group ventures in the United States at the turn of the century. In this connection, John Moody observed, "It should not be supposed, however, that these two great groups of capitalists and financiers are in any real sense rivals or competitors for power, or that such a thing as a war exists between them. For, as a matter of fact, they are not only friendly, but they are allied to each other by many close ties, and it would probably require only a little stretch

21. This analysis is based on data found in Bolsa de Comercio de Santiago, *La riqueza.*

22. Compañía Nacional de Tejidos "El Salto," *Memoria*, June 1926.

23. See Appendix 3.

of the imagination to describe them as a single great Morgan-Rockefeller group."[24]

What emerges from this is the existence of a generic economic elite whose interests were merged into industrial activities from an early date.[25] The ephemeral dominance of some landed aristocrats or the impact made by a few mid-nineteenth-century mining entrepreneurs such as Gallo or Ossa, which in all probability influenced later writers to an unwarranted degree, gave rise to the widely accepted concept of separate oligarchies. For the most part, this was not the case. One of the strengths of the Chilean oligarchy has been its flexibility and ability to transfer its capital and talent among different areas of the economy in accord with the relative opportunities offered by each.

Industry provided its incentive to many in the available high rates of return on invested capital. In the years 1915–18, the rates of return on investment in industry averaged 15.9 per cent, and throughout most of the decade 1920–30, industrial profits maintained this level, which was more than 5 per cent over that which could be earned in finance, mining, and commerce.[26]

Ownership and control of the larger and more successful enterprises was limited to a small number of individuals, a listing of whom would be almost indistinguishable from the membership rolls of the Club de la Unión, the Club Hípico de Santiago, or the Valparaíso Sporting Club. A review of the structure of ownership and control of forty-two major industrial enterprises from the late nineteenth century to the 1930s reveals that most were "closed" firms owned and managed by individuals or small groups of the oligarchy.[27] In those instances where the stock came to be more widely dispersed, as in the cases of Tejidos "El Salto," the Fábrica Italo-Americana de Paños Tomé, the Compañía de Refinería de Azúcar de Viña del Mar, or the Compañía Cervecerías Unidas,

24. Moody, *The Truth about Trusts* (New York, 1904), pp. 492–93, quoted in Peter C. Dooley, "The Interlocking Directorate," p. 320.

25. This is essentially the same situation as was to be found until the end of the 1960s. For empirically based studies of this problem, see Oscar Garretón and Jaime Cisterna, "Algunas características del proceso de toma de decisiones en la gran empresa; la dinámica de concentración"; Gabriel Gasic, "Concentración, entrelazamiento y desnacionalización en la industria manufacturera."

26. Bolsa de Comercio de Santiago, *Riqueza*, gives condensed balance sheet data for 266 companies from 1913 to 1922. Profit figures also are to be found in Ministerio de Fomento, *Monografía industrial de Chile*, p. 12, and Ministere des Relations Exterieures, *Les Capitaux au Chili*, p. 7.

27. See Appendix 3.

less stock (as little as 8 per cent in the case of the Fábrica Italo-Americana) was necessary for effective minority control to be exercised since the dominant group always held strong representation on the board of directors and controlled the proxy machinery. In the latter cases, the dominant influence most often came from the Chilean oligarchy or importing houses.

There are few stories of substantial upward mobility of Chileans of modest origin in the history of Chile's industrialization. But true to its elastic nature and its respect for wealth, the oligarchy demonstrated its tolerance for those who were successful and absorbed them into the social elite.

Such was the experience of Carlos Justiniano, who came from an unassuming family in Valparaíso.[28] As a young man he opened a small shop for the production of army and navy uniforms. Through his efforts the enterprise grew until, by the 1880s, the establishment, now known as the Taller Militar de Chile, had become the supplier of uniforms for most of the armed forces and the local police. The wealth which Justiniano had earned in industry merited him a position as director of the Sociedad de Fomento Fabril. He turned to finance and became a member of the board of the Banco de la Industria y El Comercio. In 1920, he purchased the fundo "Las Mercedes," in Graneros, and with his newly acquired status of landowner was elected a director of the Sociedad Nacional de Agricultura. He had been admitted to the most exclusive social circles; he was a member of the Club de la Unión and the Club de Septiembre, and, in 1927, was president of the executive committee of the Chilean Red Cross. In business he had associated himself with the highest levels of the oligarchy. After his enterprise had shown promise, the Johnson Gana family had gone into partnership with Justiniano. When the firm was incorporated in 1926, as the Sociedad Fábrica de Uniformes, its directorate included such outstanding members of the elite as Luis Matte Larraín, Francisco Garcés Gana, and Carlos Aguirre Luco.[29]

Carlos Werner, the man responsible for the successful expansion of the Fábrica Nacional de Paños de Bellavista de Tomé, the large woolen textile factory near Concepción, advanced in much the same fashion. Born of German parents in Osorno, Werner left there at the age of fifteen to work in the nitrate fields. Seven years later

28. Details of Carlos Justiniano's life are found in V. Figueroa, *Diccionario*, 3:588, and "Don Carlos E. Justiniano."

29. "Estatutos de la Sociedad Fábrica de Uniformes."

he had become the youngest manager of any nitrate operation in the country. In a short time he owned several nitrate oficinas and began to purchase fundos in the south. In 1904, he acquired a textile factory whose installed capacity he increased many times over through the import of new machinery. It soon became one of the largest textile operations in Chile, and he exercised almost complete ownership over the firm until his death in 1927. A prominent figure of the Liberal Party, he had been elected senator from the southern provinces of Arauco, Malleco, and Cautín the year before. Werner was described by the biographer Virgilio Figueroa as one of the wealthiest men in Chile, with numerous landholdings, factories, and mining interests, and an outstanding member of the German-Chilean colony of the south which was an integral part of the dominant sector of national society.[30]

Industry and the Importing Houses

The great trading firms of Valparaíso, Santiago, and Concepción were without doubt pedestals of Chilean economic life throughout the nineteenth century. This is quite understandable since the essence of the country's livelihood was foreign trade—the exportation of copper, gold, silver, wheat, flour, and nitrates. Most of the trade was handled by foreigners who later rose to the forefront of the Chilean aristocracy of wealth. In this fashion originated the fortunes of such families as Edwards, Lyons, Bunster, Délano, and others. Later, merchant capital intermingled with agriculture, mining, and finance. From the end of the last century, trading interests could also be clearly identified in industrial ventures. The passage of mercantile capital into manufacturing was fundamental to the evolution of the industrial sector throughout the period treated in this study.

That this occurred to any extent is contrary to the conventional interpretation of events in the Chilean economy prior to 1930. Nevertheless, the export-import interests established in Chile perceived that those factors operating after the War of the Pacific to produce changes in the economy and internal market situation were opening opportunities to which they were in a most favorable position to respond. The feedback effects upon the domestic market of foreign trade expansion, urban growth, increased demand

30. See Figueroa, *Diccionario*, 5:1,088.

for basic consumer goods, and improved transportation facilities to regions recently incorporated into the national life afforded a potential which the merchants could easily exploit.

Several advantages held by the importers favored their entry into industry. They were in possession of accumulated experience and an information network which permitted them to assess the changing conditions of domestic market demand. Their very operations in foreign trade gave them an advantage in learning alternative product specifications and production techniques. In this regard they also had more ready access to the sources of imported raw and intermediate materials which were so important in the early stage of Chile's industrialization. These contacts likewise served them in the acquisition of the necessary capital equipment.

The situation of the merchants with respect to credit was also strategic in affording them the possibility of taking advantage of entrepreneurial opportunities. Since the middle of the nineteenth century, trading firms had acted as financial intermediary institutions to agriculture and mining. As seen earlier they occupied a similar role with respect to industry. Many of the largest trading houses were foreign owned, principally by English-, German-, and American-based firms. They had access to the capital of their home offices in Europe and the United States which provided them with the funding necessary to enter industrial ventures in Chile. Among others, such were the cases of Duncan Fox y Cía., Williamson Balfour y Cía., Gibbs y Cía., Vorwerk y Cía., Wessel Duval y Cía., Grace & Co. (Chile), and Gleisner y Cía. Finally, the merchants had at their disposal a network of wholesale and retail outlets throughout the country. Thus, goods produced by enterprises in which these merchants participated had established channels of distribution ready for the marketing of the finished product.

On the other hand, there were individuals who as immigrants had worked with importing houses and had thereby acquired experience and contacts which served them later when they engaged in manufacturing. Previous experience in commerce was to be found in the original entrepreneurs of fourteen of the forty-two companies surveyed in Appendix 3.[31] In addition, examples of com-

31. These were the Compañía de Refinería de Azúcar de Viña del Mar, the Molinera San Cristóbal, the Compañía Molinera El Globo, the Compañía Chilena de Tabacos, the Fábrica de Leche de Weir Scott y Cía., the Sociedad de Paños de Tomés, the Compañía Chilena de Tejidos, the Fábrica Victoria de Puente Alto, the Sociedad Industrial de Los Andes, the Imprenta y Litografía Universo, the Compañía Chilena de Fósforos, the Fábrica de Vidrios y Cristales "La

panies in which trading houses were quite active may be seen in the cases of the Sociedad Fábrica Nacional de Paños de Bellavista and the Fábrica Nacional de Envases y Enlozados, S.A. The importance of the participation of importing houses in the founding of the paper companies of Puente Alto and Quillota was manifest. In 1905, the second year of its operation, over 90 per cent of the total stock of this company was held by mercantile interests. In all, three import houses, two Chilean-owned (although of European origin) and one German firm, were the major participants.[32]

In many cases, manufacturing involved only an extension of activities already performed by the importer. Thus, those houses which imported machinery and equipment for mining, agriculture, transportation, and industry already had workshops and foundries operating. These were necessary to assemble those products whose volume and weight made them too costly to ship in finished condition. The imported equipment was also repaired by the importer's shop, and gradually spare parts and complete units were produced by them. Orchard Hnos., Raab Rochette y Cía., and Balfour Lyon y Cía. are examples of this transformation.

Although quite plausible in general, the literature which emphasizes the competitive relation between importing and manufacturing and concludes that Chilean importers could hardly have had any interest in domestic industry encounters difficulty in the numerous cases which indicate that the contrary was true. On the microeconomic level, a wide variety of specific products existed which merchants found more profitable to produce domestically than to import.

In this respect, trading houses were in a most advantageous position. They imported the raw material directly, produced the item, and distributed the finished product. In this fashion, the British house Gibbs y Cía. invested heavily in the Fábrica Nacional de Clavos y Puntas de Alambre, formed in 1913 from the fusion of five smaller establishments which operated in Santiago, Valparaíso, and Concepción. Gibbs imported the raw material before World War I from Europe, then from the United States (through its New York offices). They were the general agents and distributors of the

Yungay," the Fábrica Nacional de Loza de Penco, and the Compañía Electro Metalúrgica.

32. The Chilean houses were Hormann y Cía. and Saavedra Bernard y Cía. The German-owned concern was Vorwerk y Cía. See Fábrica Nacional de Papeles y Cartones de Puente Alto y Quillota, "Lista de accionistas de 31 de diciembre de 1905," ANMH, vol. 2,839.

nails, spikes, and wire staples produced by the factory and also acted as the financial intermediaries of the firm, discounting its documents and providing other credit when necessary.[33]

As was seen earlier, most of the textile industry was based on the importation of semifinished goods. The majority of the major textile plants were controlled by import houses and only weaving, dyeing, printing, and other finishing touches were added. With few exceptions these ventures were quite profitable over the years, even though the sector as a whole made little contribution to the development of industry.[34]

In most instances, the importer engaged in industrial activities which were complementary to his operations; in others, the merchant branched out into new fields. The trading house of Nieto y Cía. which had been active in the exportation of foodstuffs detected a growing domestic market for processed foods. It established a canning factory for fruits and vegetables in 1902 and became one of the major producers of these goods in the country.[35] In like fashion, import houses engaged in the production of flour, oil, condensed milk, liquor, clothing, shoes, jute for bagging, furniture, and glassware.[36]

Certainly, then, no inherent conflict existed which impeded trading houses from transferring their experience and capital to industry. Moreover, the merchants themselves formed an integral component of the elite system. Not only did the fortunes of many of the wealthiest families have their origin in commerce but merchants were in turn involved in all aspects of Chilean economic life. The important firm of Besa y Cía. illustrates this. Throughout the nineteenth century it was active in mining and banking. By the turn of the century it was dominant in sugar refining and paper manufacturing. Its founder, José Besa, was one of the principal figures in the founding of the Banco de Chile in 1894. He was an active

33. "Fábrica Nacional de Clavos y Puntas de Alambre."

34. Although during the years 1914–16 the textile industry accounted for only 4.8 per cent of the total industrial labor force, by 1936–38 labor force absorption by this sector had increased to 16.3 per cent (Muñoz, *Crecimiento*, Table 3.3).

35. Sociedad de Fomento Fabril, *Exhibición*, p. 4; in 1968, this firm controlled 18.6 per cent of the total market and 34.6 per cent of the total capital and reserves in its industrial group (Gasic, "Concentración," Appendix 1).

36. Prado Martínez, *Anuario Prado Martínez: Chile, 1902*, pp. 33–50, lists major trading houses and their manufacturing interests. See also Pérez Canto, *La industria* (1896), pp. 17–18; "Las fábricas en Concepción," pp. 42–44; Soto Rojas, *Crónicas*, pp. 212–21; Márquez, *Libro*, passim.

politician and served in the national congress as deputy and senator for many years. His son, Arturo, had much the same career pattern over the period 1900–1921. He was most active in commerce and industry and on several occasions was appointed minister of state.[37] Moreover, as industrial corporations came to yield high rates of return on invested capital, trading houses began to look to them as good investments for surplus capital. Thus in 1920, the Compañía Chilena de Tejidos obtained the capital it needed for an expansion program through a sizeable sale of its new stock issue to the nitrate trading firm Buchanan Jones y Cía., whose principals engaged in the export of nitrate and the import of mining machinery and equipment. They were also involved in banking and in the manufacture of canned palm honey from their extensive landholding, the Sociedad Hacienda Cocalán.[38]

Apart from direct investment in industry by importers, equally important to the success of Chile's industrial growth were those men who had had experience in importing and then applied this knowledge to manufacturing. Many of the early entrepreneurs had first learned importing and marketing techniques. Thirty-seven per cent of the corporations surveyed in Appendix 3 owed their origin and development to men with this prior experience.

The Role of Foreign Investment in Chilean Industrialization

Among the essential ingredients of Chilean industrialization was direct foreign investment. From the late nineteenth century, foreign trading houses which had long been active in Chilean mining and as bankers to agriculture began to take an active interest in domestic manufacturing. The reasons for this extension of economic activity and the identity of these firms have been discussed. The principal import houses which had most expanded their activities into manufacturing were English-owned. Before the Great Depression they controlled factories that produced flour, rolled oats, condensed milk, vegetable oil, glassware, textiles, knit goods, and clothing. But, in addition to trading companies, European banks

37. V. Figueroa, *Diccionario*, 2:192–94; *Chile industrial y comercial* 1 (November 1908):14–15; *Estatutos de la Compañía Industrial "El Volcán."*

38. "Estatutos de la Compañía Chilena de Tejidos." See also the biographical sketches of Jorge Buchanan, Jorge Jones, and Walterio Jones in *Diccionario biográfico de Chile, 1936*, pp. 130, 378.

and large corporations made significant investments in Chilean industry.

Enrico Dell'Acqua, owner of one of the largest textile manufacturing and exporting companies of Milan, sent his representatives to Chile at the turn of the century to inquire into the possibilities of establishing a weaving mill there as he had in Brazil, Argentina, Uruguay, and Paraguay. The reports were positive, and in 1904 the Fábrica de Tejidos de Punto de G. Corradi y Cía. was founded in Santiago with venture capital provided by Dell'Acqua. This firm was later to become the Compañía Chilena de Tejidos, an important textile operation. However, like the rest of the textile industry at this stage of development, which lasted until the late 1930s, the operation was incomplete, limited to processing the imported thread spun by Dell'Acqua's Italian mills.[39]

In 1906, the Belgian textile corporation Etablissements Américains Gratry opened a branch plant in Viña del Mar to weave imported cotton thread. This mill remained under the complete control of the Belgian firm and prospered considerably. However, not all factories established with foreign capital were successful in the long run. Another cotton mill, the Chilean Mills Co. Ltd., was founded in 1900 by the English trading house Allardice & Co. Ltd. It lasted for twenty-two years but went bankrupt toward the end of the depression years 1920–22. The control of other factories which started as foreign-owned operations passed to the highest levels of Chilean oligarchy once they had proven to be worthwhile investments. Thus, the Cousiño group acquired minority control over the Compañía Nacional de Tejidos "El Salto" in 1900, after it had been developed successfully by Belgian interests.

The reverse also occurred with some frequency in the 1920s, characterized by one author as a period during which "the golden stream of foreign capital was flowing into Chile."[40] Foreign capital purchased controlling interests in factories which had been Chilean operations until then. A sample of 42 major Chilean enterprises in existence before 1932 reveals that firms using foreign capital increased from 14 before World War I to 26 in 1920–32 (Table 15). Majority control of stock was evident in five companies in the first period and nine in the second; likewise, the number of

39. González, *El esfuerzo*, p. 121. For details on Dell'Acqua's operations in São Paulo, see Warren Dean, *The Industrialization of São Paulo, 1880–1945*, pp. 55–60.

40. George Wythe, *Industry in Latin America*, p. 224.

Chilean firms with foreign ownership of 20 per cent to 49.9 per cent of the total voting stock increased from two to five.

The sources of foreign capital were varied. Aside from the trading houses, European and American industrial concerns invested directly in Chile, either establishing new branch factories or, more commonly, building on the base of existing operations. The incentive for them to do so became greater as import duties for manufactured goods underwent substantial increases in the decade 1920–30. American firms were most attracted to this type of operation. A listing of American subsidiaries active in Chile from the 1920s on

TABLE 15

FOREIGN PARTICIPATION IN SELECTED MAJOR CHILEAN MANUFACTURING ENTERPRISES

Percentage of Total Stock	Number of Firms Prior to 1914	Number of Firms 1920–32
1.0–4.9	3	4
5.0–9.9	2	6
10.0–19.9	2	2
20.0–49.9	2	5
50.0–100.0	5	9
Total	14	26

SOURCE: Based upon the sample of 42 firms in Appendix 3.

reveals that they were involved in several different areas but were especially critical in the growth industries of those years (Table 16). The automotive, airplane, radio, and sewing machine plants were mere assembly operations with minor parts produced locally. These factories avoided high tariffs by importing the item in sections and could better respond to consumer preferences in matters such as color combinations and various options.[41]

European manufacturers, on the other hand, at first seemed to favor the sale of patent rights on their production techniques for which handsome royalty payments were collected. But they also participated in the pattern of direct investment so prevalent in the 1920s. Thus, the Compañía Chilena de Fósforos, organized in 1913 from the fusion of three Chilean-owned firms and employing Swedish technology, was finally brought under the majority control of the worldwide Swedish match consortium, Svenska Tändsticks

41. Pfeiffer, "Development," pp. 193–203.

A.B., in 1927.[42] In that same year the Compañía Cristalerías de Chile entered into an agreement with the Cristalerías Rigolleau of Buenos Aires, whereby the latter would provide technical and managerial assistance for the Chilean firm. The Argentine company, which at the time seems to have been acting as an intermediary for the American corporation Corning Glass Company, sent in 1928 one of its principals, José Sabaté, to be general manager of Cris-

TABLE 16

BRANCH FACTORIES OF AMERICAN FIRMS IN CHILE, 1920–32

Company	Product
Abbott Laboratories	Pharmaceuticals, drugs
Atlas Powder Co.	Explosives
Bristol-Myers Co.	Pharmaceuticals, drugs
Curtiss-Wright Corp.	Light airplanes
E. I. Du Pont de Nemours	Explosives
Ford Motor Co.	Automobiles
General Motors Corp.	Automobiles
W. R. Grace	Textiles, sugar
The Lambert Co.	Pharmaceuticals, drugs
Otis Elevator Co.	Elevators
R.C.A.-Victor	Radios, phonographs, records
Singer Sewing Machine Co.	Sewing machines
Standard of New Jersey	Refined oil
Sterling Drug, Inc.	Pharmaceuticals, drugs
Vick Chemical Co.	Pharmaceuticals, drugs
Zonite Products Inc.	Antiseptics, drugs

SOURCE: Adapted from Pfeiffer, "Development," Table 11. This was modified on the basis of information in Dudley Maynard Phelps, *Migration of Industry to South America.*

talerías de Chile, a position he held until 1932. Later, Cristalerías de Chile entered into direct relations with Corning Glass, which acquired a quarter of its stock sometime before World War II.[43]

In addition to import houses and industrial corporations, foreign capital entered Chilean manufacturing through investments made by financial institutions and private individuals in Europe. This form of investment in Chile was not common to the United States at this time. Only the First National Bank of New York invested during the pre-Depression period and always in very limited amounts. British, German, and Spanish banking agencies were quite

42. "Estatutos de la Compañía Chilena de Fósforos"; Compañía Chilena de Fósforos, *Memorias*, ABCS, pp. 1,914–32.

43. Compañía Cristalerías de Chile, *Memorias*, ABCS, pp. 1,927–40; Pfeiffer, "Development," p. 227.

active. The first of these were represented principally by the Banco Anglo Sud-Americano Ltdo., a most important investor. The Anglo Bank directed capital to Chilean industry just before World War I, but the period of intense investment came in the years 1920–32, when the bank's portfolio contained the stock of at least twenty major Chilean manufacturing enterprises (Table 17). In some cases the bank's participation was most significant, yet it did not usually exercise active control. Content with the profits reaped from its industrial stock, the Anglo Bank delegated control of the firm to its Chilean affiliates, the Edwards.[44]

German and Spanish investments were to be found in only a limited number of firms. They were represented by both financial institutions and individuals. Most illustrative of this are the cases of the Compañía Industrial and the Compañía Chilena de Tabacos. Founded in 1901, the Compañía Industrial was one of the most important enterprises in the chemical sector of Chilean industry, with an exceptionally wide variety of products. Its principals were German-Chileans. The German trading houses of Weber y Cía. and Vorwerk y Cía. were also very active participants in the early years of the company.[45] Foreign investment always formed a significant portion of the company's capital, but it was almost entirely accounted for by German residents in Europe and by the Banco Alemán Transatlántico. In no instance did these exercise any control over the affairs of the firm. The shares were apparently acquired as sound investments by Germans with contacts in Chile (most probably the bank itself acting as trustee or on the advice of the trading houses).

The same phenomenon occurred in the evolution of the Compañía Chilena de Tabacos, with the exception that in this case the major foreign interests were Spanish banking institutions.[46] The offices of the Banco Hispano Americano in Madrid and Barcelona were the principal foreign investors from before 1914 to 1932. They were followed closely by the Banco Alemán Transatlántico. Once

44. In addition to these acquisitions, the Anglo Bank invested very heavily in the Cousiño-owned Compañía Minera e Industrial in 1926. It purchased almost 16 million pesos worth of shares, which represented 5.4 per cent of the total stock of that enterprise. See Compañía Minera e Industrial, *Memoria*, 1926, ABCS.

45. In 1901, the two import firms held two directorates and 14.7 per cent of the stock ("Estatutos de la Compañía Industrial").

46. Of course, this excludes the participation of the Anglo Bank in the 1920s, which surpassed all other foreign investors.

TABLE 17

PARTICIPATION OF THE BANCO ANGLO SUD-AMERICANO LTDO. IN CHILEAN MANUFACTURING ENTERPRISES

Firm	Year	Book Value of Invest-ment[a]	Percentage of Total Stock
Compañía de Refinería de Azúcar de Viña del Mar	1920	1,708	8.0
	1926	6,988	10.1
	1932	14,566	6.6
Compañía Molinera San Cristóbal	1932	25	0.6
Compañía Molinera "El Globo"	1920	127	2.5
	1926	486	9.7
	1932	750	15.0
Hucke Hnos. S.A.C.	1932	303	3.4
Compañía Cervecerías Unidas	1914	30	4.0
Compañía Chilena de Tabacos	1914	171	2.3
	1920	300	3.0
	1926	777	7.8
	1932	965	9.7
Sociedad Fábrica Nacional de Paños de Bellavista	1932	105	1.3
Compañía Nacional de Tejidos "El Salto"	1926	335	3.4
	1932	190	1.9
Sociedad Nacional de Paños de Tomé	1933	83	1.4
Fábrica Italo-Americana de Paños	1933	293	3.5
Compañía Manufacturera de Tomé Papeles y Cartones	1932	422	2.2
Imprenta y Litografía Universo	1912	200	9.5
	1914	230	11.0
	1920	526	52.6
	1926	204	20.4
	1929	244	24.4
Compañía Chilena de Fósforos	1920	25	0.8
Compañía Industrial	1915	28	1.4
	1920	349	5.6
	1926	45	0.8
	1932	160	2.6
Fábrica Nacional de Loza de Penco	1932	33	0.7
Compañía de Cemento "El Melón"	1926	969	4.0
	1932	511	2.1
Compañía Industrial "El Volcán"	1925	71	3.6
	1932	3	0.1
Compañía de Maestranzas y Galvanización	1922	750	27.3
Fábrica Nacional de Envases y Enlozados	1914	5	0.5
	1926	188	3.8
	1932	468	9.4
Compañía Electro Metalúrgica	1932	85	5.7
Compañía Industrial de Catres	1932	66	2.2

SOURCES: Shareholder lists of the respective companies; also see Appendix 3.

a. Expressed in thousands of current pesos.

again, this participation was made strictly for investment purposes. Control of the firm remained in the hands of the trading house Fernando Rioja y Cía., until the 1920s, at which time the Edwards clan became the major force in the company.

The Contribution of Immigration to Industrial Growth

As in other countries, immigration constituted a key element in the industrialization process of Chile. Unlike other national experiences, however, the contribution of the immigrants did not provide a substantial increase in the total population, overall market size, and supply of manual labor. The impact was primarily felt in the expansion of entrepreneurial capacity and the supply of technicians, which served to lessen the shortage of these productive factors in the country.

TABLE 18
Industrial Ownership by National Origin, Chile, 1914–25
(in percentages)

Year	Chilean	Foreign	Mixed	Corporation	Not Given	Total
1914	43.2	50.3	4.6		1.9	100.0
1915	43.1	48.2	3.8	3.7	1.2	100.0
1916	45.8	47.8	3.0	3.1	0.3	100.0
1917	44.6	47.3	3.0	4.6	0.5	100.0
1918	45.5	46.6	2.9	4.6	0.4	100.0
1919	45.7	44.7	3.1	6.0	0.5	100.0
1920	46.0	44.3	2.7	6.7	0.3	100.0
1921	46.0	44.3	3.7	6.0	0.0	100.0
1922	44.8	44.9	3.7	6.6	0.0	100.0
1923	44.9	44.8	3.8	6.5	0.0	100.0
1924	44.4	45.3	3.7	6.6	0.0	100.0
1925	42.9	46.5	3.9	6.7	0.0	100.0

Source: Table A-6.

In comparison to the native population, immigrants revealed a greater proclivity toward entrepreneurial activity. That they possessed a dynamic spirit and an aptitude for industrial ventures is strongly indicated by the empirical data. Between the years 1915 and 1925, those establishments whose proprietors were of foreign origin accounted for 44–50 per cent of the total of all manufacturing concerns in Chile (Table 18). In terms of invested capital, this represented approximately one-third of the total (Table 19). Unfortunately, the large corporate entities were grouped separately, and it is not possible to measure the extent of immigrant entrepreneurship at that level through the statistical yearbooks. The survey of firms in Appendix 3, however, reveals that the contribution of this group was important for a significant portion of the major Chilean industrial corporations, 38 per cent of which were founded by immigrants. Moreover, they remained as principal figures in the management of these concerns after incorporation in over one-quarter of the cases.[47]

TABLE 19

Industrial Capital Investment by National Origin, Chile, 1915–25
(in percentages)

Year	Chilean	Foreign	Mixed	Corporation	Not Given	Total
1915	27.2	34.1	5.1	33.3	0.3	100.0
1916	30.9	33.5	4.4	30.7	0.5	100.0
1917	31.3	33.7	3.3	31.6	0.1	100.0
1918	31.1	33.4	3.6	31.7	0.2	100.0
1919	28.1	32.3	4.3	35.1	0.2	100.0
1920	28.5	32.0	2.2	37.2	0.1	100.0
1921	27.4	30.4	4.9	37.3	0.0	100.0
1922	25.5	30.3	4.3	39.9	0.0	100.0
1923	25.8	27.9	4.7	41.5	0.0	100.0
1924	24.3	29.1	5.0	41.6	0.0	100.0
1925	26.1	30.1	3.9	39.9	0.0	100.0

Source: Table A-7.

How may this superior economic performance of the immigrants in a new productive area be explained? From a sociological perspective, it was quite common in the past to seek an answer in terms of the cultural deviance or social marginality of the minority ethnic groups. Since the traditional areas of production are generally closed to him, the immigrant often turns to commerce or moves into activities which are not filled by the dominant sector of society. Moreover, since he is of modest means, at the margin of the native community and uninhibited by its value system, the immi-

47. The companies were Compañía de Refinería de Azúcar de Viña del Mar, Compañía Molinos y Fideos Carozzi, Cervecería Anwandter, Fábrica de Cerveza de Limache, Fábrica de Cerveza Gubler y Cousiño, Cervecería Andrés Ebner, Compañía Chilena de Tabacos, Compañía Chilena de Tejidos, Fábrica Italo-Americana de Paños Tomé, Camiserías Matas y Cía., Imprenta y Litografía Universo, Fábrica Nacional de Loza de Penco, Compañía Electro Metalúrgica, Compañía de Maestranza y Galvanización, Fundición y Fábrica de "La Unión," and the Fábrica Nacional de Envases y Enlozados S.A.

grant tends to be more adventurous and opportunistic in his business dealings.[48]

This explanation generally does not apply to the immigrant entrepreneurs who came to Chile. Although many of them were connected with trade and industry, it would be difficult to argue that this was due to their condition as marginal men. On the contrary, these were the most logical activities for them to engage in since they were precisely the ones to which they had been dedicated in Europe. Immigration to Chile was always a selective process, both in fact and by design. Those who came were usually of urban bourgeois background. A government-sponsored immigration service operated during the years 1850–71 and from 1882 to the First World War. The benefits of this service varied throughout these years and ranged from obtaining work contracts in industry for the urban-bound immigrants and grants of land in the south for those who were to colonize the Valdivia area to a subsidy for the payment of passage from Europe. With regard to industry, the expressed purpose of the program and that of the entire body of legislation concerning immigration was to attract individuals with experience and skill who could fill the need for technical and managerial personnel, as well as establish their own enterprises.[49] This program never sought to bring great numbers of people to Chile; during the entire period from 1850 to 1913, only a little over 62,000 people came assisted by the Chilean authorities.[50] In addition, census data indicate that between 1885 and 1930, the number of non–Latin American foreigners living in Chile never amounted to much more than 2 per cent of the total population.[51]

The selective nature of immigration to Chile may also be appreciated by the high percentage of foreigners occupying technical positions in Chilean industry. Between 1919 and 1926, this was on the order of 40–48 per cent (Table 20). The better preparation of the immigrant worker for industry in relation to his Chilean

48. A review of the literature on entrepreneurship may be found in Alec Alexander, "The Supply of Industrial Entrepreneurship."

49. González, *La Sociedad*, p. 7; "La Sociedad de Fomento Fabril, su labor durante cincuenta años," p. 473; Teodorindo Parada, *Algunas consideraciones sobre inmigración.*

50. Time-series data of government-sponsored immigration are available in Parada, *Algunas consideraciones*, pp. 9–11, and Macchiavello, *Política económica*, p. 83.

51. Five censuses were taken during this period: 1885, 1895, 1907, 1920, and 1930.

counterpart was also evident in their occupational composition according to "blue collar" (*obrero*) or "white collar" (*empleado*) condition of employment. In 1918, of a total of 60,042 persons employed as obreros in the manufacturing sector, 98.6 per cent were Chileans, whereas foreigners represented 18.6 per cent of all those holding "white collar" positions.[52]

Immigrant entrepreneurship in Chile was supplied by the nationals of many countries rather than one particular nation. Before 1930, the British, French, German, Spanish, and Italians were all

TABLE 20
TECHNICAL PERSONNEL IN CHILEAN INDUSTRY BY NATIONAL ORIGIN, 1919–26

Year	Chilean	Percentage	Foreign	Percentage
1919	532	52.1	489	47.9
1920	610	56.7	466	43.3
1921	839	56.0	658	44.0
1922	1,168	60.2	772	39.8
1923	1,012	54.4	849	45.6
1924	1,671	53.1	1,474	46.9
1925	1,615	51.9	1,495	48.1
1926	1,597	51.9	1,479	48.1

SOURCE: Oficina Central de Estadística, *Anuario estadístico, industrias*, 1919–26.

well represented among the organizers of industrial concerns. Foreigners entered and became important in practically all areas of the economy. But, for the most part, they began in commerce and industry, later expanding into banking and agriculture. In addition to the human capital which they brought to Chile in the form of training and experience, some of the immigrants also came with funds which they had accumulated from their own enterprises in Europe.[53]

Carlos Anwandter, who has been referred to as the founder of the industrial plant of Valdivia, was such a man. He had studied pharmacy and the natural sciences in Berlin and was a deputy

52. Chile, Oficina Central de Estadística, *Anuario estadístico, industrias*, 1918, p. 25.

53. There are several valuable studies of the foreign colonies in Chile: Amadeo Pelegrini and Jorge Ciro Aprile, *El progreso alemán en América, Chile: resumen general de las actividades que ha desarrollado en Chile la colonia alemana*, and *El censo comercial-industrial de la colonia italiana en Chile*; Alberto Hoerhl, *Los alemanes en Chile*; E. Valga, *Album de la colonie française au Chili*; Dorte, *El porvenir*.

of the Prussian Diet in 1847 and a member of the Constituent Assembly of Prussia the following year. His business interests consisted of pharmacies, a brewery, and land estates. Because of the political problems in his homeland, he came to Chile in 1850 and, with the money he had taken with him, began to establish factories and other business in the Valdivia area. He was one of the first beer producers in Chile, opened a factory for the manufacture of soap and perfume, founded the first pharmacy of Valdivia, and acquired extensive agricultural holdings.[54]

Carlos Klein and José Rabinovitch, who had large foundries in Santiago, came to Chile equipped with considerable formal training in their field. They had studied at the polytechnical institutes of Stuttgart and Paris. In addition, Klein's father owned a machine factory and foundry in Germany, which also served as a base of experience and capital for the Chilean venture.[55]

Many of these immigrants of urban bourgeois background associated themselves with trading houses soon after arriving in Chile, thus broadening their range of contacts and knowledge of market conditions, opening up channels of supply and distribution, and assisting them in gaining access to credit. Augusto Gubler came to Valparaíso from Germany as an employee of the import company Hagnaner Gubler y Cía., in which his father was a partner. By 1870, he became manager of all of the company's operations in Chile. Since he had also acquired considerable experience in the beer industry in Europe and saw the potential for local production in Chile, in 1883 he used his contacts to persuade Carlos Cousiño to support him in the founding of a brewery and ice factory in Providencia, then at the outskirts of Santiago. The enterprise was a complete success. It was able to open up exports to northern countries and for a time even had a monopoly of the distribution of beer in central Bolivia.[56]

Another immigrant, Antonio Aninat, arrived in Chile around the middle of the nineteenth century and worked as a merchant for a short time. His father was the owner of a textile mill in France, where Antonio learned the trade. He opened a cloth factory near Santiago but did not have much success, so he moved to Concepción where he became the agent of a commercial house. He soon

54. "Crónica de Don Carlos Anwandter."
55. "Don Carlos Klein"; "Don José Rabinovitch."
56. Pedro Pablo Figueroa, *Diccionario biográfico de extranjeros en Chile*, p. 98.

established his own trading firm, Aninat y Cía., which grew into an important one. Later he became active in the manufacture of wine, liquors, and flour. His son took up the management of his father's business interests after returning from years of study at the Sorbonne. He expanded the family operations, moved into banking, where he was one of the principal figures of the Banco de Concepción, and held a chair on the board of the Compañía Molinera "El Globo," controlled by the British import firm Duncan Fox y Cía. He was highly regarded by Chilean society and was decorated by the French government for his services in strengthening Franco-Chilean trade.[57]

The foreign community itself was valuable to the entrepreneur in a number of ways at different stages in his career. The French, British, Italian, Spanish, and German communities, although easily identifiable as cohesive entities, were all closely associated with the Chilean upper classes through business, social, and blood ties.[58] Entry to the highest social circles of the country was thus provided for the immigrant entrepreneur. Capital also was forthcoming from the foreign communities since, in addition to the branch offices of European banks, most of them had their own ethnic-based banks.[59] Indeed, the principal figures in the immigrant-owned factories and in these financial institutions were often the same.

Fernando Rioja Medel, a Spanish immigrant eminently successful in mercantile and industrial activities, was able to obtain considerable capital from the Banco Español de Chile, which purchased over 9 per cent of the stock in the Compañía Chilena de Tabacos, controlled by Rioja. He was a prominent member of the Spanish colony and had been decorated on several occasions by the king of Spain, who had finally bestowed upon him the title of Conde de Rioja y Neila, in consideration of his efforts in behalf of Spanish-Chilean commercial relations.[60]

Finally, the foreign colonies provided the channel through which partnerships could be formed and trustworthy personnel hired. Thus, Augusto Carozzi, who began with a small food store and pasta factory in 1897, was able to develop the latter enterprise into

57. Ibid., p. 29; *Diccionario biográfico de Chile, 1936*, pp. 44–45.

58. For a contemporary account of the relations between the foreign colonies and the Chilean social elite, see Dorte, *El porvenir*, pp. 196–204.

59. For example, the Banco Francés de Chile, the Banco Español de Chile, the Banco Italiano, and the Banco Yugoeslavo de Chile.

60. See the obituary of Fernando Rioja Medel in *La Revista Comercial*, July 15, 1922, pp. 497–99.

a major industry in Chile with plants near Valparaíso and Santiago by 1926, with the capital and expertise of his six partners, all from the Italian community.[61]

From the foregoing it may be appreciated that the sources of entrepreneurship and capital for industry were multiple. A national oligarchy predominantly homogeneous in nature, with investments spread across mining, commerce, finance, and agriculture, participated actively in manufacturing as well. Foreign import houses, industrial corporations, and banks were also present at an early date, often in association with the national oligarchy. Finally, the immigrant provided another important reserve of entrepreneurs. Success, however, most often led the immigrant or second-generation industrialist to become incorporated into the ranks of the elite which had traditionally evidenced a decidedly fluid attitude with regard to social mobility. The criteria were not set according to the type of economic activity or ethnic background, but rather were based on the demonstrated business prowess of the individual. Under no circumstances should the immigrant businessmen in Chile be characterized, as has been done most recently, as "marginal men, individuals who found themselves at odds" with the prevailing values of Chilean culture and who "rejected the traditional elite's ways of doing things."[62]

A more common career pattern for the successful immigrant entrepreneur was that of Guillermo Helfmann, who arrived as a young man from Germany in 1852.[63] He was given the position of managing editor of *El Mercurio* of Valparaíso. Seven years later, Helfmann opened a trading house in Valparaíso for the importation of printing presses, newsprint, and other publishing equipment. He soon became the principal supplier to the trade and, with his accumulated experience, founded in 1870 the English language newspaper of Valparaíso, *The Chilean Times*. His capital and am-

61. Compañía Molinos y Fideos Carozzi, *Bodas de oro, 1907–1957*; Pedro Luis González, *Album gráfico de la Sociedad de Fomento Fabril*, p. 148.

62. Carl Solberg, *Immigration and Nationalism: Argentina and Chile, 1890–1914*, p. 50. Also unacceptable is his observation that Chilean culture conferred little prestige on commercial or industrial entrepreneurship, activities supposedly not suitable for gentlemen (p. 49).

63. Sources for Guillermo Helfmann's life and the history of his enterprises are V. Figueroa, *Diccionario*, 3:436–37; Imprenta y Litografía Universo, *Memorias*, 1906–32, ABCS; Invoice from Sociedad Imprenta y Litografía Universo to the Sociedad de Fomento Fabril, August, 1908, MIOPAN, vol. 1,356; and Memorandum of the Santiago Stock Exchange on the Imprenta y Litografía Universo in "Estudios," vol. 4, ABCS.

bition expanded over the years until, in 1895, he founded one of the largest publishing houses in the country, the Imprenta y Litografía Universo in Santiago. Helfmann's was an aggressive spirit. In 1906, he acquired the Litografía e Imprenta Gillet with offices in Valparaíso and Santiago and the Valparaíso publishing concern Babra y Cía. Never having deserted the importing business, he also remained the major source of imported material for the sector, and few other publishers could offer any serious competition.

In addition, he operated at the highest levels of the Chilean plutocracy. His contacts gave him access to government, which offered him the lion's share of official publications, as did the Sociedad de Fomento Fabril and numerous other institutions. He and his family maintained close association with the Edwards and other members of the Chilean elite on a social as well as a business level. They were members of the Club de la Unión and the Club de Viña del Mar, his son Federico married into the Subercaseaux family, and outstanding representatives of the elite were associated with him in his business operations.[64] Never out of touch with the Edwards, Helfmann purchased the publishing house Zig-Zag from them in 1912, and from then held a virtual monopoly in the publication of illustrated magazines. Almost from the outset, Helfmann had been associated with, accepted by, and assimilated into the highest echelons of the Chilean elite.

Illustrative of the manner in which industrial activities were accommodated with other economic interests, ostensibly in conflict with the development of domestic manufacturing, is the example of the import-export house of Weir Scott y Cía. Founded in 1856 by the English immigrant Andrew Scott, it had grown into one of the most important commercial enterprises in Chile by World War I and had become a foreign-owned entity with home offices in London. The firm had nitrate railroad lines in the north and distribution outlets in Antofagasta, Valparaíso, Santiago, Talcahuano, and Concepción. The concern owned fundos which served as a base for its condensed-milk plant founded in Graneros in 1907. It operated in close cooperation with the Sociedad de Fomento Fabril, which worked to maintain Weir Scott's markets, protected

64. Examples are Gustavo Ross Santa María and Manual Pardo Correa, who both occupied the position of president of Helfmann's publishing house before World War I. Pardo Correa has been referred to by Virgilio Figueroa as "the patriarch of Viña del Mar" (*Diccionario*, 4:468). He was one of the founders of the Valparaíso Stock Exchange and a leader of the Radical Party.

by import duties on condensed milk in the extreme south and north of the country. These markets were threatened from time to time by Ministers of Hacienda who tried to establish duty-free ports for the product in these regions. Weir Scott also owned the glassware factory "Yungay" but was not in competition with the powerful Compañía Cristalerías de Chile since the product lines were different.[65]

As stressed earlier, although their social origins were varied, as a group the industrialists were integrated into the dominant sector of society. Consequently, distinctions between the industrial bourgeoisie and other groups lack any real meaning. From the time of the War of the Pacific, modifications in the opportunity structure—the total environmental or economic structure—stimulated a demand for industrial entrepreneurs. As these changes in the economy and productive possibilities of the country occurred and were perceived by the "economic men" of the elite, they, in turn, responded by shifting and expanding their investments. But they were not the only ones in a position to take advantage of these opportunities, for the occupational backgrounds of immigrants and importers placed them in an exceptionally favored position to do so also. Since the industrial structure was essentially oriented to the final consumer in the domestic market, no conflict of interests appeared as has been stated by other writers. Moreover, all elements—immigrants, foreign investors, and national elite—tended to merge as industrial enterprise became more profitable and industry expanded.

65. Márquez, *Libro*, 1:267; *BSFF* 32 (August 1915):550; 41 (September 1924):633–34; 47 (October 1930):744–48.

5. Civil War and the Failure of Industrialists as Agents of Change

THE ASSIMILATION of industrialists into the traditional oligarchy was crucial in defining the course of industrialization and its ability to act as an instrument of institutional change. It was also decisive in determining the role of industrialists during moments of national crisis when fundamental issues concerning prevailing economic interests and the structure of power were at stake. Indeed, such a moment came during the presidential administration of José Manual Balmaceda.

Following a period of intense political strife, Balmaceda came to office in 1886 only to be overthrown in 1891. His suicide after defeat and the thousands of casualties during the eight months of conflict indicate the high stakes in the civil war. Regardless of the schools of thought to which they subscribe, virtually all students of modern Chilean events agree that the Revolution of 1891 has had a profound influence on subsequent Chilean history. The purpose of this chapter is to review the issues and examine the actions and alliances of industrialists in this crossroads of Chilean national development, to demonstrate that the existing interpretations concerning their participation are inadequate. Because the events and motives for the conflict have been examined in considerable detail elsewhere, I will present only a brief summary in order to deal more extensively with the industrialist group.[1]

Motives for the Revolution

In simplified terms, the issues which provoked the 1891 conflict were divided into politically motivated and economically motivated ones. Broadly speaking, the former interpretation may be identified with conservative analysts of the Chilean past, while the latter has primarily been the product of Marxist writers.

There were several basic issues in the political contest leading up to the violent events of 1891. First, there was conflict over principles of juridical organization, based on a growing trend to shift the focus of political power from the executive to the legislative branch of government. Balmaceda, on the contrary, intended to return Chile to the strong presidential state anchored in the Portales Constitution of 1833. Since 1861, the latter had been eroded through increasingly frequent amendments and practices by the various liberal groups in congress which sought to implant a parliamentary system. Curiously, as a member of congress Balmaceda himself had espoused this cause, but upon occupying the presidential chair, he became increasingly obsessed with the real and even greater potential power (as he viewed it) which the office presented him.[2]

Balmaceda's efforts to increase rather than diminish presidential authority were not lightly dismissed as eccentric and anachronistic by the members of an already strong and militant legislature. On the other hand, given his highly egoistic personality and tendency to enforce his goals by an escalation of arbitrary acts in the face of any congressional opposition, the majority of congressional representatives, irrespective of political party, gradually perceived him to represent a real threat to their interests and power. Thus even though he exercised the traditional practice of direct presidential intervention in national elections and was able to maintain a con-

1. An ample bibliography of the main works dealing with Balmaceda and the civil war of 1891 is to be found in Pike, *Chile*, pp. 318–22. See also Harold Blakemore, "The Chilean Revolution of 1891 and Its Historiography." The most recent additions to the literature on the subject known to me are Harold Blakemore, *British Nitrates and Chilean Politics 1886–1896: Balmaceda and North*, and Heise, *Historia*.

2. On Balmaceda's background as a proponent of parliamentarism see Heise, *Historia*, pp. 69–77.

gressional majority in the elections of 1888, by the following year practically all of his picked adherents had passed over to the opposition. According to Julio Heise, a mistaken concept of authority together with an evident lack of political acumen and flexibility prevented Balmaceda from achieving the necessary balance of forces to maintain a governmental majority in congress, as his predecessors Errázuriz, Pinto, and Santa María had done.[3]

The increasingly arbitrary and authoritarian behavior of the president in imposing institutional changes in government was enmeshed with political matters. One of these was the fear of certain political parties that they would lose the gains they had made in specific areas of political dispute. Another matter was that the Conservatives, seeking to utilize whatever influence the church still held at the local level to advance their interests, supported a plan to establish a political structure based on autonomous municipalities. No doubt, they were also distrustful of Balmaceda's efforts at the time to reconcile himself with the church. Remembering him as a promoter of anticlerical legislation, the Conservatives interpreted this as an attempt to better his political image at their expense.[4] On the other hand the Radical Party had made considerable headway in recent local and provincial elections. If they could end presidential intervention, the Radicals felt certain of bringing a sizeable component to congress. But an unfriendly central government with the authority and the disposition to intervene in elections promised a barren political future for them.

The final point of political contention involved personalities. As the 1891 election drew closer the Liberal National Alliance, which had supported Balmaceda, was splintered by the resurgence of conflict among several factions of different candidates. Most factions were particularly outraged when Balmaceda began to groom a close collaborator and cabinet member, Enrique Salvador Sanfuentes, to succeed him in the presidency. Harold Blakemore informs us that "though the idol of some sections of the Government Liberal Party, Sanfuentes was 'cordially detested' by the other Liberal groups, which were in any case already at loggerheads with Balmaceda because of his apparent neglect of their political interests and his predilection for personal adherents."[5] In view of such opposition, Balmaceda denied the existence of any "official"

3. Ibid., p. 80.
4. Pike, *Chile*, p. 41.
5. Blakemore, *British Nitrates*, p. 116.

candidate and Sanfuentes withdrew his candidacy upon accepting the post of Minister of Interior in May 1890. Nonetheless, by that time, the Nationals, the Radicals, and other Liberal factions did not trust either Balmaceda's word or Sanfuentes' gesture, and opposition mounted. But Balmaceda continued his obstinate policy of building up a personal political party—a vain obsession which finally caused Sanfuentes himself to break from the ranks of the president's supporters.[6]

All of these issues involved a contest for political power at either the institutional party or strictly personal level; it served to divide the oligarchy into a patchwork of affiliations. The political conflict was essentially a struggle within the traditional ruling elite, with no participation of the masses. As an integral part of the dominant sector of the population, industrialists once again were not distinguished by their participation in a single party or faction. On the whole, their political interests were represented by the widespread coalition which gradually united to overwhelm Balmaceda, whose base of support was diminishing, and finally stopped the president's drive toward authoritarianism. The political interpretation of events and actors is inadequate, though, as it leaves unexplained important forces put into motion against Balmaceda for nonpolitical reasons.

These forces are related to the other basic set of issues which were at play—economic interests. It is on this point that Marxist writers have attempted to demonstrate the existence of a nationalist industrial bourgeoisie acting in union with Balmaceda as champions of a new middle class to transform the social and economic order on the European model.

To a significant degree, Balmaceda's announced program was the precursor of economic planning efforts and policy issues which have dominated development in twentieth-century Chile. His policy statements were strongly nationalistic and were based on a state-directed and state-supported program of modernization. His administration antagonized foreign interests by proposing to nationalize the nitrate territory railway, then owned by British interests, and by planning to use the still extensive public reserves of nitrate lands to regulate both the production and sale of that re-

6. Sanfuentes' alienation was provoked by Balmaceda's appointment in October 1890 of "a new cabinet consisting solely of unswerving personal adherents," chief among whom was Domingo Godoy, a man not adverse to the use of force to beat down opposition (ibid., pp. 184–85).

source. Later, the government encouraged private domestic companies to buy the public reserves, to which foreign interests were denied access, and thereby increase domestic participation in nitrate production and exportation.

On the other hand, domestic oligarchic interests were directly threatened by Balmaceda's plans concerning the future use of nitrate revenue and the proceeds of the export duty on nitrates. First, he proposed to establish a state central bank based on nitrate revenues. Until then, private banks had used this income to follow an increasingly inflationary note-issuing policy, which favored the heavily mortgaged oligarchy and the exporting interests whose income was received in foreign currency and whose costs lagged behind the general increase in the price level. The central bank, however, would have exclusive responsibility for note issue. Forced savings generated by the state-controlled growth of the money supply would allocate more resources to the public sector for the expanded public works program sponsored by Balmaceda. Moreover, he proposed to use the central bank to stimulate development through low-interest, broad-based loans which would lessen the power of private financial interests and reduce the advantage of those who enjoyed privileged access to bank credit.

Second, Balmaceda intended to use the nitrate export duty income for special national development projects such as road building, railway construction, and expansion of the educational system. His stated plan was to cover the costs of regular government administration and ordinary services through a series of additional internal taxes which would transfer resources from the higher income groups to the lower. As a consequence of these policies, Balmaceda antagonized the most powerful vested interests in the country. Dominant elements of Chilean society viewed his administration as a direct threat to their sources of wealth, income, and traditional life style which could be preserved only through the defeat of any proponents of such a program.

The Role of the Industrialists in the Civil War

As mentioned, the main economic interpretation of the Civil War of 1891 stems from Marxist thought, particularly from the works of Hernán Ramirez Necochea and Marcelo Segall.[7] They both uti-

7. Hernán Ramírez Necochea, *Balmaceda y la contrarrevolución de 1891*; Marcelo Segall, *Desarrollo del capitalismo en Chile*. See also Véliz, "La mesa," p. 236.

lize supposed differences in the economic activities and interests of the opponents as basic units of analysis. Ramírez concludes: "Two forces were active in the country: on the one hand, there are the old landowners, the commercial and financial bourgeoisie and English imperialism. These elements were something like an omnipotent trinity which obstructed the possibilities for developing the national economy; their presence and action would tend to perpetuate the feudal relations prevalent in the countryside, to make Chile an appendage of British expansion and to subordinate it to the whims of imperialism. In opposition to these sectors were several social levels. Among these incipient and still weak groups we may mention the following: (1) the industrial bourgeoisie . . . (2) the middle sectors . . . and (3) the proletariat."[8]

To indicate the existence of an industrial sector spurring national development, these authors refer to the existence of numerous factories and single out as prime examples the Compañía de Refinería de Azúcar de Viña del Mar and the foundries of Lever Murphy and Balfour Lyon.[9] The years of the administration of José Manuel Balmaceda are precisely those which are identified as the only moments in Chilean history when a nationalist industrial bourgeoisie may be found, a group dedicated to the development of new productive forces in the nation and identified in its ideology with the need for far-reaching changes in the Chilean social order. The moment of crisis came with the Civil War of 1891 and, it is argued, the results of this conflict sealed the course of Chilean development in the twentieth century by destroying the existence of this nationalist group of industrial entrepreneurs. From then on, industry came under the control of the "financial and commercial capitalists" who opposed any transformation of the structure of power and were incapable of making industry an instrument for national economic development.

This interpretation rests heavily on the supposition that no structural links existed between the industrial sector and the dominant elements of Chilean society. But, as has been seen, the relationship among industry, commerce, finance, and the foreign sector were always strong. The foreign concerns Alsop y Cía. and Kendall y Cía. were the first financiers of Julio Bernstein's sugar refinery in

8. *Balmaceda*, pp. 199–202. For the same identification of groups by economic activity, see Segall, *Desarrollo*, p. 172.

9. Hernán Ramírez Necochea, *La guerra civil de 1891: antecedentes económicos*, pp. 189–90; Segall, *Desarrollo*, p. 174.

Viña del Mar; Arturo Besa, proprietor of the large commercial firm Besa y Cía., was vice-president of the refinery from 1889 to 1920. The principal furniture manufacturer was the import house Muzard, and in the flour-milling industry the English occupied a cardinal position. Among the first three presidents of the SFF before 1891 were Agustín Edwards Ross, Ramón Barros Luco, and Domingo Matte Pérez, all outstanding figures in finance, commerce, and agriculture. It should be noted that the first two were among the most active leaders in the formation of the anti-Balmaceda movement. Finally, the European immigrants, who were, upon reaching Chile, characteristically urban bourgeois, for the most part assimilated into the upper classes of Chilean society if their entrepreneurial activities met with success.

Even more noticeable than these contradictions is the number of factual errors in the evidence presented to sustain this generally accepted interpretation. According to Segall, the entrepreneurs of heavy industry followed "the fate of their agrarian representative"; they became outcasts for their activities during the war. As proof, he offers the case of the foundry of Lever Murphy which, he affirms, could no longer obtain the public contracts it had had before the war; consequently, the enterprise deteriorated. Nevertheless, in spite of the vengeance and extreme reprisals taken upon the supporters of Balmaceda, no important foundry or metalworking factory was touched by the Constitutionalist looters.

On the contrary, Ricardo Lever found it necessary to expand his plant to meet the orders he received after the war. With respect to contracts to produce locomotives for the state railroads, he and the other foundry owners generally received orders with the same degree of inconsistency as before.[10] A description of the Lever Murphy foundry published in January 1893 reported that the establishment "has recently undergone considerable expansion and important improvements which place it at the level of a truly great industrial enterprise."[11]

10. Reference is made to "inconsistency" because not even during the Balmaceda administration did the foundry owners receive a steady stream of government contracts under circumstances in which they were able to compete favorably with foreign firms. Thus, in 1889, the government purchased 45 British and 5 American locomotives as well as 200 flatcars through the British trading house Antony Gibbs y Cía. See Chile, Ministerio de Industrias y Obras Públicas, *Boletín*, 1889, 2:111–12.

11. "Una visita a Caleta Abarca," p. 6.

In 1892, Lever Murphy, Balfour Lyon, and Hardie y Cía. received contracts from the government for 500 freight cars of 8-, 12-, and 15-ton capacity, and in 1893, Lever Murphy won a public bid to build 12 locomotives for the state railroad.[12] In 1898, congress employed the national factories for the construction of rolling stock for the value of 1,450,000 pesos distributed by firm according to the figures in Table 21. Finally, in early 1900, Lever Murphy was given an important contract to build a 625-ton ship to be used by the navy for lighthouse and buoy tender work.[13]

TABLE 21
RAILROAD CONTRACTS CONCEDED TO NATIONAL FOUNDRIES, 1898

Firms	Locomotive	Tenders	Passenger Cars	Freight Cars	Value[a] (000)
Lever Murphy	10	10		70	520
Balfour Lyon			18	10	154
Hardie y Cía.			15	33	286
Tomás Stillman				220	490
Total	10	10	33	333	1,450

SOURCES: *BSFF* 15 (April 1898):110–12; Ministerio de Industrias y Obras Públicas, *Memoria*, 1898, p. 77.
a. Expressed in current pesos.

But perhaps the most interesting indication that there was no nationalist industrial bourgeoisie in Chile at the end of the last century is the fact that eminent personalities of the industrial sector in the SFF and even the so-called progressive agriculturalists with whom Balmaceda has been identified fought actively in the ranks of the Constitutionalists against their president. A director of the Sociedad Nacional de Agricultura from 1895, Ascencio Bascuñan Santa María, was also one of the most dynamic directors of the SFF. He served as vice-president of the association in 1892 and as president from 1912 to 1917. Bascuñan is representative of the progressive agriculturalists who became enterprising industrialists. A professional engineer, he directed the construction of numerous state railroad lines before the revolution, processed canned palm honey at his hacienda, Las Palmas de Ocoa, and even devised a method to transform palm leaf fibers into cardboard, water-resistant corrugated roofing sheets, and weaving material for fur-

12. "Locomotoras para los ferrocarriles del estado."
13. "La construcción naval en Chile."

niture.[14] But during the Civil War he was an officer in the anti-Balmaceda forces and distinguished himself in the battles of Concón and Placilla.

Maximiliano Errázuriz, a director of the SFF, one of the principal wine producers of the country and proprietor of the vast mineral foundry at Guayacán, is called by Segall one of the outstanding examples of the national bourgeoisie. Errázuriz, who also owned important mines near Coquimbo and Lebu was, however, among the principal investors in the Banco Nacional de Chile, of which he was president. Another member of the board of this bank was José Besa, one of the leaders of the rebel forces. In support of his statement that the industrialists followed the fate of Balmaceda, Segall sustains that Errázuriz retired in disillusionment to his landholdings in Panquehue. Given his background and the fact that the biographical dictionaries report that he died in 1890, one year before Balmaceda's downfall, it is difficult to picture Errázuriz' participation in behalf of Balmaceda during the crisis.[15]

On the contrary, in commenting upon the retaliation against members of the opposition by partisans of the Balmaceda administration, José Miguel Yrarrázaval informs us that "In the middle of January, 1891, the establishment belonging to the succession of don Maximiliano Errázuriz in Lebu was razed. The coal which had been mined was burned, the mine, locomotives, machines and water conduits were destroyed; the railway line was torn up and all the tools stolen. This involved damage which the chief engineer of the establishment estimated to be in the order of 1,250,000 pesos."[16]

Moreover, those industrialists who were active in politics and in the Revolution of 1891 appear with great frequency in the anti-Balmaceda faction. Men such as Ramón Barros Luco, Pedro Ewing, Guillermo Anwandter, Benjamín Dávila Larraín, Ismael Valdés Valdés, Pedro Lucio Cuadra, and Carlos T. Rabinet, all of whom had manufacturing interests, allied themselves with the Constitutionalist cause.[17]

Finally, an examination of the behavior of the SFF does not reveal any sign of a position which might be interpreted as forth-

14. V. Figueroa, *Diccionario*, 2:163–64; "Una nueva industria"; Laso, *Catálogo*, p. 157.

15. V. Figueroa, *Diccionario*, 3:65–66; Banco de Chile, *Banco de Chile, 1894–1944, reseña histórica*.

16. Yrarrázaval, *El Presidente Balmaceda*, 2:382.

17. *Memorandum de la revolución*.

coming from a national bourgeoisie group. Not only did Balmaceda fail to receive active support from this institution, but, on the contrary, evidence exists to suggest that the association was in opposition to the president. Having at its disposal all the elements with which to launch a strong campaign of public support in behalf of Balmaceda, the SFF discontinued publication of its monthly *Boletín* until Santiago came under rebel control. Then, in the first issue after its reappearance, the journal referred with a certain disdain to the "dictatorship" which the country had just experienced.[18] Certainly, silence is the least that could be expected from Balmaceda's sympathizers after his tragic death. The repudiation of his cause on the part of the association is clearly seen in the meetings of the executive council. On its own initiative, the council voted to refuse acceptance of the state subsidy which was due it "during the period of the dictatorship"; it manifested that those funds had to come from an administration legally constituted by congress, i.e., Balmaceda's adversaries.[19]

I conclude that the interpretation which touts the existence of a nationalist industrial bourgeoisie which supported Balmaceda in the struggle against the forces of "bankers, miners, merchants and the English" is erroneous. It misleads one into believing that industrialists were fulfilling the role of agents of change conventionally ascribed to them, when, if anything, the reverse was the case. As an integral part of the oligarchy rather than as a separate group, industrialists tended to oppose Balmaceda simply because the interests of that dominant group which represented the pinnacle of wealth and power were being threatened on both the political and the economic level simultaneously.

18. "Los trabajos de la Sociedad," p. 6.

19. Consejo Directivo de la Sociedad de Fomento Fabril, Acta del 25 de septiembre de 1891, "Libro de Actas," ASFF. See also "Memoria de la Sociedad de Fomento Fabril que corresponde a 1891," p. 129.

6. The Evolution of Industrial Concentration: Monopoly and Oligopoly, 1918-1937

ARISING in a traditional society, intimately linked with a generic national elite, and dependent upon foreign hegemony, Chilean industry did not challenge the traditional interests of the dominant forces in Chilean society. On the contrary, it buttressed the existing power structure. Rather than provide a "growth pole," manufacturing served to preserve the life style of the oligarchy and channel the income generated from its output to those who already composed the highest income groups of the country. This was made possible principally because of the high degree of concentration in Chilean industry. The monopoly rents which accrued to the oligarchy who invested in manufacturing thus served to maintain or intensify the distorted structure of national income distribution and later overall development. The purpose of this chapter is to prove the existence of this monopolistic and oligopolistic pattern in industry from the early stage of its development and to show that the major firms involved were those intimately linked with the national elite. In correlative fashion, the goal of this group was not to create an efficient industrial sector, eventually to be competitive on an international scale in those areas where comparative advantages could be applied, but rather the enhancement of a traditional life style.

Since the beginning of the last decade a central theme of the literature on Chilean industry has been the high degree of concentration which characterizes it. In reviewing the period between 1937 and 1957, Ricardo Lagos has shown the existence of a process which tended toward ever increasing monopolization of the sector.[1] The major part of his study, however, is directed to the latter date, and he provides a detailed examination of the situation according to different industrial groupings. At a much more highly disaggregated level of analysis, others have focused only on the final years of the decade 1960–70, and have proven industrial concentration to be much more intensive than had been believed. Many more industries were involved. These, in turn, were interlocked and entwined among themselves at the corporate level to form a convergence of power among an exceptionally small group of individuals and firms.[2] Existing without effective controls, this monopolistic situation is believed by many to have aggravated the current major problems in Chilean development. Just as the industrialization process itself was touted as a creature of the depression years, so this process of concentration is viewed as arising from that time.

In view of the fact that industrialization matured long before 1930, and many of its characteristics had crystallized before then, it is not unlikely that monopolistic and oligopolistic practices were also well advanced at an early date. This proposition is very plausible, given the assimilation of industry into the sphere of influence of the oligarchy, the restricted access to capital, and the structure of the industry's output itself, which was directed to the final consumer and the limited internal markets, especially that of the growing urban middle sectors.

A comparison of the empirical evidence for 1918 and 1937 bears out this observation. Since labor is the only factor of production for which comparable data are available, it was utilized to measure

1. Lagos, *La industria*, passim. The term monopoly is used in a broad sense and includes situations which are both strictly monopolistic and oligopolistic. More exactly, monopoly is defined as "a market in which virtually all of a commodity is provided by a single seller. An oligopoly is a market in which there are but a few firms, each of which recognizes that its actions have a significant impact on the price and supply of the commodity." See Robert Dorfman, *Prices and Markets*, p. 22.

2. Gasic, "Concentración"; Garretón and Cisterna, "Algunas características"; E. Acevedo and H. Vergara, *Algunos antecedentes sobre concentración, participación extranjera y transferencia technológica en la industria manufacturera chilena*.

concentration. Given the relatively labor intensive nature of Chilean manufacturing in this period, this technique is economically defensible, although obviously the possession of comparative material regarding capital, total assets, total output, and sales would have been more desirable. The statistical yearbook's volume for industry in 1918 and the industrial census of 1937 provide data on industrial establishments according to the number of workers employed.[3] These include all workers for 1937, both white collar employees and blue collar workers, but only the latter for 1918. Thus, the effect would be to underestimate the degree of concentration in 1918, since white collar employees would probably be found in greater proportion in the larger firms for reasons of administration, distribution, etc.

Five categories were utilized in both years by the Chilean Statistical Office, but the firms were grouped somewhat differently according to the number of persons employed, as may be seen from the classification.

Categories	1918 Industrial Yearbook	1937 Industrial Yearbook
	obreros	empleados and obreros
1	6–10	6–10
2	11–40	11–25
3	41–100	26–50
4	101–200	51–100
5	over 200	over 100

For purposes of immediate comparison of all Chilean industry in these two years, these categories may be consolidated into three broad sets with the percentage of establishments and workers which corresponds to each.

Size of firm according to number of workers	Percentage of establishments		Percentage of all workers	
	1918	1937	1918	1937
6–10	61.8	41.3	14.8	9.8
11–100	34.9	53.1	42.0	42.8
over 100	3.3	5.6	43.2	47.4
Total	100.0	100.0	100.0	100.0

3. The sources for the following analysis are Chile, Oficina Central de Estadística, *Anuario estadístico, industrias, 1918*, p. 81, and Chile, Dirección General de Estadística, *Censo industrial y comercial, 1937*, pp. 22–27.

This reveals a larger percentage of smaller establishments in 1918 than in 1937, and they were using relatively more labor. The changes evidenced during the period with regard to small- and medium-sized firms permit one or both of two possible interpretations. Either a number of the smaller concerns had grown into medium-sized operations and/or the establishment of a greater number of medium-sized firms with more capital-intensive production methods is indicated as manufacturing became more attractive. In any event, a higher degree of concentration existed in 1918. In that year 3.3 per cent of the total number of establishments were employing 43.2 per cent of all manual laborers. In 1937, a considerably greater percentage, 5.6 per cent of the largest enterprises, was required to account for 47.4 per cent of manual and nonmanual employees. As indicated, the concentration shown among the largest firms in 1918 in all probability is conservative since it excludes nonmanual personnel.

TABLE 22
CONCENTRATION IN CHILEAN INDUSTRY 1918 AND 1937, ACCORDING TO CUMULATIVE PERCENTAGES

	1918		1937	
Category	Establishments	Workers	Establishments	Workers
1	61.8	14.8	41.3	9.8
2	90.5	39.8	75.9	27.0
3	96.7	56.7	88.3	39.9
4	98.3	67.0	94.4	52.6
5	100.0	100.0	100.0	100.0

SOURCE: See p. 107*n*2.

A more precise and graphic presentation of the degree of concentration existing in Chile around the end of World War I compared with that of the late 1930s may be provided by the construction of a Lorenz curve. This device measures the cumulative percentage relationships between two variables, one on each axis. In this case the variables are the cumulative percentages of establishments and of labor. A completely uniform distribution would appear as a straight line of 45 degrees. The more hollow the curve, the more unequal is the distribution. The cumulative percentages for all of Chilean industry, 1918 and 1937, are arranged in Table 22 according to the five categories given above for each year.

The existence of a high level of concentration is evident in both years. An examination of the figures in the last category for 1918 (which includes only establishments with over 200 workers) reveals that 1.7 per cent of the firms employed 33 per cent of the manual labor force for all industry. In 1937 (when the final category included all establishments with over 100 workers), 5.6 per cent of the firms absorbed 47.4 per cent of the total industrial labor force. From these data the Lorenz curve may be drawn, the results of which appear in Figure 1; it depicts a slightly more intense degree of concentration for 1918.

It is possible to summarize the extent of inequality represented in the Lorenz curve in a single coefficient. For this purpose, a Gini

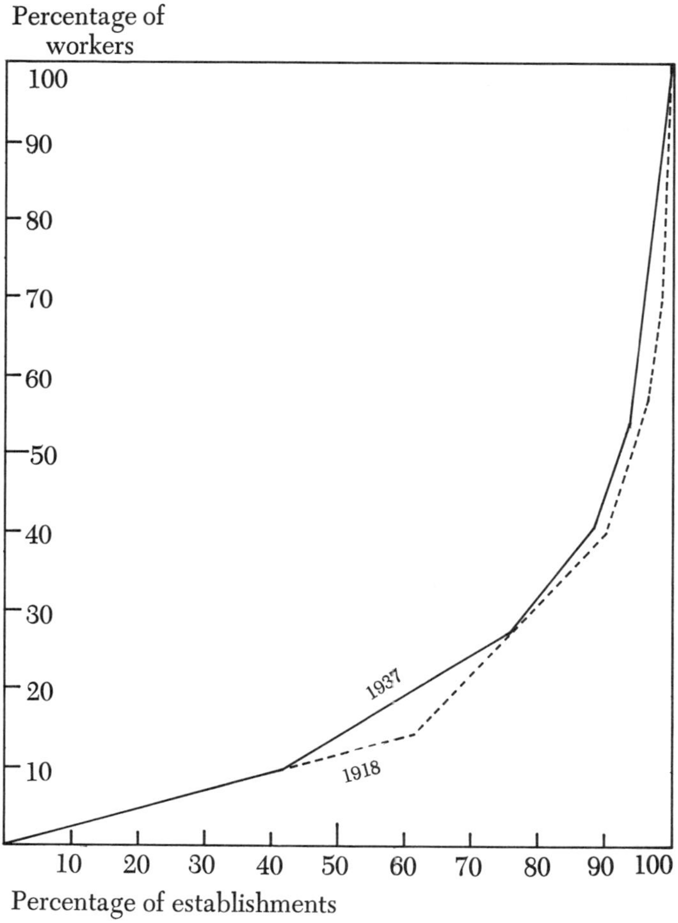

Fig. 1. Industrial concentration for all manufacturing, Chile, 1918 and 1937

coefficient was calculated. This is simply the ratio of (a) the area between the Lorenz curve and the diagonal line of perfectly equal distribution to (b) the area under the line of perfectly equal distribution. As the coefficient approaches 1.0, the degree of concentration increases. For 1918, this calculation yielded a coefficient of concentration of 0.64; in 1937, it was 0.61; and for 1957, Lagos has found it to be 0.71.[4]

Under the somewhat arbitrary but generally accepted assumption that a coefficient over 0.50 is indicative of a fairly high level of concentration, it may be concluded that from the perspective of labor input, Chilean industry was characterized by an advanced state of concentration at least as early as World War I. This concentration was slightly over that found in 1937, but with respect to 1957, the long-run trend was toward increasing monopolization in manufacturing.

In Figure 2, the level of analysis is carried to a sectoral level, and the Lorenz curves for seven industrial sectors are presented. These were chosen to compare the levels of concentration for important industries and because the firms in each of them which accounted for the existence of monopolistic situations were most often those which have been identified as being controlled by the oligarchy and foreign capital interest.[5]

The structure of the food, beverage, paper and printing (principally the latter), and construction materials industries was as concentrated in 1918 as it was in 1937, or slightly more so. Notable changes are evident in the tobacco, textile, and clothing industries. As the textile industry began to develop, especially after the depression, it assumed the same monopolistic structure as the other manufacturing sectors of importance. Clothing, on the other hand, gave way to the entry of a large number of medium-sized firms.

Tobacco provides an interesting case in that it appears that concentration declined considerably between 1918 and 1937. In fact, this did not occur and the curve is misleading. This problem derives in part from the shortcomings of the tool of analysis being used. Since the Lorenz curve deals with percentages and not the absolute number of firms, it obscures measurement somewhat. Yet

4. Lagos, *La industria*, p. 74.

5. Certain sectors closely identified with the oligarchy were not included in this analysis because only several firms existed in the entire industry. Thus, glass and pottery were excluded. Most of the factories operating in this sector belonged to the Compañía Cristalería de Chile and the Fábrica Nacional de Loza de Penco.

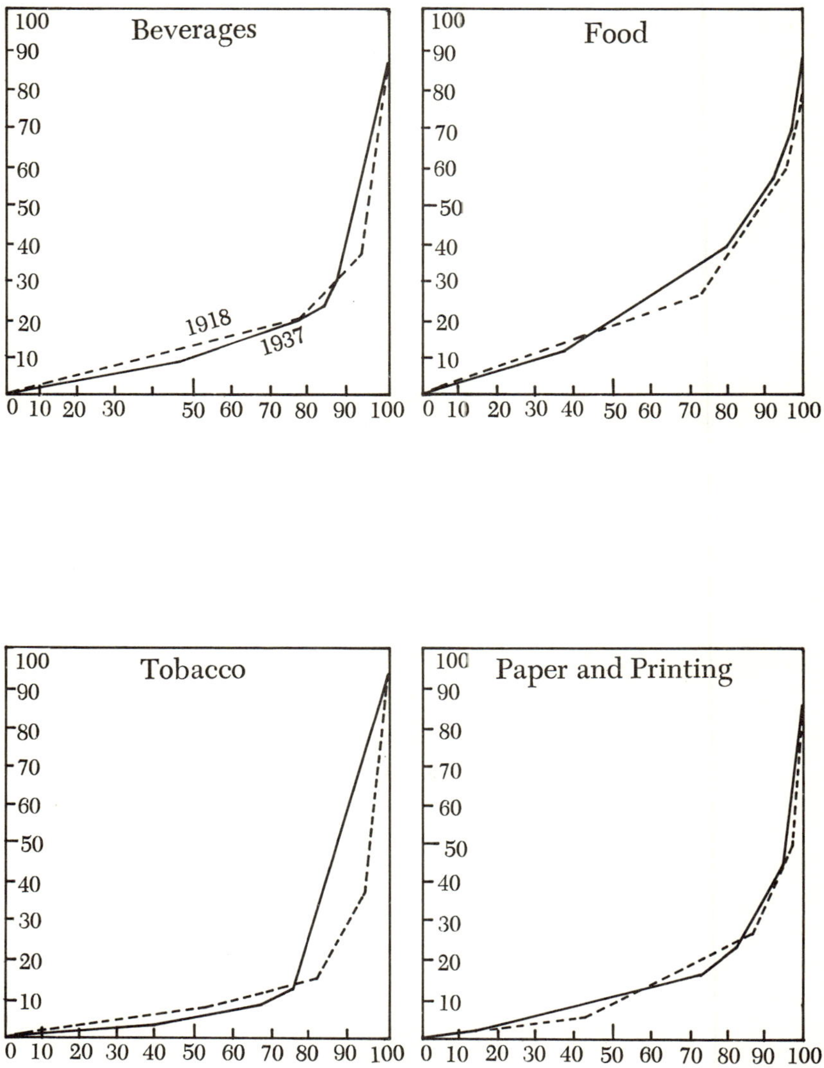

Fig. 2. Industrial concentration for selected sectors, Chile, 1918 and 1937. SOURCE: Table A-8.

Fig. 2—*Continued*

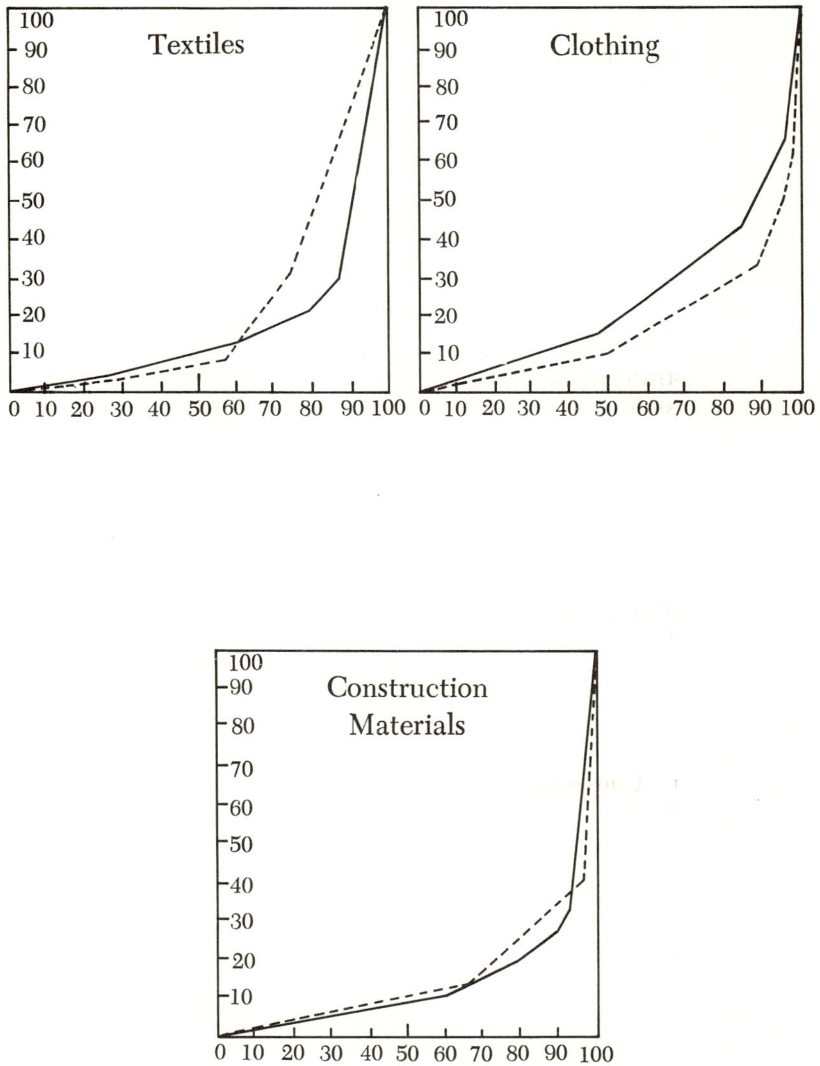

it is the only device known to me which can be applied to the available evidence so as to be able to discern the nature of the process underway. Data are not available to measure the percentage of workers employed by the largest companies down to the smallest in diminishing order of size. If this were possible, much of the distortion would be removed. Furthermore, this type of analysis still operates at a level of aggregation which conceals important aspects of the monopolistic nature of Chilean industry. The tobacco sector, for example, included a number of firms producing a variety of articles; the most interesting for my purpose here is cigarette production. This was the main item processed by one of the most important monopolistic firms of Chile, the Compañía Chilena de Tabacos. Moreover, the other firms in this sector, many of which began after World War I, were not capital intensive and tended to use more labor.[6] Obviously, this distorts the use of labor force at a sectoral level as an index with which to gauge industrial concentration.

Other indicators are needed. Capital, production, and sales figures would have been particularly useful. Regrettably, such data are either unavailable or presented in such a form that the more incisive instruments of analysis cannot properly be applied to them.

It is possible, however, to gain an overall idea of the extent of industrial concentration, at a much more disaggregated level, in specific production lines by the use of the monetary resources wielded by certain firms. This is done in Table 23 for sixteen industries and twenty corporations. Information on the total assets and fixed capital investments of firms forthcoming from their balance sheets was compared with the same items for specific industries as they appeared in the industrial yearbook for 1920. Certain firms had several factories which produced a number of products and published only consolidated balance sheets. This resulted in the total assets of the firm exceeding those of the sector to which it was assigned. In these cases, however, through contemporary accounts, the firms could be identified as exercising monopolistic or oligopolistic power.[7] Consequently, rather than present the actual amounts and percentages which might be misleading, it was decided to indi-

6. Arnoldo Rivera, *La industria del tabaco en Chile*, p. 14.

7. Examples are the Compañía Cervecerías Unidas, which had a number of product lines, i.e., soft drinks and ice, as well as products for its own consumption, such as sulfuric acid, and the Compañía Industrial de Catres, which produced other furniture items; but in the bed industry only three factories existed, all of which were owned by this company.

cate the situation in each industry by the broad categories of high, medium, and low degrees of concentration. Where one or several large enterprises account for over 50 per cent of the total assets and fixed capital investment of a given industry, a high degree of concentration was deemed to exist; between 20 and 50 per cent it was considered to be medium, and under 20 per cent, low.[8]

From Table 23, it is evident that, from the perspective of financial power, a high degree of concentration was characteristic of most of the industries surveyed. The only exceptions appear to be the flour, ship-building, and paper industries. Large mills existed in the flour industry, but since many of these were unincorporated enterprises, the situation of this industry is not clear. Of a total of 156 industrial mills, only two, both controlled by British trading houses, accounted for a considerable percentage of the industry's total assets (21 per cent). Yet there is no additional information to suggest that an oligopolistic condition existed, so it must be concluded that this industry was not marked by any significant degree of concentration. In paper manufacturing, the Compañía Manufacturera de Papeles y Cartones had been organized only that year. Thus, it did not yet evidence the monopolistic position which it later acquired, but this was not long in coming. From the very outset, the "papelera" started with a capital base which made it dominant in the paper industry under any circumstances.

The Steps to Industrial Domination

Although the macroeconomic analysis has shown that concentration was quite advanced at an early stage of Chile's industrialization, it does not afford insight into the process through which this state of affairs was reached. It does not identify those enterprises which were dominant or trace the development of their monopolies to uncover continuity or change in the structure of power in a particular industry. This can only be done by following the case histories of the companies most representative of those which ruled

8. Although only one or two factories accounted for all of the total assets and capital investment of a particular industry, these were not included if the industry was small, with very limited productive capacity and unable to satisfy a significant portion of domestic market demand. In such cases, foreign imports were most important and so a situation of industrial concentration with monopolistic characteristics could not be said to exist. An instance of this situation is the condensed milk industry, where only one factory, that of Weir Scott, existed and accounted for only a portion of domestic demand.

TABLE 23

INDUSTRIAL CONCENTRATION ACCORDING TO TOTAL ASSETS AND FIXED CAPITAL, 1920

Industry and Major Firms	Degree of Concentration According to	
	Total Assets of Specified Firms[a]	Fixed Capital of Specified Firms[a]
Sugar	High	Medium
Compañía de Refinería de Azúcar de Viña del Mar		
Flour	Medium	Low
Compañía Molinera San Cristóbal		
Compañía Molinera "El Globo"		
Vegetable oil	High	High
Compañía Industrial		
Beer	High	High
Compañía Cervecerías Unidas		
Tobacco	High	High
Compañía Chilena de Tabacos		
Woolen cloth	High	High
Fábrica Nacional de Paños de Bellavista		
Sociedad Nacional de Paños de Tomé		
Knit goods	High	High
Compañía Nacional de Tejidos "El Salto"		
Sociedad Manufacturera de Tejidos		
Compañía Chilena de Tejidos		
Shirts	High	High
Camiserías Matas y Cía.		
Paper	Medium	Medium
Compañía Manufacturera de Papeles y Cartones		
Printing	High	High
Imprenta y Litografía Universo		
Soap and perfume	High	High
Compañía Industrial		
Cement	High	High
Compañía de Cemento "El Melón"		
Glass	High	High
Compañía Cristalerías de Chile		
Beds	High	High
Compañía Industrial de Catres		
Metal containers and enamelware	High	High
Fábrica Nacional de Envases y Enlozados		
Ships	Medium	Medium
Astilleros Las Habas		

SOURCES: Chile, Oficina Central de Estadística, *Anuario estadístico, industrias,* 1920, and the annual reports of the specified firms.

a. Less than 20 per cent of industry total is considered a low degree of concentration, between 20 and 50 per cent medium, and over 50 per cent high.

industry. The history of the rise to a monopoly position of the major Chilean enterprises makes comprehensible the goals and values of the industrialists themselves and demonstrates that the primary consideration was to dominate an internal market from a secure position free from competition. Once this objective was attained and the means to maintain the life style to which the oligarchy had long become accustomed were assured, very little interest was shown in further growth or expansion into foreign markets.

One of the first oligopolies to be established was that of sugar refining. From the late nineteenth century only two refineries operated in Chile, the Compañía de Refinería de Azúcar de Viña del Mar (CRAV) and the Refinería de Azúcar de Penco, located near Concepción.[9] Since both were faced with very stiff competition from imports, especially that of German beet sugar, an oligopolistic market could not be said to exist from the beginning. In 1892, however, the interests of the refineries were defended in congress by representatives of their respective principals: Besa y Compañía and the German import house of Mauricio Gleisner y Compañía, as well as by the Sociedad de Fomento Fabril.[10] The results of this lobbying were a series of tariff changes beginning in 1893 which afforded the national refineries effective protection for a number of years. Between 1892 and 1895, sugar imports dropped by 75 per cent. After having passed several years of instability and slow growth, CRAV began to enter a period of rapid expansion in 1893. From 1894, high dividends were paid regularly to its shareholders.[11]

A gentleman's agreement was made with the Penco refinery according to which the Chilean market was cut into two parts: all to the south of Talca belonged to Penco and the region from Talca to the north (by far the most important market) went to CRAV. Thus, all competition between the two was avoided and a monop-

9. Several efforts were made at refining beet sugar in a way which would draw entirely on domestic raw materials, but these were not successful. It was not until the Chilean Development Corporation opened a beet-sugar mill and refinery, in 1952, that the dependence of the Chilean sugar industry on imports dropped by 50 per cent.

10. "Protección a la industria de refineración de azúcar." Gleisner owned the Penco refinery. Once again the instance arises in which an importer perceived greater profits in completing the transformation process domestically, in this case with imported Peruvian sugar, than from importing the finished product.

11. CRAV, *50 años*, p. 19.

oly came into being.[12] As early as 1902, the Viña and Penco refineries were attacked by the influential newspaper *El Ferrocarril* of Santiago, which accused them of exacting monopolistic profits. Even Jorge Hormann, a spokesman for the industrial sector, who replied in defense of the refineries, was forced to concede that the prices of national sugar were somewhat high and admitted that CRAV's management had no trouble at all in paying the stockholders fat dividends of 16 per cent annually.[13]

By 1904, the price of sugar had risen substantially. This provoked more criticism of the two national refineries. It also motivated a group of Spanish and Italian retail merchants of Santiago who had the financial backing of the Banco Español-Italiano to organize their own refinery, the Compañía Internacional Azucarera de Santiago.[14] As soon as the enterprise began to show promise, CRAV decided that the precedent was not a good one for them. A fierce campaign was launched against the Santiago refinery and by 1912, its owners were persuaded that the earnings made by their company did not warrant the struggle against CRAV. In that year they agreed to turn over the Santiago refinery to CRAV in return for the latter's stock whose capital base at the time was in pounds sterling rather than in unstable Chilean pesos.[15]

After CRAV came under the control of the Edwards in the early 1920s, it was decided that the time had come to dominate the entire national market. To this end the Penco refinery was absorbed in 1923. Apparently, the only other product competitive for CRAV was granulated sugar produced by twelve small- to medium-sized sugar-washing plants and also that imported from Perú. Most of this type of sugar, which was not as sweet as the refined variety, was used by other industries rather than for direct consumption.[16] But one grade of it, the *Sindicato* type, was popular among the low-income groups of the population who could not

12. Letter from Carlos Zañartu, vice-president of the SFF, to Ricardo Salas Edwards, Minister of Hacienda, December 31, 1917, published in *BSFF* 25 (March 1918):209–11; "Fábricas en Penco"; Galdames, *Geografía*, p. 189.

13. Jorge Hormann, "Las refinerías de azúcar."

14. Vicuña Pérez, *Proteccionismo aplicado a la industria chilena*, p. 25; "Nueva refinería de azúcar La Internacional."

15. CRAV, *50 años*, p. 23. In this period of inconvertibility, paper money, and inflation, the directorate of CRAV changed its capital base to pounds sterling in 1898. Apart from its products, lucrative earnings were made by the company through frequent foreign exchange operations. See CRAV, *Memorias*, 1898, 1920.

16. Hormann, *Chile industrial y económico, 1897–1917*, pp. 68–72.

afford CRAV's expensive refined sugar. To capture this market CRAV began to distribute Sindicato granulated sugar in 1922, and within a couple of years closed out competition from imports. Domestic competition in this line was overcome by the end of the decade with the purchase of the Valdivia plant of Hoffmann Hnos.[17]

In the meantime, one of the larger sugar-washing plants decided to test its luck against CRAV and expanded its operations into the production of refined sugar. This was done in 1921 by Hucke Hermanos y Compañía, a manufacturer of chocolate and candy.[18] Even though Hucke's output was miniscule alongside that of the Viña refinery, it was located in Valparaíso at the doorstep of CRAV's operations and in the middle of a superb urban market. This affront to CRAV's supremacy was not to be tolerated. In its 1923 annual report, CRAV's board of directors declared war on Hucke. In retaliation, CRAV opened up a factory for the production of chocolate and caramels, Hucke's main line. This measure brought success. By 1928, Hucke had tired of the unequal match and agreed to accept stock in CRAV and the sugar company's chocolate plant in exchange for its refinery and the promise not to encroach upon CRAV's enclave in the future.[19]

Although the Compañía Cervecerías Unidas (CCU) was the dominant force in the beverage industry of the Central Valley long before World War I, several other sizeable breweries operated in the southern provinces and produced for the lucrative market in the mining centers of the north. The CCU originated in 1902 from the fusion of two large enterprises in Santiago and Limache (near Valparaíso) controlled by the Cousiño and Edwards families.

By World War I, after a little more than a decade of highly profitable operations, the CCU was in a position to initiate its campaign of expansion to dominate the entire national market. The first move was made in 1916. In that year alone three of the larger competitors were absorbed by the CCU.[20] Of these, one, the Cervecería Andrés Ebner, located in Santiago, had been practically an appendage of the CCU for some years before. This occurred after

17. CRAV, *Memoria*, 1924, *50 años*, p. 35; see also the price listing for the various grades of sugar in *La Revista Comercial*, 1920–27.

18. This was a separate entity from the biscuit and cookie enterprise, Hucke Hermanos S.A.C., although both were owned by the same family.

19. CRAV, *Memorias*, 1922–29; *La Revista Comercial*, November 3, 1928, p. 57232; CRAV, *50 años*, p. 32.

20. Compañía Cervecerías Unidas, *Memoria*, 1916.

1906; when searching for expansion capital, the Ebner family sold out controlling participation in the firm to Carlos Cousiño.[21] The Ebner factory was a valuable acquisition since it was a major soft drink producer and held licenses from several foreign concerns to manufacture their beverages in Chile.[22] The other two firms taken over by the CCU in 1906 were the Cervecería Calera in the north and, in Valdivia, the Cervecería Anwandter, the oldest existing brewery in the country.

In 1917, the Cervecerías Unidas opened up a large warehouse in Antofagasta to centralize the distribution of beer to the nitrate workers. Acquisitions continued: between 1923 and 1932 the CCU had acquired breweries in Antofagasta, Santiago, Talca, Concepción, and Osorno.[23] Thus, with the exception of some small operations scattered across the country, by the depression years practically all of the beer and soft beverages produced in Chile came from the plants of the Compañía Cervecerías Unidas.[24]

The power exerted by the CCU, however, extended directly to other industries which dealt with it. Decisions made by its directorate often had repercussions across the economy and conditioned the development of enterprises which also exercised monopolies in key industries. This occurred with the Compañía Cristalerías de Chile in which the Cousiños and Edwards were most influential through stock held by the CCU and direct family participation.[25] By the end of World War I, the glass industry had become highly concentrated. Only a few factories existed in all of Chile. Of these, Cristalerías (then known as the Sociedad Fábrica Nacional de Vidrios) was the largest with two plants in Santiago. It increased productive capacity throughout 1916–17, and began to produce neutral glass in addition to its output of colored glass. In late 1917,

21. See the analysis of the Cervecería Andrés Ebner in Appendix 3.

22. One of the most popular of these was Bilz, a widely consumed beverage (*Chile industrial y comercial*, May 15, 1911, p. 53).

23. The breweries and dates of acquisition by the CCU were Sociedad Cervecerías de Concepción y Talca (1923), Fábrica Antofagasta ex-Mitrovich Hermanos (1927), Cervecería Santiago (1930) (which was dismantled and its installations distributed among the other CCU breweries), and Fábrica Osorno, ex-Jorge Aubel (1932). See Compañía Cervecerías Unidas, *Memorias*, 1923–32.

24. There is no reason to believe that the situation reached by the depression years was any different from that existing in the 1950s when the CCU supplied about 97 per cent of Chilean beer consumption (U.S. Department of Commerce, *Investment*, p. 125).

25. Between 1916 and 1920, the Compañía de Cervecerías Unidas held between 20 and 50 per cent of the total voting stock in the glass company; see Tocornal, *Exposición*, pp. 3, 10.

it purchased the old glass factory which the Cervecerías Unidas had in Rancagua. The following year, the Sociedad Manufacturera de Vidrios, in Santiago, was acquired by Cristalerías. With this structure the corporation became the largest glass manufacturer in Chile with a virtual monopoly over the production of glass containers for the beverage, foodstuffs, pharmaceutical, and toiletry industries.[26]

In spite of this, Cristalerías was highly dependent on Cervecerías Unidas, its major customer. So much of its output was destined for CCU beer and soft drink bottles that the company was hard pressed to meet the orders of other customers.[27] Moreover, disputes arose on several occasions between members of Cristalerías' board of directors and the CCU. These disputes were occasioned by disagreements over prices and the desire of Cristalerías' management to service the wine industry and to diversify into new product lines which would develop the glass industry further in Chile and diminish CCU's dominance over Cristalerías. The fear of the beer company was that if Cristalerías were to achieve independence, it would use its own dominance of the glass industry to dictate monopolistic prices to Cervecerías Unidas and would not meet the ever increasing demand of that company for bottles. As a result of these conflicts, Cervecerías Unidas forced substantial changes in the board of directors of Cristalerías in 1916 and 1921.[28] Only when the directorate headed by Ricardo Lyon, a personal representative of the controlling interests of CCU, took over and expanded the productive capacity of glass containers sufficiently to guarantee ample supply of bottles was Cristalerías permitted to embark upon its long-delayed program of diversification. By 1932, in addition to a wide variety of glass containers, it offered such products as electric insulators, glass plates and other household glassware; it was about to begin the manufacture of light bulbs

26. In 1924, the Vicuña Mackenna plant alone was producing 50,000 glass containers daily. By 1926, all production of standard glass containers (principally beer, wine, and soft drink bottles) was completely automatic (Sociedad Fábrica Nacional de Vidrios, *Memorias*, 1914–26).

27. In 1920–21, the orders of Cervecerías Unidas accounted for almost 50 per cent of the stock of Cristalerías. And from the beginning of 1921 to the middle of 1923, operations in the major plants of the glass company had to be suspended because of the closing of many nitrate oficinas which in turn resulted in a sharp decline in beer consumption. See Tocornal, *Exposición*, pp. 12–14, and Sociedad Fábrica Nacional de Vidrios, *Memorias*, 1921–23.

28. Tocornal, *Exposición*, pp. 3–11.

and had plans to develop the manufacture of plate glass.[29] The monopoly of Cristalerías advanced with its product line. Although a couple of other firms opened in the glass industry, competition was assiduously avoided through the simple expedient of each new concern laying claim to a specific glass products field so they would not overlap each other or transgress upon Cristalerías' domain.[30]

In tobacco, the dominance of the Compañía Chilena de Tabacos can be traced back to 1909, the year of its incorporation. The base for this corporation was a union of the powerful Compañía General de Tabacos owned by the trading house of Fernando Rioja y Compañía and the major commercial agencies which distributed its products.[31] Established in 1897, the Compañía General de Tabacos had easy access to capital for the importation of Bonsack automatic cigarette-making machines.[32] The company grew rapidly: in 1904, it reported net profits equal to 32 per cent of its total invested capital and reserves. In that year also it added fourteen new Bonsack machines and five more were on order.[33] Its largest competitor, Carrera y Compañía, of Valparaíso, opened in 1908 with only four Bonsack machines and was not able to last out the year before being absorbed into the newly formed Compañía Chilena de Tabacos. Numerous producers who could not afford to automate their production lines were forced out of business. One of these, the Fábrica de Tabacos "La Intimidad," founded in 1880, employed 140 workers in 1911, the year it ceased operations.[34]

Other entrepreneurs who had automated their factories encountered difficulties in marketing their cigarettes since the major distributors were working exclusively with the Compañía Chilena de Tabacos. Before 1916, all of them had sold their factories to the

29. Sociedad Fábrica Nacional de Vidrios, *Memorias*, 1922–24; Cristalerías de Chile, *Memorias*, 1930–34.

30. Thus, the English-based trading house Weir Scott established the Fábrica de Vidrios y Cristales La Yungay to produce fine glassware, and later Vidrios Planos Lirquén was formed to specialize in the manufacture of flat and construction glass.

31. *Estatutos de la Compañía Chilena de Tabacos.*

32. Invented in 1881 by an American, James Bonsack, this machine represented a technological breakthrough in the manufacture of cigarettes. Until then, cigarettes were made by hand and a skilled worker could make no more than 300 per day. The Bonsack machine could manufacture over 200 cigarettes per minute.

33. Compañía General de Tabacos, *Balance de 31 de diciembre de 1904*, ANMH, vol. 2,839.

34. *Chile industrial y comercial* 2 (September 1909):28; 3 (May 1911):19.

Compañía Chilena de Tabacos, which then became the only cigarette manufacturer in Chile.[35]

This situation lasted until 1921, when the British American Tobacco Company established a branch plant in Valparaíso. The two firms divided the Chilean market between them until the Edwards group which controlled the Compañía Chilena de Tabacos decided to merge with the British firm in 1936. With this fusion, the Compañía Chilena de Tabacos, in which the British held majority interests, maintained an uninterrupted and absolute monopoly over the Chilean cigarette industry.

In these circumstances of a highly concentrated industrial structure, cases of restriction of trade were not uncommon. In 1925, Oriana Silva, who owned a clothing factory, went to the executive committee of the Sociedad de Fomento Fabril to plead her case. She had recently won a public contract to provide uniforms to the army, but her cloth orders were refused by the Sociedad Nacional de Paños de Tomé and the Fábrica Nacional de Paños de Bellavista. Since these were the only companies manufacturing cloth which met the specifications required by the army, she lost the contract. The explanation behind all this was that she was infringing upon the market in which Justiniano, Johnson y Compañía had long held a monopoly. As was shown in chapter 4, this enterprise was begun by Carlos Justiniano who, after having achieved success, affiliated himself with the highest levels of the economic elite. By 1926, a director of his enterprise was Carlos Aguirre Luco, who also happened to be president of the Sociedad Nacional de Paños de Tomé. Another important shareholder was Carlos Werner, owner of the Fábrica Nacional de Paños de Bellavista. Needless to say, both textile companies had an agreement with Justiniano not to supply cloth for military uniforms to any other firm.[36]

Occasionally a monopoly was totally in foreign hands and adversely affected the development of another industry. This occurred with the entry of the United Shoe Machinery Company into Chile in 1907. It quickly maneuvered itself into the position of sole supplier of machines and equipment to the footwear industry. Only capital equipment forthcoming from the American company could

35. Rivera, *La industria del tabaco en Chile*, pp. 13–14.

36. Consejo Directivo de la Sociedad de Fomento Fabril, Acta del 30 de diciembre de 1925, "Libro de Actas del Consejo Directivo," ASFF; "Estatutos de la Sociedad Fábrica de Uniformes," *Diario Oficial*, October 29, 1926, pp. 2,699–706; Sociedad Nacional de Paños de Tomé, *Lista de Accionistas*, March 15, 1926, ABCS; also see Appendix 3.

legally be used in Chile. This was achieved through the registration of numerous broadly worded patent rights on all aspects of the shoe-manufacturing process in Chile which made it illegal for machinery other than that of United Shoe to be used in the country.[37] Moreover, machinery was not sold to the Chilean manufacturers; it was only rented and a fee exacted for each pair of shoes produced. The entire Chilean shoe industry was thus placed in a position of complete dependence on the American corporation.

In spite of having been one of the earliest and most important sectors, by this time the shoe industry had little power. Many small- and medium-sized manufacturers existed but had little influence. On the other hand, in 1914, about half a dozen large producers of footwear existed, but these were appendages of major tanning enterprises which were more interested in maintaining their lucrative export market for leather. Since the latter was going through a period of crisis during the years 1910–15 due to substantial declines in the orders from Germany, their major customer, the owners of these enterprises were totally committed to the struggle to protect current profits in that area and were not very concerned with the long-term consequences of recent developments in a domestic industry which was then of minor importance to them.[38]

It was not until 1928 that the Chileans reacted. In that year the United Shoe Machinery Co. requested that the period of one of its patents be extended from fifteen years to twenty. When consulted by the Ministry of Fomento, as was normal procedure on issues concerning industrial patents, the SFF opposed the extension and launched a public campaign against the United Shoe monopoly. The executive committee of the manufacturers' association sustained that the shoe industry was being harmed by a situation in which it was forced to rent at excessive rates machinery made by one foreign corporation which sought only to maintain its monopoly through the acquisition of an endless series of extensions on its patents.[39] The government refused to grant twenty-year pat-

37. Between 1907 and 1911 alone, 39 patents were registered by United Shoe. See Chile, Ministerio de Industrias y Obras Públicas, *Registro general de patentes de invención, 1840–1912.*

38. "Medidas de protección a la curtiduría nacional"; León Bonder, "La industria de curtiduría en Chile y sus derivados."

39. Consejo Directivo de la Sociedad de Fomento Fabril, Acta del 22 de junio de 1928, "Libro de Actas del Consejo Directivo," ASFF; Sociedad de Fomento Fabril, "Memoria, 1928," *BSFF* 46 (January 1929):25.

ents to United Shoe and the SFF continued its attack on the company. In 1930, Camilo Carrasco Bascuñan, president of the SFF, asked the Minister of Fomento to put an end to the monopoly by restricting further extensions of the patents and reviewing the legality of the existing contracts of the American firm with Chilean shoe manufacturers for the rental of machinery. He expressed the hope that in this manner the Chilean producers would be able to escape from the control of United Shoe and acquire their equipment elsewhere under conditions more advantageous to them.[40]

Suddenly, however, the campaign against United Shoe ceased; the SFF did not touch upon the issue again, in either its *Boletín* or in the meetings of the executive committee. Perhaps it was merely coincidental that the end of the SFF pressure against the company occurred very shortly after United Shoe, which had never been a member of the association, joined its ranks. In any event, the Chilean shoe industry remained dependent upon this monopoly until the 1960s.

In the chemical products industry, concentration evolved at an early date. Founded in 1901, the Compañía Industrial engaged in a continual program of expansion and absorption of other factories. By 1916, it was the only company left producing vegetable oils for industrial use which benefited from the increased duty levied that year on the importation of oils. In addition to vegetable oils, it produced a wide variety of goods, including artificial fertilizers, glue, stearine candles, glycerine, perfumes, soaps, and detergents. The market for most of these goods was dominated by the Compañía Industrial which had acquired its competitors' factories in Santiago, Viña del Mar, Concepción, and Coronel, only to close down all plants except those in Santiago and Viña del Mar before 1930.[41]

The decade which began in 1920 saw the consolidation of numerous other monopolies. At the beginning of that year the Compañía Chilena de Fósforos took over the factories of its only remaining competitors which by then were at the verge of bank-

40. Letter of Camilo Carrasco Bascuñan, president of the SFF, to Luis Matte Larraín, Minister of Fomento, September 26, 1930, published in *BSFF* 47 (September 1930):700–701. Carrasco Bascuñan himself had no participation in the shoe industry. He had organized Laboratorio Chile, one of the largest pharmaceutical companies in Chile, and was a prominent lawyer and landowner.

41. Compañía Industrial, *Memoria, 1915*; *Compañía Industrial, 1900–1964*, passim.

ruptcy. Working with modern Swedish equipment and under license to the international match corporation, Svenska Tändsticks, A.B., the match factory at Talca was able to increase its production to meet the total demand of the country and close down the plants of its former competitors in 1921.[42] In the paper industry, the Compañía Manufacturera de Papeles y Cartones, which began operations as a result of the fusion of two firms in 1920, was able to command a dominant position by 1926. At that time practically all the domestic production of paper was forthcoming from this company's mills.[43] The production of beds and many other articles of furniture was concentrated around the output of the Compañía Industrial de Catres, by the end of World War I.[44] At this same time no other national firm could compete with the vast capital and modern technology employed by Cemento El Melón which supplied cement for all the public works of the country and, with the assistance of a 35 per cent increase on the duty of imported cement, was able to supplant foreign competition completely.[45]

The unchecked rise of industrial concentration was sensed by contemporary observers in Chile, some of whom openly opposed what they considered to be a dangerous process. Restriction of trade, price-fixing, and monopolistic profits were denounced in the Chamber of Deputies in 1928 by the Tariff Committee of that house. Specifically mentioned were the sugar, cement, woolen textile, artificial fertilizer, and match industries, but the situation was declared to be the same in many other sectors.[46] Charges were even made that the match factory which had long existed in Santiago remained idle because its owners preferred to receive 90,000 pesos a year from the Compañía Chilena de Fósforos to keep the plant closed than to compete.[47]

The Tariff Committee generally approved the increases in import duty which had been proposed by the government of Carlos Ibáñez, but asked that steps be taken to stop the abuses committed

42. Compañía Chilena de Fósforos, *Memorias*, 1920–22.

43. Compañía Manufacturera de Papeles y Cartones, *Memorias*, 1920–30; statement by Luis Matte Larraín, general manager of the paper company, in the Consejo Directivo de la Sociedad de Fomento Fabril, Acta del 12 de octubre de 1926, "Libro de Actas del Consejo Directivo," ASFF.

44. Pedro Luis González, *Chile industrial, 1918*, pp. 18, 99.

45. Compañía de Cemento El Melón, *Memorias*, 1922, 1930, 1931; "La Sociedad Fábrica de Cemento El Melón," *BSFF* 42 (April 1930):224–26.

46. Congreso Nacional, Cámara de Diputados, *Boletín de las sesiones extraordinarias, 1927–1928*, 2:1667–79.

47. Ibid., pp. 1,675–76.

by manufacturers who had created monopolies with the assistance of protectionist measures. The interests which benefited from these enterprises were much too strong by then, however, and no measures were adopted to control their activities or to counteract the aggravating effects of monopoly profits on the distorted pattern of income distribution. When the only serious challenge in Chilean history finally arose against the power structure which the industrial monopolies buttressed, the consequences were staggering. It is significant that chief among the firms singled out by the administration of Salvador Allende to pass under state control were most of the enterprises identified in this study as monopolistic before the depression years.[48]

48. See *El Mercurio*, Santiago, January 15, 1972, pp. 17–18.

7. Industry and the State

An assumption, if not always explicit, of the conventional interpretation of Chilean industrialization has been that industrialists were generally at the margin of the center of political power until the administration of Pedro Aguirre Cerda (1938–44). With the Popular Front government, it is argued, industrial development became a national goal and industrialists supported by governmental policy became the dominant pressure group in the country. The coming to power of the Radical Party is supposed to have galvanized the rebellion against the landed aristocracy. Industrialization was viewed by leftist elements as a vehicle for "depriving the landlords of political power."[1] This view of conflict among groups representing different economic interests is a corollary of the assertion that Chile did not industrialize until after the first several decades of this century because only then did there arise pressure groups powerful enough to insist that industrialization be a national goal and to exact the necessary protectionist legislation from congress.[2]

1. Markos Mamalakis, "Public Policy and Sectoral Development—A Case Study of Chile, 1940–1958," in Mamalakis and Reynolds, *Essays*, p. 17.
2. Véliz, "La mesa," p. 239.

I do not propose that industrialization was a national goal before the Depression to the extent that it was in the years following it. Nor do I claim that manufacturing was considered the leading sector of the economy as, in later years, it was perceived by prevailing opinion. But the difference cannot be attributed solely to the crisis or later political changes. The principal manifestations of the country's commitment to industry in the 1930s were a protectionist policy more stringent than ever, promotion. of private enterprise through credit facilities, government contracts and exchange controls, and the direct participation of the state in industrial ventures. Yet industry was a vibrant sector before those years. And, clearly, the oligarchy was not compartmentalized according to economic activity but rather moved its resources freely according to fluctuations in the rate of return. If an expanding economy, rising incomes, urbanization, and a growing middle class made industrial consumer goods profitable for the elite to manufacture, it would seem odd if pressure groups were not at work in congress to obtain the protection and stimulus necessary to ensure them dominion over domestic markets. Moreover, as will be seen, a definite trend toward higher duty on imported manufactured goods was evident from the late nineteenth century. Government intervention, even to the extent of the establishment of public enterprises, was not unusual. What is suggested, therefore, is that the principal effect of the Great Depression (in which Chile's foreign trade collapsed but not her industrial sector) was to hasten the final stage of development of a process which, for a variety of reasons, had been ongoing for years and was close to maturity by 1930.

If industrial interests as a whole were to be represented before the public, an institutional base was essential. This was provided after 1883 by the Sociedad de Fomento Fabril. Until the turn of the century it was composed of approximately 175 individual and corporate members. Most of the largest enterprises were affiliated. But concurrent with the economic boom of 1904–5, its membership lists climbed sharply. At this time the SFF began a campaign to attract medium-sized manufacturers, and membership rose from 221 in 1903 to 735 in 1904. Nor did the SFF cease to grow with the depression of 1906–7. In 1907, it had 1,178 members. Throughout the 1920s total membership stabilized around 1,050, but this figure does not include the associates of the Cámara Industrial de

Valparaíso or the Cámara Industrial de Valdivia, which were correspondent organizations affiliated to the SFF.[3]

The SFF had numerous spokesmen in congress and before the government. Of the 146 men who served between 1883 and 1930 on its executive council, 36 per cent held high public office either as congressional deputies, senators, or ministers of state.[4] Far from being at the margin of the political power center, by the first decade of the twentieth century, industrialists had at their disposal an organization for effective pressure group action.

From the outset the SFF adopted an open policy of assisting all entrepreneurs in their struggles with the state bureaucracy, especially with regard to the entry of capital goods into the country. Each year the executive council supported innumerable petitions which were sent to congress through the association for the exemption of duty on a particular shipment of machinery or raw materials. Often the society was called upon to intercede before the Minister of Hacienda or the Director of the Customs Service in behalf of an industrialist who complained that his importation of raw material had been charged the same duty as that of the finished product. But important as was this daily labor of the SFF, and although these petitions at times occasioned heated congressional debates, they all formed part of the national Chilean pastime of the *trámite*, albeit at a rather high level. The trámite, a harrowing obstacle course of bureaucracy, in effect functioned as the court of first instance in the interpretation and enforcement of the nation's laws and regulations. It has always been a part of every Chilean's life, but in this instance, successful manipulation of the bureaucratic machinery was an attribute of individuals or groups which had at least a foothold in the mainstream of power. The annual reports of the SFF during its first twenty years indicate that the association was an effective agent for industrialists in these matters. After 1897, it had a permanent representative on the powerful Tariff Assessment Revisory Committee (Comisión Revisora de la Tarifa de Avalúo), which was responsible for adjusting the appraised value of a commodity upon which the ad valorem duty would be levied.[5]

3. Sociedad de Fomento Fabril, "Memoria," *BSFF* 42 (January 1925):22.

4. It should be recalled that 17.4 per cent of 207 directors of manufacturing corporations in 1922 were also identified as major political officeholders. See Table 14.

5. *BSFF* 43 (May 1901):282–83.

On another level, that of obtaining lasting protectionist legislation, the most important industrialists often preferred to lobby congress directly in these early years in addition to having recourse to the services of the SFF. Thus, the Viña and Penco sugar refineries represented themselves before the Senate to obtain a higher tariff for refined sugar and lower duty on imported raw sugar at the same time that the SFF was working in their behalf.[6] This was only natural, given the powerful interests which controlled the major industrial enterprises. Nonetheless, as the SFF came to institutionalize its channels of communication with congress, especially toward the end of the decade 1900–1910, the larger enterprises tended to rely more on the association as their spokesman before congress, the authorities, and the public, rather than to operate on their own. By then the access of the association to the legislature had been formalized; it testified before the appropriate committee on bills relating to industry and was often requested to submit reports stating its views on legislation under debate.[7] This process coincided with a growing stratification within the directorate of the SFF. In 1911, the composition of the executive council was revised to include as permanent members all those who had served on the committee for twelve years in addition to the twenty directors who were elected for two-year terms.[8] This reform was later criticized by a few industrialists on the grounds that it would result in a closed hierarchical power structure and impede changes in leadership within the organization.[9] But opposition was slight, and by the 1920s, over one-third of the executive council were lifetime directors.

At this time the larger enterprises were receiving considerably more attention and benefiting more from the SFF's efforts than other member firms. In recognition of this, those firms with a capital investment of over 300,000 pesos were required to pay 100 pesos annual dues, whereas smaller industries were charged only 30 pesos. Moreover, to help pay the costs involved in the intensive campaign for tariff changes, launched in the 1920s, those firms

6. Congreso Nacional, Senado, *Boletín de las sesiones extraordinarias, 1897,* pp. 98, 540, 701.

7. Even more, the efforts of the SFF were recognized as an important element in obtaining for a number of industries the highest level of protectionism permitted by the 1897 tariff. Ministerio de Industrias y Obras Públicas, *Memoria,* 1898, p. 19.

8. "Junta general extraordinaria de socios en 8 de septiembre de 1911."

9. "Junta general de socios en 6 de enero de 1912," p. 145.

which were to benefit most from the SFF's project were assessed an additional yearly quota after 1924 which ranged between 200 and 500 pesos. Among the companies which paid this were the five largest textile firms, the Viña sugar refinery, Cemento El Melón, the *papelera*, Cristalerías de Chile, and the Compañía Industrial.[10]

By 1924, the SFF had local councils or affiliate organizations throughout the country, in Antofagasta, Valparaíso, Talca, Concepción, Temuco, Valdivia, Osorno, Puerto Montt, and Punta Arenas. In reference to this expansion of the SFF, its importance as a national representative of industry was explicitly recognized by Arturo Alessandri in his presidential message of 1924.[11] Concurrent with these developments was the expansion of formal relations with state administrative and policy-making bodies. This began with major reforms in the public administrative apparatus, the culmination of a long process of increasing direct state intervention in the internal economic activities of the country, which may be traced back at least as far as the creation of the Ministry of Industry and Public Works in 1887. These reforms came with greater frequency in the 1920s, particularly during the administration of Carlos Ibáñez (1927–31).[12]

During this period, there was increasing decentralization of the state machinery as new ministries appeared and specialized agencies were created.[13] By 1925, the SFF had become a voting member of the Consejo de Vías de Comunicación, which set freight rates on the state railroad, the Consejo de Agricultura, the Consejo de Enseñanza Comercial, the Central Bank, and the Consejo de Vigilancia de las Fábricas y Maestranzas del Ejército.[14] In 1927, the Ministry of Development (Fomento) was established with responsibility for agriculture, industry, public works, and transportation. Manufacturing was given special consideration in this min-

10. Consejo Directivo de la Sociedad de Fomento Fabril, Acta del 24 de octubre de 1924, "Libro de Actas del Consejo Directivo," ASFF; Sociedad de Fomento Fabril, "Memoria," *BSFF* 42 (January 1925):23.

11. Presidencia de la República (Arturo Alessandri), *Mensaje presidencial de 1924*, pp. 148–49.

12. See Germán Urzúa Valenzuela and Anamaría García Barzelatto, *Diagnóstico de la burocracia chileña (1818–1969)*, pp. 54–55, 69–71.

13. Some examples are the reorganization of ministries to form the Ministry of Development and the Ministry of Agriculture, the creation of the Central Bank, the Superintendency of Banks and Insurance Companies, the Superintendency of Nitrate and Iodine, the Caja de Crédito Agrario, the Caja de Crédito Minero, and the Industrial Credit Institute.

14. *BSFF* 42 (1925):55, 236–37, 700, 702.

istry through the creation of the Dirección General de Industrias Fabriles. This marked the first time that a high-level governmental agency was exclusively dedicated to secondary industry. The first Minister of Development was Adolfo Ibáñez (no relation to the president), the owner of an important trading house in Valparaíso, who had several industrial interests. One of his first acts was to require all formal contacts between the manufacturing sector and the state to be channeled through the SFF or its correspondent organizations. Industrialists would no longer be permitted to represent themselves directly before state agencies.[15] The result of this was to greatly fortify the role of the SFF as intermediary between government and industry.

From the outset of the administration of Carlos Ibáñez, the annual reports of the SFF reflect an atmosphere of complete mutual understanding between the association and the government. Within two years after his rise to the presidency, in addition to the representation in state agencies already mentioned, the SFF was on the directorate of several policy-making governmental boards, the Central Bank, the General Customs Commission, the Institute of Industrial Credit, the National Commission on Coastal Shipping, and the Commission of the Reform of Social Security Laws.[16] In early 1928, a highly protectionist tariff was passed by congress, raising duties and authorizing the president to make additional increases. The SFF was very influential in drafting the provisions of this law and was able to obtain subsequent higher duty for a number of articles through its relations with the executive branch and the Customs Commission which "cooperated fully, never losing sight of the protectionist spirit of the Tariff."[17]

Tariff Legislation

After the War of the Pacific, four general tariff reforms were passed by congress, in 1897, 1916, 1921, and 1928, each with a gradually higher level of protection, the 1928 tariff being as protectionist as those measures taken after the Great Depression. Of equal importance, however, were a number of specific modifications to the general law. Together with the tariff reforms, these changes, which affected only certain products, provide insight into

15. Sociedad de Fomento Fabril, "Memoria," *BSFF* 45 (January 1928):4, 24.
16. Ibid., *BSFF* 46 (January 1929):29.
17. Ibid., p. 3; "Memoria," *BSFF* 47 (January 1930):3–5.

the manner in which specific industries were able to obtain ample protection from the international market of manufactured goods. The pattern of development of both also illustrates the changing relative importance of the criteria upon which Chilean tariff legislation was based: defense of the balance of payments, fiscal revenue, and industrial expansion.

The conventional interpretation of Chilean industrialization tends to view its process of growth as almost accidental. Impressed by the devastating effects of the Great Depression on Chile's foreign trade, advocates of industrialization see it as a "watershed" period for most of the economic life of the country. Industry, it is argued, rose as a result of the measures taken during the 1930s; yet the protectionist instruments invoked then were not principally directed toward the encouragement of industrialization but toward the defense of the balance of payments.[18] It is true that after 1931 the comprehensive system of multiple exchange rates and import restrictions had a more favorable balance of payments as the major objective. No doubt, also, the collapse of the mining-export sector which, together with the government, composed the real foundation of the Chilean economy, marks the depression years as the beginning of a new phase in the country's economic history.

Nevertheless, industry was the least affected of all sectors. It was momentarily jolted by the economic disruption which crossed the world. Production declined somewhat, but in 1933 and 1934 it had reached and overtaken the levels attained in 1929 and 1930, which were the highest registered until then.[19] This ability to weather the years of worldwide economic disorder could hardly have been the result of government policy, no matter how severe the program adopted.

It is a well-known fact that Chilean fiscal revenue always depended largely on foreign trade for the fees collected from duties imposed on exports and imports. Moreover, with the exception of the 1928 tariff, all general increases in levies on imports from the War of the Pacific coincided with economic recession and balance of payments problems. In 1896, however, for the first time, the issue of protecting domestic industry as an end in itself became a major point of discussion in the debates on the tariff reform bill presented to congress.

18. Aníbal Pinto, "Political Aspects of Economic Development in Latin America," in Véliz, *Obstacles*, p. 10.

19. Muñoz, *Crecimiento*, Table II–2.1 and p. 45.

The prelude to this bill was a severe contraction of economic activity, a consequence of world-wide recession and the 1895 law which re-established the convertibility of Chilean currency into gold. The latter has been judged by nearly all students of Chile's long courtship with inflation as "one of the most disastrous monetary operations of all time."[20] The world price level for Chile's principal exports fell rapidly in 1894, 1895, and 1896. From an average quotation in the London market of 14 pence in 1893–94, the peso was revalued to 18 pence by the government and made convertible. Immediately a drain on the gold reserves of the country began, reaching crisis proportions in 1896.

To counteract this process, President Federico Errázuriz Echaurren introduced a bill which would do several things: it would change the basis for fixing the value of a foreign trade commodity from pesos of 38 pence to pesos of 18 pence, increase the export tax on nitrate and iodine, raise the import duty to a maximum of 60 per cent ad valorem, and increase the number of articles upon which high specific duties were placed. Until this point the highest ad valorem category had been 35 per cent. The expressed intention for placing goods in these categories, however, was to stimulate the development of national industry rather than to provide revenue,[21] but many congressmen felt that fiscal income should be the overriding objective of the law. They believed that, although the high specific duties as well as the 60 per cent category were not exactly prohibitive, there would be relatively little income from import duty on the products to be included in these groupings; therefore they objected to extending this protection to more than a few goods. The Tariff Reform Committee of the Chamber of Deputies called for extreme caution in order to reconcile the two positions, pointing out that "so long as our tributary system cannot be transformed to tax everyone directly on the basis of his possessions, customs duty must be considered as the principal and most constant source of public income."[22]

Eliodoro Yáñez, a member of the congressional committee, agreed that policy measures specifically designed to support the

20. Albert Hirschman, *Journeys toward Progress*, p. 231; also see Fetter, *Monetary Inflation in Chile*, pp. 98–117.

21. "Mensaje del Presidente de la República que remite un proyecto de ley que modifica la tarifa de avalúo," in Congreso Nacional, Cámara de Diputados, *Boletín de las sesiones extraordinarias, 1895–96*, pp. 806–13.

22. "Informe de la comisión encargada de informar sobre el proyecto," ibid., 1896, p. 627.

development of national industry were gaining more adherents. He referred to other steps which might be taken in behalf of industry, such as direct production subsidies which had been recommended by the committee itself.[23] Most of the debate, however, did not revolve about whether or not the 60 per cent duty would adversely affect public revenue, but rather centered on the protectionist motives behind it.

A nerve had been touched by the administration's insistence that manufacturing merited the active support of the state. This was the principle of economic liberalism which still held the allegiance of many politicians in the Parliamentary Period. It had been only a decade since Marcial González, one of the major proponents of laissez-faire, had passed away; and Zorobabel Rodríguez, another of the prolific spokesmen for this economic stance, still functioned as chief of the Superintendency of Customs. The real issue at debate was the maintenance of economic liberalism in the face of growing acceptance of the principles of economic nationalism and state interventionist theories of Friedrich List.[24] This was most clearly expressed in the speeches of such staunch opponents of the tariff as Enrique Mac Iver or in the statements of its supporters, men like Eliodoro Yáñez, Carlos Palacios, and Jorge Huneeus.

Like so many aspects of the Parliamentary Period, the major currents of opinion on the conflict between the principles of free trade and protectionism could not be distinguished by party affiliation. On the contrary, the Radical Party, the bulwark of nineteenth-century Chilean liberalism, was divided on this issue. Two of its most prominent members, Enrique Mac Iver (president of the party) and Jorge Huneeus (its secretary) met head-on in defense of their diametrically opposed views. The cause of moderate protectionism was evident to some degree in virtually all parties. The recent platforms of the Liberal, Radical, Liberal Democratic, and Chilean Democracy parties all agreed in principle on the need to stimulate manufacturing through tariff reforms.[25]

But in practice, earlier proposals to increase the duty on imported manufactured goods through a total revision of the existing legislation were not generally supported.[26] Not until the economic

23. Ibid., 1896–97, p. 50.
24. Ibid., pp. 31–39, 44–57, and 1896, pp. 453–55, 493–96.
25. Ibid., 1896–97, pp. 116–17.
26. The SFF had presented tariff reform proposals in 1887, 1889 and 1894, but none of these was ever seriously considered by congress.

crisis was the political atmosphere appropriate to permit the issue to be fully aired in congress, and it was only after several months of intense debate that the law was passed in December 1897, under pressure exerted by the recently elected President Errázuriz, who had emphasized industrial development in his campaign.[27]

On the other hand, substantial modifications of the duty imposed upon a single commodity were passed without such extensive battling. Of course, this had not occurred often, and since it involved the vested interests of powerful groups of capitalists, such measures were not viewed as major attacks on the structure of economic liberalism. Protectionism of this sort was usually accomplished through the imposition of specific duties which were usually much higher than the 60 per cent ad valorem category sought in the general tariff reform of 1897.[28] Thus, in 1893 congress levied a specific duty on sugar: the tax on refined sugar was 8.20 pesos per 100 kilograms and 4 pesos for an impure variety of granulated sugar used as raw material by the Chilean refineries. This differentiated tax was of great value to the domestic refineries. Years before, in 1878, beer producers had received similar protection.

These changes were passed without substantial opposition in congress; so were bills such as one in 1898 which proposed duty-free entry of cotton thread until 1920 or one in 1899 which, for a period of three years, would increase the duty on finished cotton goods to 60 per cent of their value. Supported by the large import houses which had knitwear factories, the latter bill passed easily through congress. It greatly helped these enterprises to increase their total output without the need to develop a fully integrated cotton textile industry. Although opposition to the 60 per cent category in the 1897 general tariff return was too great to permit more than 35 per cent on imported knitwear, in 1899 the domestic producers of these goods were able to persuade congress to afford them the higher protection for three years.

Once the debate over protectionist versus free trade principles in the general reform bill had ended, attention shifted to the problem of which goods would be placed in each category and the amount of increase in specific duty which would be allowed. The reaction of those who had supported free trade was much stronger

27. See Jaime Eyzaguirre, *Chile durante el gobierno de Errázuriz Echaurren, 1896–1901*, pp. 86–88.

28. Congreso Nacional, Cámara de Diputados, *Boletín de las sesiones extraordinarias, 1896–97*, pp. 423–26.

in this instance than it had ever been when a single commodity was being considered for increased import taxation.[29] As a result, the final version of the bill as approved by both houses of congress was slightly less protectionist than the draft which was originally forwarded by the Committee of the Chamber of Deputies with respect to certain specific duties, particularly those on sugar and beer. On the other hand, a larger number of products were included in the 60 per cent category, and a wide variety of raw and intermediate materials were freed from all duty payments or charged only 5 to 15 per cent.[30]

All contemporary observers generally agreed that a number of industries were favorably affected by the tariff of 1897. Among those products specified were stearine candles, refined sugar, beer, cigarettes, knitwear, footwear, brown paper and cardboard boxes, clothing, hats, printed material, pharmaceutical goods, wine, processed food, and furniture.[31] But in retrospect this law was viewed by industrial spokesmen as a "rather timid experiment," especially years later when the ad valorem duty charged was calculated on outdated assessed values which did not reflect rising world prices for manufactured products.[32]

Some of the industries producing basic consumer goods protected by high tariffs which permitted the formation of monopolistic markets received a setback during the administration of Pedro Montt (1906–10). This was a period of economic crisis (1906–8), and one in which the "social question" was reaching its climax. It was the era in which Alejandro Venegas wrote *Sinceridad: Chile íntimo en 1910*, a scathing comment on the misery of the working class, placing the blame for those conditions on the oligarchy. As Chile suffered from an ever increasing inflation, real wages fell and price levels rose sharply. A series of bloody strikes and riots broke out across the country. First came the Valparaíso port strike

29. Congreso Nacional, Senado, *Boletín de las sesiones extraordinarias, 1897–98*, passim.

30. A general duty of 25 per cent was the basis of the law; 59 articles were placed in the 60 per cent category, 117 in the 35 per cent level, 54 were charged 15 per cent, 66 received only 5 per cent duty, a specific duty was applied to 28 products, and 118 items were duty free. See Ricardo Anguita, *Leyes*, 3:400–407.

31. Sociedad de Fomento Fabril, "Memoria," *BSFF* 18 (February 1901): 31–42; Jorge Hormann, "Efectos de la ley de impuestos del 23 de diciembre de 1897; el progreso de la industria nacional."

32. Pedro Luis González, "Protección y libre cambio." Also see Jorge Hormann, "La reforma del arancel aduanero."

of 1903, then the Santiago meat riot of 1905 which claimed the lives of several hundred people. The scene was repeated the following year in Antofagasta and culminated in the Iquique massacre of 1907, when military intervention resulted in almost a thousand civilian casualties in a matter of minutes.

Shaken by the course of events, Pedro Montt had introduced a bill in congress which would reduce the import duty on articles of prime necessity.[33] This was passed in December 1907, almost two years after its initial presentation to congress, which moved in the lethargic pace so common to Parliamentary Period legislatures, prodded only by the mounting tension of 1907. Among its most important provisions was the freeing of duty payment on all meat imports and the granting of authority to the president to reduce by up to 50 per cent the tariff rate applied to sugar, knitwear, clothing, all woolen goods, low-cost unassembled houses, and corrugated sheets of galvanized iron.[34]

Regarding the rising cost of living, even the SFF had to admit that the price of nationally produced consumer goods was a contributing factor.[35] The sugar refineries were the favored target of the attacks on protection for domestic manufacturing. They were considered an artificial industry which relied on imports for all raw materials and many other inputs. Moreover, the monopolistic position they enjoyed because of the high tariffs was especially resented.[36]

In 1908, President Montt exercised the authority granted him by congress and considerably reduced the duty on the articles specified. The results had an almost immediate effect at the microeco-

33. Presidencia de la República (Pedro Montt), *Mensaje presidencial de 1907*, p. 29.

34. Anguita, *Leyes*, 4:219–20. My own view of the Parliamentary Period conforms to the general negative impression of it held by historians. This is contrary, however, to the positive interpretation of political development during the period given by Julio Heise in *Historia*. His carefully researched and stimulating works may well provide the flagstone for a complete revisionist study of the period. Nonetheless, much more systematic research is required especially into the economic and social forces at play.

35. Letter dated May 12, 1906, from Enrique Budge, president of the Sociedad de Fomento Fabril to Abraham Ovalle, Minister of Industry and Public Works, MIOPAN, vol. 1,356.

36. Letter dated January 23, 1906 from Abelardo Nuñez, acting president of the Sociedad de Fomento Fabril, to Belfor Fernández, Minister of Hacienda, ANMH, vol. 4,346. Also see Congreso Nacional, Cámara de Diputados, *Boletín de las sesiones extraordinarias, 1903–4*, passim, as well as debates in the Chamber of Deputies and the Senate, which occurred with some frequency in 1905 and 1906, on the sugar industry.

nomic level. The galvanized iron-factory at Viña, for example, could not continue operations. Others felt the impact of tariff reduction but were able to survive. The sugar refineries suspended dividends momentarily, and the knitwear factories had some difficulties but overcame them. In such cases, the success of the firms in withstanding the competition of foreign imports may be related to the fashion in which Montt implemented the law, buffering its effects against important enterprises.

For example, although the duty on refined sugar imports was reduced by 32 per cent, as the type of sugar approached that which was the principal raw material for the refineries, the reduction grew until it reached 50–55 per cent for brown and totally impure sugar (*chancaca*). This lessened the effect of the tariff change on the Viña and Penco refineries since it reduced their production costs considerably.[37] It was unquestionably a compromise, designed to lower the price of sugar without damaging the interests which controlled the refineries. Still, in this manner, Chile as a whole was obliged to pay an indirect subsidy to these enterprises. As a result of the presidential maneuver, a significant source of public revenue, duty collected on imports, was lowered.[38] Later, after the crisis, the refineries were able to make further gains. It was not unusual for certain import houses to take advantage of the differential tariff by importing full-refined sugar labeled as granulated. In 1911, the SFF reached an agreement with the customs service to apply strict control over the entry of sugar by spot checks of the saccharine content of the merchandise.[39]

With respect to the knitwear industry, Montt decided to reduce the duty paid on finished products from 35 per cent ad valorem to 25 per cent, a decrease of only 28 per cent, far less than the 50 per cent change authorized by the law. This did not appreciably affect the industry which, in any event, received its stimulus from the duty-free status of cotton yarn; it was able to obtain a greater degree of protection in January 1914 with the application of a specific duty to imported cotton products.[40]

37. *BSFF* 36 (September 1919):543–52.

38. Vicuña Pérez, *Proteccionismo*, pp. 24–31.

39. Letter dated July 10, 1911 from Enrique Budge, president of the Sociedad de Fomento Fabril, to Enrique Rodríguez, Minister of Hacienda, ANMH, vol. 3,152.

40. Pedro Luis González, "Las fábricas de tejidos de punto"; Sociedad de Fomento Fabril, "Memoria," *BSFF* 48 (January 1931):11.

Until the 1920s, public revenue continued to be the major consideration whenever a general tariff reform was debated in congress. Protectionism was of secondary concern. The trend toward a shift in priorities, however, may be traced throughout this period, with the pendulum gradually swinging toward acceptance of protection for domestic industry as a goal for national economic development. In 1911, President Ramón Barros Luco proposed a 10 per cent general surcharge on all imports, including those which were previously duty free, to lessen the deficit in the national budget. This was rejected by the industrial and mining sectors alike, since it would have raised the price on raw materials, coal, and petroleum. In view of this opposition an overall increase of only 5 per cent was decreed in 1911.[41]

In 1909, the SFF began to apply pressure for a complete revision of the 1897 tariff. Years passed before either the government or congress showed any serious interest in the matter, but in the economic crisis of 1914–15, the situation changed. The administration gave its total support to a tariff reform which would eliminate many loopholes in the 1897 law. As the Minister of Hacienda Ricardo Salas Edwards explained, "In establishing new tariff rates the general goal which we have had in mind has not been to increase the customs duty. This has been done only for a small number of items with the object of assisting those particular industries which have shown themselves capable of survival with the aid of a protective tariff. The major goal of this bill is to make the collection of customs duty more effective by applying the system of specific duty and, as a principal point, the formal incorporation of the 5 per cent surcharge decreed by special laws. The object of the 5 per cent tax is to repay the loan for military expenditure and to overcome the budget deficit."[42]

The provisions for specific duties were regarded in the Senate as too protectionist, and the proposed tax for a number of items was deemed too high. It was generally felt that if national industry were to be protected, it should be limited to those industries which used mostly national raw materials and which were not artificially sustained by the tariff provisions which favored them.[43] Conse-

41. Jorge Hormann, "El impuesto adicional de diez por ciento."

42. Congreso Nacional, Cámara de Diputados, *Boletín de las sesiones extraordinarias, 1913–14*, p. 2571.

43. Congreso Nacional, Senado, *Boletín de las sesiones extraordinarias, 1915–16*, passim.

quently, the Senate voted to reduce the duty on many commodities approved by the Chamber of Deputies. In view of this, a special session of the SFF was called to discuss a course of action. The alternatives for the industrialists were either to "have the Chamber of Deputies insist on passage of the bill in the form approved by that body or push for the swift enactment of the reformed bill."[44] The latter strategy was chosen inasmuch as the executive council felt that the law at least did away with the assessment rate (*tarifa de avalúo*) which had always been an obstacle to obtaining the most effective protection afforded by past laws.[45] The belief was also expressed that defects in the current bill could certainly be patched up through later remedial legislation. Consequently, the bill went through without further delay and was promulgated in April 1916.

As a result of the next major depression, only several years later, President Juan Luis Sanfuentes presented a bill in 1920 for an overall increase in the tariff of 30 per cent, with the exception of such basic consumer items as rice, coffee, sugar, and vegetable oils. The congressional committee which reviewed the bill, however, recommended a one-year increase of 60 per cent on "luxury" goods. But as the debate advanced in the Chamber of Deputies and the Senate, it became apparent that protectionist interests were going to take advantage of the moment to enact a law most favorable to those industries which had not been able to obtain the high level of protection long afforded such sectors as beer and sugar.[46]

Although the need to increase fiscal revenue was still used as the fundamental pretext for reform, by that time protectionism was a principle openly accepted by most congressmen as national policy. At no point in the debate was the issue of protectionism ever ques-

44. Consejo Directivo de la Sociedad de Fomento Fabril, Acta del 4 de febrero de 1914, "Libro de Actas del Consejo Directivo," ASFF.

45. Among the complaints of industrialists with regard to the tarifa de avalúo was that it was not revised often enough to reflect the rising prices of imported manufactured goods. Moreover, domestic producers charged that the system permitted easy evasion since customs officials could be bribed to classify merchandise in a category at which a lower ad valorem rate was charged than should have applied to the item.

46. The industrialists of Valparaíso, among which the most important was the Compañía de Refinería de Azúcar de Viña del Mar, felt that it was not prudent in 1920 to press for higher levels of protection than the overall 50 per cent increase, since it might cause the general worker discontent of that year to be directed against them. In 1921, however, conditions appeared more propitious to seek higher duty on some goods. See "Reunión del Consejo Ejecutivo de la Cámara Industrial de Valparaíso."

tioned; on the contrary, a number of politicians spoke vigorously in its behalf. Representative of this position were the views expressed by Deputy Miguel Luis Yrarrázaval: "Not only is it necessary to consider the increase in state revenue in this type of legislation, but principally national industry should be taken into consideration. Let them be favored by the law so that they may be able to rise and prosper."[47] Throughout the proceedings the SFF directed itself to congress to obtain more extensive protection. At one point, when it appeared that the knitwear industry was going to be excluded from any increase since the government had neglected to request it, the association successfully petitioned the Senate to amend the bill in favor of this industry.[48] As passed in February 1921, the law was well received by the SFF. The new tariff established a general increase of 50 per cent on most imports, except certain primary materials and capital goods, a rise of 100 per cent on such consumer goods as canned and processed foods, biscuits, perfumes, toys, soft drinks, candy, and chocolate, and 200 per cent on such articles as beer, wines, and liquors.[49]

The final step toward the imposition of a tariff whose objectives were exclusively protectionist came with the passage of the 1928 customs act. This measure was first conceived in 1923 by Arturo Alessandri who "felt that the 1921 law did not go far enough to protect national industry."[50] Consequently, the administration appointed a commission of industrialists and merchants in August 1923 to undertake an exhaustive study of the issue "on the basis of an open and resolute policy of protection to national industry."[51]

After two years of study, a bill was presented to congress by the government in August 1926. It was turned over to a joint congressional committee which made its recommendations in February 1928. Debates on the proposed measure had begun in January of that year, and after reception of the joint committee's report, the bill was approved almost immediately by both houses.[52] The only

47. Congreso Nacional, Cámara de Diputados, *Boletín de las sesiones extraordinarias, 1920–21*, p. 623.
48. Congreso Nacional, Senado, *Boletín de las sesiones extraordinarias, 1920–21*, p. 241; also *BSFF* 38 (January 1921):10.
49. Pedro Luis González, "Derechos de aduana: el recargo de cincuenta por ciento."
50. "Informe de la comisión mixta de senadores y diputados," in Congreso Nacional, Senado, *Boletín de las sesiones extraordinarias, 1927–28*, p. 748.
51. Ibid.
52. Congreso Nacional, Cámara de Diputados, *Boletín de las sesiones ex-*

opposition raised was in connection with granting more protection to industries which operated under monopolistic conditions. Of course, congress responded quickly to the wishes of the administration. This was the period of "one-man rule" in Chile, when Carlos Ibáñez established a virtual dictatorship over the country after having forced out of office Emiliano Figueroa, a weak president who had been little more than a figurehead for a government controlled by the strong-willed colonel as Minister of the Interior. As indicated, the industrial sector had found Ibáñez to be an energetic guardian of its interests. In the presidential message of May 1929, he took care to stress "the constant attention which manufacturing has received on the part of the executive branch," thus underscoring the dominant position which this sector had achieved.[53]

Not only did the tariff of 1928 substantially raise the duty on a wide variety of goods produced domestically, but it authorized the president at his discretion to increase the rates up to 35 per cent further. Within the next two years, Ibáñez frequently invoked this provision, so that before Chile felt the impact of the Depression, the duty on hundreds of commodities had risen considerably.[54]

In summary, a steadily increasing trend toward acceptance of protectionism may be noted from the tariff of 1897 which, although granting only moderate protection, may be considered a landmark in protectionist sentiment. Through later general and partial revisions of the law, certain industries, all of them producing for the final consumer, were able to thrive. Clearly, until 1921, the occasion to legislate for overall higher duties depended to a great extent on the condition of national finances. But by then, free trade was not seriously considered as a viable economic principle by politicians.

Legislation in behalf of industrial development was a slow process, but in the vacillating, seemingly aimless atmosphere that prevailed over Chilean politics during the Parliamentary Period, issues were usually resolved through crisis or mere default to the expanding bureaucracy. Basic social and economic problems were avoided

---

traordinarias, 1927–28, pp. 1667–79; Senado, *Boletín de las sesiones extraordinarias, 1927–28*, pp. 929–33, 954–60, 962–63, 1088–94.

53. Presidencia de la República (Carlos Ibáñez), *Mensaje presidencial de 1929*, p. 37.

54. Between 1928 and 1931, the total average increase in duties amounted to approximately 71 per cent and affected 73 per cent of the total import trade. P. T. Ellsworth, *Chile, An Economy in Transition*, p. 50.

whenever possible.[55] On the other hand, the first administration of Arturo Alessandri was almost completely taken up with a continual struggle for reforms in behalf of labor and the middle class, military intervention in government, and the drafting of a new constitution. Until Carlos Ibáñez had assured himself undisputed control over the nation, the issue of higher duty for manufacturing could hardly have overriding priority even though it had been considered for action since 1923. In any event, the measures adopted up to 1928 had responded to the demands of those who were at the centers of national power. As industry was being transformed into the dominant sector of the economy, this process reflected the changing interests of the oligarchy. Carlos Keller, one of the more prolific writers on twentieth-century Chilean social evolution, openly charged in 1931 that the steps taken to stimulate industry until then "had not been with the object of propelling national development . . . but with the sole intention of favoring certain parties."[56]

Direct State Promotion of Industry

On the nature of relations between the private sector and the state in the span 1891–1930, Keller indicated two periods. The first extended across the Parliamentary Period until 1924, and he saw the beginning, after 1924, of a new era. Among those who led the military revolt of 1924 were two figures of great future political importance, Carlos Ibáñez and Marmaduque Grove, both of whom by then were sensitive to the social demands of the country. Keller depicted the first period as one in which private industry courted the state mainly through "*un santo en la corte.*" In vivid satire, he wrote, "Not many years have gone by since advertisements in the newspapers could be seen which read something like the following: 'to establish first-class enterprise, partner needed—preferably Senator of the Republic.' "[57] In this manner individual firms were assured special privileges, tariff increases, state contracts, and so on. After 1924, the state began to invest directly in industry,

55. Although this is a familiar criticism of the Parliamentary Period, it is interesting to note that spokesmen for the industrial sector also lashed out at the vacuous legislative efforts of the era, condemning the exaggerated amount of time spent in debate over unimportant issues while meaningful bills were pigeonholed for years. See Pedro Luis González, "La labor parlamentaria"; Hormann, *Chile*, p. 63.

56. Keller, *La eterna crisis*, p. 18.

57. Ibid., p. 157.

and such operations as the Fábricas y Maestranzas del Ejército (FAMAE) were distributing plows, agricultural equipment, and other products to the open market in direct competition with certain types of private enterprises.[58] But in 1931, Keller felt that the earlier tendency was still quite strong. Actually, what impressed him most about the second half of the decade 1920–29, apart from the open military intervention in the affairs of state, were the numerous social and labor laws promulgated in 1924. The enactment of this legal industrial relations system, finally consolidated in 1931 into the first labor code in the Western Hemisphere, resulted from over "two decades of intellectual ferment and political debate."[59]

With regard to overall industrial evolution, Keller's suggestion of the beginning of a new era in 1924 is not off the mark. During the 1920s, but especially in the second half of the decade, Chile witnessed the elaboration of a series of measures which formed the embryo of post-1940 economic planning. The policy base for tariff legislation had reached a point when it was primarily protectionist. The Industrial Credit Institute had been established. Reforms in state administrative machinery had created the Ministry of Development in 1927, with the new Department of Manufacturing an important component. The department was explicitly charged by Ibáñez with lowering or completely suppressing the importation of a great number of manufactured products. These measures were but a part of the six-year program announced by the president for stimulating the expansion of domestic industry.[60] From 1926, the number of decrees and laws which pertained to state activity in the Chilean socioeconomic system proliferated to such a degree that in 1929, the administration felt it necessary to commission the publication of a systematic code of these laws.[61]

The aspect which perhaps most clearly revealed the extent to which active state collaboration in national industrial development had advanced in the decade of the twenties was the creation of

58. Pedro Luis González, "Las industrias fiscales"; see also *BSFF* 56 (1934): passim.

59. Morris, *Elites*, p. xv.

60. This policy of government intervention may be seen in Presidencia de la República (Carlos Ibáñez), *Mensaje presidencial de 1927*, pp. 35–39. Later presidential messages rounded out the Ibáñez program for industrial development, although it was not so completely formalized as those elaborated in the period following the creation of the Chilean Development Corporation (CORFO) as a result of the catastrophic earthquake of January 1939.

61. Guillermo Gandarillas, *Legislación sobre fomento de las industrias minero, agrícola y fabril.*

the Compañía Electro Siderúrgica e Industrial de Valdivia in 1926 (ESVAL). Although the Chilean government had been concerned with the development of basic industry since 1889, the first serious step came in 1905 when the French firm Schneider Creusot took an active interest in the possibilities of producing iron and steel in Chile.[62] A blast furnace began operation at Corral, the port of Valdivia, in 1910, but the production process which used charcoal rather than coal was found to be unsuited to Chilean conditions and the venture was ended the following year. The role of the state in this enterprise was marginal in any event. The Chilean government had promised to ensure the provision of ample firewood from a national forest reserve and to guarantee a 5 per cent minimum return on invested capital, but it never made good on its commitment.[63]

The issue of basic industry remained untouched until the administration of Arturo Alessandri. In 1923, the president sent a bill to congress which provided a generous government subsidy for up to ten years to any firm producing iron and steel domestically.[64] This move stimulated a group of private investors to purchase the Corral blast furnace the following year, but their intentions are questionable. The newly formed company claimed that it would establish a hydroelectric plant and employ a new and different production system using national bituminous coal which was then suitable for making metallurgical coke. But the capital actually paid in by these private investors covered little more than the purchase price of the old blast furnace (3,250,000 pesos). Chilean manufacturers were unwilling to invest in stock issues for basic industry with anything more than token participation. In fact, the enterprise was never designed to be financed from private Chilean sources. The board of directors began to search for a formula to provide the proper mixture of foreign and government financing to bear the burden of risk which such a venture entailed.

In a way, foreign interests were already involved, if only indirectly. In 1914, Schneider Creusot had been able to salvage some of its investments by negotiating a contract between the Bethlehem-

62. Charles Vattier, *L'Avenir de la metallurgie du fer au Chile*. This was one of four studies which the Chilean government commissioned Vattier to do on the possibilities of national production of iron and steel.

63. Sánchez Hurtado, *Evolución histórica de la industria siderúrgica*, pp. 121–23.

64. Presidencia de la República (Arturo Alessandri), *Mensaje presidencial de 1924*, p. 145.

Chile Iron Mines Co. and the Chilean government. Bethlehem leased the French company's iron deposits at El Tofo near La Serena, and the Chilean government ratified this arrangement which had had initial duration of over ninety years.[65] Mining operations began in 1921, and until 1952, all Chilean production of iron ore came from the operation of the Bethlehem-Chile Iron Mines Co. This was the source of the raw material upon which Chile's basic industry would depend for many years.

More directly, the ESVAL management negotiated a loan for 30 million pesos from E. H. Rollins & Sons, a New York investment bank, but this was subject to the willingness of the Chilean government to accept responsibility for the repayment of the loan. In December 1926, congress passed Law 4110, which initiated the process through which the state would participate in the establishment of basic industry in Chile. The law provided state guarantee of the loan and conceded 24,000 acres of national forest land near Valdivia to the firm. But in return, three state representatives appointed by the president were to be on the company's board of directors. All plans for production techniques, construction projects, and contracts had to be submitted to a government committee for approval. In addition, actual implementation of the law would be forthcoming only after the company's dealings up to that point had been approved by a special commission appointed by the government.[66]

Although Ibáñez particularly wanted to add steel production to the Chilean industrial plant, he did not want to act in haste and decided to appoint a commission to prepare an exhaustive report on the venture before committing the government. The results of this investigation prompted him to decree the postponement of the state guarantee for ESVAL in September 1928.[67] The commission made several rather spectacular findings. In return for nonmonetary services and contributions of water reserves to the company, the original board of directors had reserved almost 9 million pesos worth of shares for themselves, representing over 14 per cent of the company's initial capital stock. Ibáñez denounced this maneuver since it would have allowed a small group of individuals who

65. Sánchez, *Evolución*, p. 123.
66. "Ley N° 4110," *Diario Oficial*, December 30, 1926, pp. 3,574–76.
67. "No se concede la garantía del estado a la Compañía Electro Siderúrgica de Valdivia."

had not made significant investments in the venture to make enormous personal profits before the company had even constructed its plant. Moreover, actual private investment in the firm was very small, not meeting the amount stipulated in Law 4110, most of it taken up by foreign interests who would effect payment of the stock only when the Chilean government actually cosigned the pending 30-million-peso loan.[68]

Thus, just as before, private Chilean entrepreneurs were either unwilling or unable to develop basic industry. On the other hand, they were quite willing to act as intermediaries and managers of the venture, acquiring substantial gains while the state absorbed all the risks.

Now aware that the president's great interest in establishing a steel industry during his administration did not outweigh his insistence that this be accomplished under stringent government supervision of the company's affairs, ESVAL's directors requested further negotiation on the matter to arrive at a "second-best" solution for themselves.[69] This came with Law 4600 of June 1929, but was something of a disappointment to the management. According to its provisions the total capital of the company was to be 60 million pesos, of which the state would purchase four shares for each one paid in by a private investor. Stock held by private investors was preferred to some extent. Such issues would receive up to 8 per cent annual dividends when these were declared before the state could claim any share of the company profits. A production subsidy was established and the president was authorized to increase the duty on imported iron and steel. Management of the firm was to be in the hands of the state. Of a total of eight chairs on the board, six were to be occupied by government representatives.[70] Such a law did little to attract private capital, and the government finally had to take over the company completely in 1934.[71]

68. Ibid.
69. "La industria siderúrgica de Chile."
70. Gandarillas, *Legislación*, pp. 237–38.
71. The year before, ESVAL had begun to produce pig iron and its rolling mill soon began to turn out about 10,000 tons of steel a year. Yet it was always a financial disaster. The company's income statements reported losses in almost every year until 1958, when it was finally closed down and total responsibility for steel production turned over to the state-owned Compañía de Acero del Pacífico located near Concepción.

The strong commitment of Chilean industrialists to consumer goods which had relatively short gestation periods dissuaded most of them from basic industry or, for that matter, from the production of tools and machinery for industrial use. From the outset, the SFF gave no support to the petition of foundry owners that the machines and tools which they produced be given some degree of protection. On the contrary, the association proposed that all such articles be admitted duty free. This caused discord in the SFF when the law of August 1889, proposed by the association, was passed, exempting all machines and tools from the payment of import duty.[72] On the other hand, most of the foundry owners who had proven their worth over the years through the production of locomotives and rolling stock for the state railroads were forced out of business in the long run. The main reason was the sporadic nature of the orders they received, whose conditions with respect to deadlines could be met only by continuous assembly-line production. In turn, given the inconsistent nature of state policy toward the national foundries, specialization could hardly be maintained, and production on a custom basis was the best that could be offered.[73] Finally, in 1921, the state decided that it would order those articles not supplied by imports or by ELECMETAL from FAMAE, the immense factory operated by the army.[74] Consequently, with the exception of a couple of enterprises such as ELECMETAL which specialized in specific steel pieces for the railroads, the rest of the foundries turned to the production of fabricated metal products, traditional tools, and simple machinery. In this atmosphere of resignation, the conditions for expansion of heavy industry and for firms to delve into the possibilities of developing new types of capital equipment were not present. Thus, the line of least resistance was followed and most of the sector's expansion was related to the production of consumer-oriented metal products. By 1930, the SFF's registry of industrial establishments listed only three major foundries in existence. Of these, only two

72. Consejo Directivo de la Sociedad de Fomento Fabril, Acta del 22 de julio de 1887, "Libro de Actas del Consejo Directivo," ASFF; letter dated June 1, 1888, from Santiago foundry owners to the Sociedad de Fomento Fabril, published in *BSFF* 5 (June 1888):248–51; "Liberación de derechos de internación."

73. Antonio Subercaseaux, "La administración de los ferrocarriles del estado"; *BSFF* 26 (May 1909):222–23; González, *El esfuerzo,* p. 152; although orders to national producers were made on a regular basis from 1909 to 1914, this practice had been discontinued by 1916.

74. Consejo Directivo de la Sociedad de Fomento Fabril, Acta del 15 de julio de 1921, "Libro de actas del Consejo Directivo," ASFF.

were privately owned and survived principally through contracts with the state railroads for a limited number of items.[75]

With regard to the manufacturing community as a whole, it must be said that little interest was shown for the development of basic industry or the capital goods sector. If anything, a certain antagonism may be sensed, explained by the feeling of the vast majority of established industrialists, who were committed to the production of consumer goods by means of imported machines and production techniques, that the development of domestic basic industry would tend to increase the cost of those capital goods which could be imported with little or no duty payments. Journalists, politicians, and technicians, rather than industrialists, filled the ranks of those who argued in behalf of basic industry. Intellectuals, not entrepreneurs, looked to the future evolution of industry in relation to national development instead of the preservation of current profit margins. On the other hand, if the state was intent on creating iron and steel industries with large payments for the use of privately held water, mineral leases, or the parceling out of lucrative directorates, such opportunities were not to be missed by those who were in a position to gain with no personal investment required or risk incurred.

75. These were FAMAE, ELECMETAL, and SIMA, which was owned by Guillermo Díaz. See "Rol de industrias," passim.

8. Industrialization and the Course of Chilean Development

THE GENESIS of industrialization in Chile may be traced back to the War of the Pacific. Developments in mining, transportation, and agriculture and demographic changes altered the productive possibilities of the country in favor of domestic manufacturing. Rising national income, concentrated markets, and an expanding urban middle class created a demand for a wide variety of industrial products. In response to the changing conditions of the economy, Chilean industry grew considerably. The secondary sector evolved in its productive system from an essentially artisan, pre-factory stage to a semi-complete industrial plant which, to a certain degree, created linkages extending across its own sector and to other areas of the economy. By World War I, industry was mature enough to respond adequately to market fluctuations and to embark upon large-scale import substitution. In terms of its degree of modernization and its growth rate, domestic manufacturing exhibited considerable vigor.

But throughout the period until the Great Depression, this development was highly dependent upon foreign trade fluctuations, to the extent that the evolution of Chilean industry was largely a function of export cycles and the capacity of the country to import. The latter was particularly important since, at least until the 1930s, the lifeblood of industry was the flow not only of capital goods but also of raw and intermediate materials. To a great extent this reflected the nature of Chilean industrialization, which was almost totally oriented towards the final consumer. Beginning with items of daily consumption, manufacturers gradually expanded the metallic industry, but their output was primarily consumer durables. No base of heavy industry was permitted to prosper, no autochthonous source of technological progress developed. To enter these areas would have meant substantial investments and long periods before there were profitable results. Private industrialists did not wish to wait—they wanted profits quickly, and they sought and gained sufficient protection to establish captive markets for the kinds of production which could be attempted with minimal risk.

Although diversified and technically advanced, Chilean industry did not become a "growth pole" for development. It was incapable of transmitting innovation and progress to the rest of the economy, as it was expected to do, or to the nation to initiate a self-sustained, autonomous process of growth. In the Chilean case, one must question the validity of the conventional reasoning of economic planners who envision the function of industrialization in teleological terms essentially the same in all countries and points of time. This case also makes comprehensible the frustration which often emanates from recent literature dealing with the industrialization process in Latin America.[1] Government authorities expected industry to develop the country by releasing it from dependence on the foreign sector, i.e., the exportation of raw materials. It was to diversify production and contribute to the growth rate of the gross domestic product. Indeed, manufacturing did broaden the productive base, to a point, and on the basis of its growth rate could be termed dynamic. But just as Chile never established adequate "rules of the game" for the nitrate and copper producers, asking only a limited tribute from them rather than integrating the sector into the national economy, so also nothing more was required from industry than that it expand in aggregate terms. The problem of its relation to national development was poorly conceived.

Only in the most vague and ill-defined terms was manufacturing

1. See Osvaldo Sunkel and Pedro Paz, *El subdesarrollo latinoamericano y la teoría del desarrollo*, and Andrés Bianchi, ed., *America Latina, ensayos de interpretación económica.*

expected by the proponents of industrialization to break somehow the "resilient traditional structure of institutions, hierarchical arrangements and attitudes."[2] In fact, it ended by buttressing them, since it did not evolve in such a fashion as to provide the mechanisms, incentives, institutions, and framework whereby social and economic modernization could be effected.

In the final analysis, the root of the problem was to be found not so much at the macroeconomic level as in those aspects which related to the dominant values of a traditional society—the social origins of Chilean entrepreneurship, the national power structure, and institutional change. This raises the broader question of what is understood by the term "development." Gunnar Myrdal has defined the process as the "movement upward of the entire social system."[3] This system involves a number of basic features which are interrelated: output and incomes; conditions of production; the consumption patterns of the various groups of people; consumption provided collectively; educational and health facilities and levels; the distribution of power in society; and, more generally, economic, social, and political stratification; institutions and attitudes toward life and work; and, finally, as an exogeneous set of factors, policy measures adopted in order to change any of the previous endogenous elements.

The identification of development with economic growth is by now too discredited to merit refutation, however much influence the concept may still exert in national planning and political discourse. Definitions that retain the central position of economic growth and its aggregate indicator, per capita income, while grafting on requisites of structural change and a few "social" or distributional objectives are also inadequate. This approach alone does not offer a satisfactory solution to the conceptual problem touched upon in the Preface to this study. The determination—a natural one—to quantify development and measure "rates of progress" obviously should be a foremost concern of analysts, planners, and policy makers. But this has too often resulted in an unfortunate predisposition to restrict the vision of development to only that which can be measured. In this connection the identification of development with industrialization may be criticized because it concentrates attention on one requisite, which cannot meaningfully

2. Claudio Véliz, ed., *Obstacles to Change in Latin America*, p. 1.

3. Myrdal, "What is Development?," p. 729. See also his *Asian Drama: An Inquiry into the Poverty of Nations*, 3:1860.

be considered developmental when it is accorded an overriding and indiscriminate priority.

Development may be more adequately viewed according to two complementary analytical sets: as a perceived advance toward specified ends based on societal changes, and as the system of interrelated societal changes that underlies and conditions the feasibility of the advance.[4] The first perspective assumes that there is human capability to shape the future for human ends. It also implies that the existing society has the right and the ability, through general *consensus* or through *agents* claiming to represent the best interests of the society, to make choices and enforce sacrifices in the name of development. The choices are envisaged as feasible rather than utopian. They must fall within limits fixed by development processes and capabilities in the second set.

The second analytical set assumes that development is an intelligible phenomenon susceptible to diagnosis and to objective propositions concerning the interrelations of factors and the probable wider consequences of change in or action on key components of the system. This view is similar to the process which Myrdal defines. Under this conception, development may at different times become more spontaneous or more subject to public policy decisions; more integrated or less integrated; more or less investment-oriented or consumption-oriented; more or less autonomous or dependent at the national level. The components of development as an objective system can, in principle, be determined empirically. This may not be completely feasible in practice, however, even through the implementation of shadow-pricing and the analysis of relative social opportunity costs to quantify the relationships in any broad spectrum of developmental objectives and means.

Development is inescapably societal, although, for various analytical purposes, economic, social, and political aspects are legitimately treated separately. Both of the analytical sets designed for looking at development emphasize structural change and imply that growth is not equivalent to development. If attention is confined to the second set, one may conclude, as Myrdal does, that certain things that happen in a society and certain induced policy measures are exogenous. They fall outside the developmental system of interactions or are not related to them in any way likely to

4. For the following discussion of development analysis, I am indebted to ideas and observations made by Marshall Wolfe, director of the Social Development Division of the United Nations' Economic Commission for Latin America.

affect significantly the future course of development change. The first way of looking at development implies a different criterion for relevance, namely, that the content of "development" reflects the values and preferences of the dominant social forces. Anything to which these forces (be they an association of persons, social groups, or institutions) really accord a high value will, in practice, affect the whole system and will have to be taken into account within development analysis.

From this perspective, I do not consider development to be a single uniform process or dimension of change nor do I assume that "development" means the transformation of the countries now labeled "developing" into replicas of countries now labeled "developed." All national societies will be developing, or trying to, during the foreseeable future and, at the same time, will be trying to cope with the contradictions and disadvantages that arise from their developmental processes. There is no reason to expect their efforts to lead to uniform futures, or to final resolution of their struggles in a utopian state of "being developed."

The high-income industrialized societies in both the "capitalist" and the "socialist" styles have encountered multiple crises—of values, of resources, of capacity of their dominant forces to accomplish their declared aims, of ability to maintain high levels of employment and consumption except at the price of inflation, stagnation, and environmental degradation—that have shaken their self-confidence and partly discredited them as models for development or modernization.

Rather than concentrate on production or industrialization as an end in itself, attention should be drawn to what people do, what they receive through income, services, and subsidies and how they participate in the societal processes of political power, production, and distribution. This approach means an effort to identify and understand the interrelationships of all significant components of development systems in order to define the effective areas of intervention of human agents of change and the obstacles which confront them in the movement toward an acceptable and viable style of development.[5]

5. Most simply, a style of development may be assessed according to its *acceptability* in terms of the importance it gives to human well-being and equity, and its *viability* in terms of its compatibility with the various kinds of resources that can be mobilized by the national society as needed if it is to function and grow over the long term without breakdown. Thus, I am looking at the extent

Although I have criticized the commonly expressed opinion that makes industrialization practically synonymous with development, it must be admitted that in fact a viable style of development is hardly conceivable, except in certain small and highly specialized national economies, without considerable industrial growth. Nevertheless, it does not follow that industrial growth of any kind and at any cost contributes to a viable style of development. Assumptions of this kind have led a number of Latin American countries into traps which have bred considerable disillusionment with industrialization as the major strategy of development.

In the case of Chile, industrialization positively affected aggregate levels of output and incomes and certain technical conditions of production. But by the other factors which constitute the critical elements by which national change in the direction of an acceptable and viable style of development is appraised, Chilean industry was clearly dysfunctional.

This is understandable in light of the identity of those who were at the forefront of the individual effort. From the outset the industrialists were intimately involved with the homogeneous economic elite which composed the dominant element of national life. A separate group united by a new economic activity and by the same aspirations did not emerge to make demands upon society which would imply transformation of traditional institutions. For this reason, the conflict between the entrepreneurial bourgeoisie and the existing oligarchy, commonly believed to be inevitable in the industrialization of a nation, did not occur.

On the whole, this situation was countenanced by the state, first through the lethargy of the Parliamentary Period when powerful interest groups could obtain the necessary degree of protection and government assistance to successfully develop their ventures.

---

to which a given course or style of development enables a society to function over the long term for the well-being of all of its members. Obviously, a style may be viable but not acceptable if, for example, it entails the continuing impoverishment or oppression of part of the society. On the other hand, the reverse may be true if, for example, the style neglects the requisites in productive capacity for the consumption and welfare aspirations it stimulates. Viability is much more difficult to assess than acceptability since it is affected by many contingencies that cannot be accurately weighed and are usually made evident only through historical examination. In any event, a style of development both acceptable and viable demands that society direct production systematically to basic human needs, that it seek productive techniques that minimize environmental deterioration and waste of resources, and that it maximize the creative involvement of human resources.

Then in the 1920s, especially during the administration of Carlos Ibáñez, the state was not only sympathetic to the manner in which domestic manufacturing had evolved, but actively, if unconsciously, encouraged essentially the same form of elitist, dependent, monopolistic industrial growth. Basic industry could be had if the state would pay for it and bear the risks involved. However, even the implantation of basic industry itself was unsatisfactory since it merely added to the aggregate economic product but lacked any capacity eventually to transform social attitudes and broaden the participation of people in the decisions which would affect Chile's future style of development. The state-owned iron and steel industry achieved little except to provide raw material for a growing consumer durables sector which, in turn, would only meet the demands of the urban middle class without exposure to foreign competition.

For the most part, before the 1920s had ended, the essential characteristics of Chilean industry for the next forty years were well developed. Some of these, such as monopolistic structure and complete dependence on foreign technology and investment, had crystallized even earlier. Indeed, in too many respects the industrial profile of Chile had at an early date grown to resemble its image of later years.

A direct relation may be drawn between this pattern of Chilean industrialization and the contemporary mass urban poverty which has become increasingly critical as a result of the large rural-urban migrations following World War II. The close interrelation of concentrated manufacturing, technological dependence, and the influence of transnational interests was important because of the implications for the type of products made, the productive systems employed, and the consequent labor-absorptive capacity of industry. A well-known characteristic of Chile (and Latin America in general) is the failure of the secondary sector to adequately absorb the large and fast-growing urban labor force, resulting in high levels of underemployment for the heads of urban households.[6] From its beginning, Chilean manufacturing was heavily dependent upon foreign technology, and an indiscriminate reliance on determined suppliers of technology and production systems became

6. Since they usually cannot "afford the luxury" of a long search for the "right job," heads of households are much more affected by underemployment than by unemployment, which is the typical plight of youth and women in the urban labor force.

institutionalized over the years. But the technological packages received have been geared typically to an economy where labor, not capital, is the scarce factor. This is the reverse of the Chilean situation and its needs.

Of equal importance, technological advance did not come in a continuous fashion, but rather in the form of intermittent, unequal waves directed especially to monopolistic enterprises. Such a form of introducing technical progress has been largely responsible for the creation and encouragement of a heterogeneous growth structure affecting the combinations of capital and labor used in the productive process.

As a result, underemployment and poverty exist to a great extent because productivity (and income) differentials between the large modern firms and the small traditional factory or workshop are continuously coming into existence. This is due to the existence of differential rates of transfer and diffusion of technology and organization. Since the successive waves of modernization affect only certain enterprises rather than the entire sector, or even branches of production, in some cases the productivity and income gap closes only extremely slowly, while in others it even tends to widen. In such fashion the perdurable and resilient character of structural heterogeneity has arisen in the industrial sector as well as in the national economy (given the generic nature of the Chilean oligarchy). This trait has been buttressed both economically and politically by those privileged groups of society which participate in the "modern" patterns of industrial production and consumption. Simultaneously, the majority of the population has continued to engage in activities of relatively low productivity with concomitant low and often unstable or fluctuating incomes. This situation is coupled with the distorted pattern of income distribution and the tenuous power base of those at the lower levels of economic and social structure. Because the industrialists from their social origins formed an integral part of the summit of the national configuration of power, they were able to maintain and expand this type of industrial growth. Consequently, the resources of Chile were not allocated according to their real social opportunity costs, but rather were used to satisfy the values and lifestyle demands of a traditional minority.

Appendix 1. Statistical Tables

TABLE A-1

Growth and Distribution of Chilean Exports, 1870–1930

(in millions of pesos of 18d)

Year	Mineral Products	Agricultural Products	Manufactured Products	Other	Total
1870	41.6	21.0		2.8	65.4
1871	42.2	31.6		5.9	79.7
1872	47.5	35.3	1.9	9.0	93.7
1873	45.3	32.8	1.2	12.6	91.9
1874	41.4	39.6	0.7	0.1	81.8
1875	45.1	27.6	0.7	0.1	73.5
1876	49.7	22.7	0.7	0.2	73.3
1877	39.1	21.3	0.6	0.1	61.1
1878	38.5	19.1	0.5	0.1	58.2
1879	48.1	23.4	0.2	0.1	71.8
1880	79.8	20.5	4.5		104.8
1881	99.5	16.0	5.8		121.3
1882	120.4	18.9	6.3		145.6
1883	132.9	20.1	7.1		160.1
1884	98.0	12.7	4.6		115.3
1885	85.4	12.9	4.1		102.4
1886	85.1	16.4	4.4		105.9
1887	104.3	16.9	3.2		124.4
1888	133.4	15.1	3.8		152.3
1889	119.1	11.6	4.4		135.1
1890	128.5	9.4	4.1		142.0

Continued

TABLE A-1—*Continued*

Year	Mineral Products	Agricultural Products	Manufactured Products	Other	Total
1891	108.2	22.9	5.4		136.5
1892	108.4	21.3	3.7		133.4
1893	124.2	21.7	3.3		149.2
1894	129.4	16.3	3.7		149.4
1895	127.0	16.2	4.1		147.3
1896	128.9	19.4	5.0		153.3
1897	115.7	13.6	5.6		134.9
1898	126.8	20.0	5.3		152.1
1899	137.8	16.3	4.8		158.9
1900	151.6	10.6	4.1		166.3
1901	158.9	9.5	3.2		171.6
1902	158.6	13.3	3.5		175.4
1903	170.9	18.9	4.4		194.2
1904	195.5	21.5	5.0		222.0
1905	220.2	17.8	5.8		243.8
1906	252.1	14.5	4.2		270.8
1907	241.9	17.8	4.8		264.5
1908	271.3	28.4	5.0		304.7
1909	243.8	35.5	4.6		283.9
1910	269.1	26.4	6.6		302.1
1911					
1912	336.0	32.9	8.2		377.1
1913	346.2	34.6	10.4		391.2
1914	255.4	30.7	8.3		294.4
1915	273.0	39.3	9.8		322.1
1916	446.9	41.6	17.4		505.9
1917	614.9	70.0	21.5		706.4
1918	644.7	79.2	39.6		763.5
1919	184.1	83.1	32.3		299.5
1920	660.7	84.9	33.3		778.9
1921	331.5	46.0	30.8		408.3
1922	284.8	30.3	15.4		330.5
1923	480.5	37.5	18.6		536.6
1924	507.7	75.2	17.6		600.5
1925	522.8	78.3	21.8		622.9
1926	416.0	54.6	12.6		483.2
1927	479.0	52.7	19.9		551.6
1928	552.2	72.9	21.1		646.2
1929	675.2	67.5	21.5		764.2
1930	370.1	54.2	17.8		442.1

SOURCE: Chile, Oficina Central de Estadística, *Anuario de comercio exterior*, 1870–1930.

TABLE A-2

GROWTH AND DISTRIBUTION OF CHILEAN IMPORTS, 1880–1920
(in millions of pesos of 18d)

Year	Consumer Goods	Raw Material	Capital Goods, Transport, and Communication	Fuel	Other	Total
1880	22.8	31.0	1.9	3.3	5.9	64.9
1881	30.8	40.7	3.5	3.9	3.7	82.6
1882	38.3	54.4	5.1	4.8	4.5	107.1
1883	38.8	55.9	5.7	3.9	9.5	113.8
1884	41.4	49.3	9.5	4.0	7.3	111.5
1885	30.5	38.2	6.4	3.8	5.7	84.6
1886	35.6	45.5	4.2	2.9	4.6	92.8
1887	37.1	49.8	7.2	2.9	5.5	102.5
1888	43.9	59.8	12.0	7.1	4.7	127.5
1889	47.8	61.8	13.7	6.4	6.4	136.1
1890	45.9	61.9	21.4	6.8	6.4	142.4
1891	44.2	58.7	16.5	8.7	5.7	133.8
1892	54.0	80.7	14.8	6.6	7.9	164.0
1893	46.2	67.3	16.2	7.2	6.2	143.1
1894	35.0	51.5	12.3	10.0	5.2	114.0
1895	45.3	69.8	11.4	9.8	7.9	144.2
1896	49.9	67.5	12.0	11.7	14.9	156.0
1897	47.4	67.5	7.6	8.8	6.8	138.1
1898	31.6	44.5	4.2	13.2	8.7	102.2
1899	31.1	48.4	6.3	12.6	7.9	106.3
1900	39.6	63.9	7.2	13.7	4.1	128.5
1901	43.2	69.4	11.1	14.6	1.0	139.3
1902	39.1	61.4	15.6	15.2	1.1	132.4
1903	44.0	67.8	13.0	16.0	0.8	141.6
1904	45.1	74.2	20.6	16.5	0.8	157.2
1905	49.5	85.8	26.4	24.7	1.0	187.4
1906	64.8	95.7	40.6	22.4	0.7	224.2
1907	80.3	118.1	49.7	33.1	1.4	282.6
1908	63.0	96.4	57.6	39.8	1.6	258.4
1909	65.5	118.7	29.5	36.8	1.5	252.0
1910	76.0	134.4	30.8	41.6	2.0	284.8
1911						
1912	90.7	134.8	48.5	38.4	2.5	314.9
1913	102.8	135.3	45.7	43.8	3.9	331.5
1914	98.7	98.7	29.1	41.3	2.0	269.8
1915	57.1	60.4	15.3	19.5	0.9	153.2
1916	69.6	102.8	23.1	26.3	0.7	222.5
1917	100.3	163.3	49.8	24.1	1.3	338.8
1918	117.3	201.5	54.1	20.9	1.2	395.0
1919	125.5	185.9	61.2	14.7	0.1	387.4
1920	155.5	204.4	52.9	25.6	2.2	440.6

SOURCE: Chile, Oficina Central de Estadística, *Anuario de comercio exterior*, 1880–1920.

TABLE A-3
GROWTH AND DISTRIBUTION OF CHILEAN IMPORTS, 1880–1920
(percentages)

Year	Consumer Goods	Raw Material	Capital Goods, Transport	Fuel	Other	Total
1880	36.4	49.5	3.1	5.3	5.7	100.0
1881	37.3	49.3	4.2	4.7	4.5	100.0
1882	35.6	50.6	4.7	4.5	4.6	100.0
1883	34.1	49.1	5.0	3.4	8.4	100.0
1884	37.1	44.2	8.5	3.6	6.6	100.0
1885	36.0	45.2	7.6	4.5	6.7	100.0
1886	38.4	49.0	4.5	3.1	5.0	100.0
1887	36.1	48.6	7.0	2.8	5.5	100.0
1888	34.4	46.9	9.4	5.6	3.7	100.0
1889	35.1	45.4	10.1	4.7	4.7	100.0
1890	32.2	43.5	15.0	4.8	4.5	100.0
1891	33.0	43.9	12.3	6.5	4.3	100.0
1892	32.9	49.2	9.0	4.0	4.9	100.0
1893	32.3	47.0	11.3	5.0	4.4	100.0
1894	30.7	45.2	10.8	8.8	4.5	100.0
1895	31.4	48.4	7.9	6.8	5.5	100.0
1896	32.0	43.3	7.7	7.5	9.5	100.0
1897	34.3	48.9	5.5	6.4	4.9	100.0
1898	30.9	43.5	4.1	12.9	8.6	100.0
1899	29.3	45.5	5.9	11.9	7.4	100.0
1900	30.8	49.7	5.6	10.7	3.2	100.0
1901	31.0	49.8	8.0	10.5	0.7	100.0
1902	29.5	46.4	11.8	11.5	0.8	100.0
1903	31.1	47.9	9.2	11.3	0.5	100.0
1904	28.7	47.2	13.1	10.5	0.5	100.0
1905	26.4	45.8	14.1	13.2	0.5	100.0
1906	28.9	42.7	18.1	10.0	0.3	100.0
1907	28.4	41.8	17.6	11.7	0.5	100.0
1908	24.4	37.3	22.3	15.4	0.6	100.0
1909	26.0	47.1	11.7	14.6	0.6	100.0
1910	26.7	47.2	10.8	14.6	0.7	100.0
1911						
1912	28.8	42.8	15.4	12.2	0.8	100.0
1913	31.0	40.8	13.8	13.2	1.2	100.0
1914	36.6	36.6	10.8	15.3	0.7	100.0
1915	37.3	39.4	10.0	12.7	0.6	100.0
1916	31.3	46.2	10.4	11.8	0.3	100.0
1917	29.6	48.2	14.7	7.1	0.4	100.0
1918	29.7	51.0	13.7	5.3	0.3	100.0
1919	32.4	48.0	15.8	3.8	0.0	100.0
1920	35.3	46.4	12.0	5.8	0.5	100.0

SOURCE: Table A-2.

TABLE A-4

CAPITAL-OUTPUT RATIOS FOR SELECTED CHILEAN PRODUCT LINES, 1910

Product Lines	Total Capital : Gross Value Added (I)	Fixed Capital : Gross Value Added (II)
Mills	2.75	1.09
Sugar	1.68	0.86
Vermicelli	2.85	1.48
Biscuits	1.67	1.14
Canned fruits, vegetables	3.82	2.39
Canned meat, shellfish	2.79	1.46
Chocolate	2.94	1.13
Vegetable oil	9.37	4.86
Animal oil	2.66	1.15
Condensed milk	0.75	0.59
Beer	2.83	1.52
Gaseous beverages	1.94	1.11
Cigarettes, cigars	1.76	0.87
Woolen woven cloth	2.42	1.26
Cotton woven cloth	5.40	2.13
Wool, cotton mill products	2.52	0.67
Cotton knitwear	2.76	1.51
Ready-made clothing	1.07	0.24
Shirts	2.20	0.51
Hats	3.18	0.77
Footwear	1.56	0.41
Tanned leather	2.93	1.07
Processed wood	2.15	0.87
Furniture, upholstery	1.35	0.41
Paper, cardboard	2.88	1.60
Stearine candles	2.16	0.77
Synthetic fertilizer	1.14	0.36
Matches	2.46	1.61
Soap	1.92	0.47
Gunpowder, explosives	2.07	1.40
Glassware	2.55	1.30
Cement	7.94	7.17
Foundry products	2.08	1.35
Shipyard production	1.97	1.08
Bedsteads	1.70	0.45
Tin containers, glazed ironware	2.54	1.31
Machines, tools	3.12	1.70

SOURCE: Table A-5.

TABLE A-5

Capital and Gross Value Added for Selected Chilean Industries, 1910
(in current pesos)

Industry	Number of Establish-ments	Total Capital (000)	Fixed Capital (000)	Gross Value Added (000)
Food products	274	116,987	53,957	48,653
Flour mills	174	63,412	25,227	23,047
Sugar refineries	8	26,558	13,646	15,832
Vermicelli factories	34	4,812	2,491	1,687
Biscuit factories	14	4,163	2,843	2,489
Fruit, vegetable canneries	22	5,700	3,572	1,492
Meat, shellfish canneries	12	6,937	3,627	2,485
Chocolate factories	4	374	144	127
Vegetable oil factories	2	2,006	1,041	214
Animal oil factories	3	2,876	1,249	1,082
Condensed milk factories	1	149	117	198
Beverages	232	29,709	16,104	11,146
Beer factories	62	25,652	13,791	9,057
Gaseous beverage factories	170	4,057	2,313	2,089
Tobacco products	23	5,073	2,556	2,883
Cigarette, cigar factories	23	5,073	2,556	2,883
Textiles	6	8,473	3,892	2,344
Woolen woven cloth factories	3	2,704	1,409	1,117
Cotton woven cloth factories	2	5,019	1,983	930
Wool, cotton mills	1	750	500	297
Clothing and footwear	89	31,565	9,343	17,649
Cotton knitwear factories	7	4,839	2,648	1,750
Ready-made clothing factories	10	3,644	809	3,399
Shirt factories	23	3,671	846	1,669
Hat factories	10	4,879	1,189	1,536
Footwear factories	39	14,532	3,851	9,295
Leather products	132	29,723	10,876	10,158
Tanneries	132	29,723	10,876	10,158
Wood products and furniture	308	28,028	10,797	14,596
Sawmill, wood-finishing factories	131	22,275	9,052	10,346
Furniture, upholstery factories	177	5,753	1,745	4,250
Paper	7	2,716	1,510	944
Paper, cardboard factories	7	2,716	1,510	944
Chemical products	79	10,751	5,265	5,181
Stearine candle factories	15	3,726	1,327	1,728
Synthetic fertilizer factories	4	279	87	244
Match factories	4	2,252	1,470	915

Continued

TABLE A-5—*Continued*

Industry	Number of Establishments	Total Capital (000)	Fixed Capital (000)	Gross Value Added (000)
Soap factories	46	3,203	1,512	1,669
Gunpowder, explosives factories	10	1,291	869	625
Nonmetallic mineral products	6	8,121	6,019	1,906
Glassware factories	3	3,324	1,690	1,302
Cement factories	3	4,797	4,329	604
Metallic products	90	18,520	10,289	8,416
Foundries	58	8,445	5,470	4,065
Shipyards	18	2,711	1,385	1,375
Bedstead factories	5	1,888	498	1,110
Tin container, glazed ironware factories	7	1,525	786	600
Machine, tool factories	2	3,951	2,150	1,266
Total	1,246	289,666	130,608	123,876

SOURCE: Oficina Central de Estadística, *Anuario estadístico, industrias,* 1910.

TABLE A-6

INDUSTRIAL OWNERSHIP BY NATIONAL ORIGIN, CHILE, 1914–25
(number of firms)

Year	Chilean	Foreign	Mixed	Corporation	Not Specified	Total
1914	727	846	77		33	1,683
1915	1,003	1,121	89	87	27	2,327
1916	1,159	1,211	75	80	8	2,533
1917	1,179	1,250	79	120	13	2,641
1918	1,238	1,268	78	126	12	2,722
1919	1,265	1,237	87	166	14	2,769
1920	1,323	1,273	77	193	8	2,874
1921	1,323	1,274	105	172		2,874
1922	1,313	1,316	110	195		2,934
1923	1,385	1,383	118	202		3,088
1924	1,395	1,426	116	208		3,145
1925	1,335	1,446	120	209		3,110

SOURCE: Chile, Oficina Central de Estadística, *Anuario estadístico, industrias,* 1914–25.

TABLE A-7

INDUSTRIAL CAPITAL INVESTMENT BY NATIONAL ORIGIN, CHILE, 1915–25[a]
(000)

Year	Chilean	Foreign	Mixed	Corporation	Not Specified	Total
1915	108,654	136,197	20,480	133,045	1,390	399,766
1916	134,204	145,416	19,084	133,293	2,469	434,466
1917	150,242	161,900	15,905	151,510	490	480,047
1918	157,304	168,866	18,396	160,084	1,055	505,705
1919	161,893	186,526	24,638	202,230	1,424	576,711
1920	179,354	201,463	13,965	234,235	326	629,343
1921	188,861	209,925	33,509	257,541		689,836
1922	192,822	228,829	32,398	301,782		755,831
1923	227,237	245,540	41,308	365,122		879,207
1924	244,668	292,111	50,230	418,132		1,005,141
1925	279,356	322,283	41,347	427,617		1,070,603

SOURCE: Chile, Oficina Central de Estadística, *Anuario estadístico, industrias,* 1915–25.
a. Expressed in current pesos.

TABLE A-8

CUMULATIVE PERCENTAGES OF ESTABLISHMENTS AND WORKERS IN SELECTED INDUSTRIES OF CHILEAN MANUFACTURING, 1918 AND 1937

1918		1937	
Establishments	Workers	Establishments	Workers
Beverages			
76.4	19.4	46.5	8.5
92.7	36.0	77.5	19.7
96.6	50.5	84.5	25.5
97.7	58.8	87.3	29.0
100.0	100.0	100.0	100.0
Food			
71.1	25.9	37.7	11.8
95.5	59.6	79.1	38.7
98.6	72.2	91.9	55.5
99.2	78.6	96.9	68.9
100.0	100.0	100.0	100.0
Tobacco			
53.3	6.3	40.0	2.6
82.2	16.5	46.7	3.5
95.5	38.6	66.7	8.0
95.5	38.6	73.3	11.5
100.0	100.0	100.0	100.0

Continued

TABLE A-8—*Continued*

1918		1937	
Establish-ments	Workers	Establish-ments	Workers
Paper and printing			
42.5	6.5	16.4	2.0
84.3	27.0	72.7	18.4
96.1	43.5	81.8	24.5
97.4	47.0	96.4	44.0
100.0	100.0	100.0	100.0
Textiles			
18.5	1.2	25.0	3.3
55.6	9.1	59.5	12.9
66.7	20.4	81.7	24.9
77.8	36.8	86.5	30.4
100.0	100.0	100.0	100.0
Clothing			
50.3	10.6	47.5	12.9
89.4	36.2	77.4	30.0
94.7	47.6	86.1	40.9
96.9	57.9	95.6	64.6
100.0	100.0	100.0	100.0
Construction materials			
66.2	13.8	58.3	10.7
93.6	34.1	81.3	18.5
95.2	38.1	88.8	24.4
98.4	61.8	94.1	32.9
100.0	100.0	100.0	100.0

SOURCE: Chile, Oficina Central de Estadística, *Anuario estadístico, industrias, 1918*, p. 81; Chile, Dirección General de Estadística, *Censo industrial y comercial, 1937*, pp. 22–27.

Appendix 2. The Measurement of Industrial Growth, 1895 to World War I

THOSE who have previously attempted to assess the intensity of the industrial process underway prior to World War I have used a wide variety of techniques that range from those that are totally qualitative and impressionistic to those employing a detailed analysis of the time series data which may be found.[1]

After examining the appraisals of the source materials made by informed contemporary observers and participants in the data collection services, I concluded that the use of those industrial statistics for the preparation of elaborate indices measuring the year-to-year growth of production, capital investment, and employed labor is a futile effort leading to illusory results. Two questions may be raised concerning the use of available time series for the purpose of marking the flow of Chilean industrial evolution during the period from the first industrial census in 1895 to 1913 or, as is most

1. An example of the former type is Véliz, "La mesa." A mixture of impressionistic observations and quantitative evidence, although without much effort expended on the meaning of the statistics presented, is to be found in Pfeiffer, "The Development," and Oscar Alvarez Andrews, *Historia del desarrollo industrial de Chile*. The only detailed quantitative analysis of industrialization before World War I is Marcello Carmagnani, *Sviluppo Industriale e Sottosviluppo Economico, Il Caso Chileno (1860–1920)*.

common, comparing the early period with the war years, 1914–18. These issues refer to the accuracy and the comparability of the data.

There is no way to evaluate the former; it is a defect that was present then and is also present in the statistical collection of today. On the other hand, the comparability of the data which encompass this period may be subjected to several contemporary assessments upon which our judgments may be based. Responsibility for data collection was in the hands of the SFF until 1910, after which the task went to the Chilean government's Bureau of Statistics. Since participation in the first industrial census of 1895 was voluntary and the industrialists feared a relation between their replies and future tax levies, their answers were most incomplete. Indeed, the lack of cooperation on the part of the industrialists is constantly referred to in the letters which the SFF received from those charged with gathering the information across the country.[2]

The next effort at raising an industrial census came in 1906–7, and once again cooperation of the industrialists was voluntary. It is not surprising to find that the 1906–7 data are useless for making comparisons with subsequent data on even the most general levels, since insufficient funding for the census severely curtailed its coverage. Only sixteen provinces were included, and Valparaíso, one of the major industrial centers at the time, was unexplainably excluded.[3] Furthermore, criteria for census coverage varied from one province to another: in Santiago, all establishments with less than four workers were excluded; in Aconcagua, less than three workers was the dividing line; in other provinces, all enterprises were included regardless of size.[4]

As mentioned, the only source who attempts to construct a time series of production levels from the late nineteenth century to 1918 is Marcelo Carmagnani. The problems in the use of the 1895 and 1906 data have already been dealt with. In addition, I find curious discrepancies between Carmagnani's published figures and the data found in the original sources. Thus, using the figures published in the 1907–8 *Boletín de la Sociedad de Fomento Fabril*, Carmagnani reports only 2,253 establishments with a total of 42,691

2. "Correspondencia," *BSFF* 12 (1895), passim.

3. Included in that census were the provinces of Aconcagua, Santiago, O'Higgins, Colchagua, Curicó, Talca, Maule, Linares, Ñuble, Concepción, Bio-Bio, Arauco, Malleco, Cautín, Valdivia, and Llanquihue. Missing were Tacna, Tarapacá, Antofagasta, Atacama, Coquimbo, and Valparaíso.

4. Sociedad de Fomento Fabril, *Estadística industrial.*

employees for 1906, whereas the SFF's annual report for the year 1908, in reference to the same period and even after disregarding all small shops of less than four workers, gives results for the 16 provinces of 2,829 factories with 51,353 employees.[5]

Most of Carmagnani's emphasis, however, falls on the period 1910–18. The object of his approach is to examine the effects of World War I on Chilean domestic industry. Once again it should be noted that no other student in this problem area has been able to quantify changes in the production levels from 1910, the year in which annually published data first appeared, to 1918.[6] In my opinion the problem remains unsolved. This conclusion is based on the fact that not only are serious errors to be found in the data, but that the nature of these errors varies erratically from one year to the next so that no basis exists for uncovering a systematic bias to which appropriate corrections may be applied.

Thus, the 1910 law which placed the responsibility for gathering industrial production data in the hands of the Oficina Central de Estadística carried out reorganization of the statistical services with a considerable degree of confusion. Moreover, since the criterion for reporting remained the tax roll law of 1866, the director of the state statistical office, Valentín del Campo, in the introduction to the 1911 industrial yearbook warned the user against having much confidence in the published results.[7] Each year, until 1914, more establishments were reported, but this reflected more

5. Carmagnani, *Sviluppo*, pp. 173, 179; Sociedad de Fomento Fabril, "Memoria, 1908," *BSFF* 26 (January 1909):53. It should be noted that similar discrepancies also are to be found for the years 1911–13.

6. I am aware of the time series produced by Mario Ballesteros and Tom Davis, which begins in 1908. However, the value of this measurement of output for this early period has been conclusively discredited by Oscar Muñoz, who points out a basic error in their use of the same 1916 production figure for the years 1913–15; apparently they did not have access to the data for those years. Furthermore, they underestimate the distortions caused by the reporting problems in the results published from 1907 to 1914 as discussed in this text. See Mario Ballesteros and Tom E. Davis, "The Growth of Output and Employment in Basic Sectors of the Chilean Economy, 1908–1957"; Muñoz, *Crecimiento*, p. 35.

7. Chile, Oficina Central de Estadística, *Anuario estadístico, industrias, 1911* (no page number). Until the year before, the reporting of industrial statistics was carried out by the SFF. In the introduction to the 1910 report, Manuel Muñoz, Chief of the Industrial Statistics Section, cautioned the reader in a similar fashion and added that small shops were grouped together and reported as one unit in order to fill in specific product categories for certain areas. See Sociedad de Fomento Fabril, *Estadística industrial de la República de Chile* (1910), pp. iv, vii.

comprehensive coverage rather than accelerated growth in industry. The preface to the 1912 yearbook informed its readers, "The present statistical yearbook contains data from 6,215 industrial establishments, that is 493 more than appeared in last year's Industrial Statistics. This difference is not due to enterprises founded during 1912 as might be thought, but rather to firms which already existed and which had never been included because of insurmountable difficulties."[8]

TABLE A-9

CHILEAN INDUSTRIAL ESTABLISHMENTS, 1910–18[a]

	Factories	Artisans Operations and Small Shops	Total
1910			5,415
1911			5,684
1912			6,173
1913			7,731
1914	1,683	2,470	4,153
1915	2,330	4,288	6,618
1916	2,533	4,140	6,673
1917	2,638	5,544	8,182
1918	2,720	4,651	7,371

SOURCE: Sociedad de Fomento Fabril, *Estadística industrial de la República de Chile* (1910); Chile, Oficina Central de Estadística, *Anuario estadístico, industrias*, 1911–18.

a. Gas and electric firms are not included.

In 1913, an entirely new industrial roll was prepared, a new questionnaire was issued, and the data were collected by officials of the state statistical office itself rather than, as in the past, the municipalities. As may be appreciated from Table A-9, coverage consequently increased by 1,558 establishments from 1912 to 1913. Finally, an important modification was introduced in the 1914 publication on industry which for the first time separated factories from small shops and craftsman operations. The definition of these categories is not given but probably followed the practice of the time of reporting as a factory any establishment with five or more people working in it. This last change also upset the 1914 reporting, and that year's publication mentions that sizeable omissions are present, a fact which is evident in the 46 per cent decline in the total number of establishments reported.

8. Chile, Oficina Central de Estadística, *Anuario estadístico, industrias*, 1912, "Consideraciones generales" (no page number).

Further observation of Carmagnani's approach to measuring output up to the end of World War I reveals another flaw of a simpler if equally fatal nature. The base year upon which his production index series is built is 1918, and the aggregate industrial output is shown to fall from 1,409,800 pesos (6d.) in 1917 to 1,096,600 pesos (6d.) in 1918. Summation of the ten product sectors, however, reveals an arithmetic error, since the total for 1918 according to his published figures is really 1,801,400.[9] The latter figure, which shows an increase from 1917 to 1918, corresponds to the trend found in the industrial yearbooks themselves, as well as that noted by other authors. But reconstruction of Carmagnani's index would not correct for the shortcomings inherent in the source material which are beyond remedy.

A Forecast Equation for Aggregate Chilean Industrial Production, 1880–1913

Although relatively rich in historical statistics, especially compared with other countries, Chilean sources of economic data for the nineteenth century present numerous difficulties, particularly with regard to secondary industry. In addition to the problem caused by the lack of or noncomparability of manufacturing data, it should be noted that most of the available time series extending across the period of interest refer only to foreign commerce or to fiscal and monetary areas which, in any event, have largely monopolized the economic historiography of Chile until very recently.

Nevertheless, the dependence of Chilean industry upon the foreign sector prior to the Great Depression, as indicated in chapter 1, provided the empirical base for independent variables of meaningful economic content which could be used in least-squares multiple regression analysis to forecast the trend of aggregate Chilean industrial output before World War I.[10] To the series of total exports and the importation of raw intermediate goods for Chilean

9. Carmagnani, *Sviluppo*, pp. 169–70.

10. A detailed explanation of the technique employed, as well as the tests applied for statistical acceptability of the regression equations, is to be found in Edward J. Kane, *Economic Statistics and Econometrics, An Introduction to Quantitative Economics*, chaps. 11, 14. Also see Hubert M. Blalock, *Social Statistics*, chaps. 17–19. The use of the least-squares technique in the context of this work was suggested by Joseph Mullen and closely follows his application of it which is to be found in his dissertation, "Energy in the Japanese Economy, 1878–1965," chap. 6 and app. 1.

manufacturing was added protectionist tariff legislation in the form of a dummy variable. If significant legislation occurred in a given year, the existence of this variable as operating was included in the computer program; otherwise, it was not. This approach was adopted as the most conservative since the effectiveness or intensity of the effect of legislation, which was often complex, including specific as well as ad valorem tariffs, could not be gauged adequately for the lifespan of the regulation. Finally, a time trend variable was included. The purpose of using this variable is straightforward. It is a proxy variable whose purpose is to remove, from what would otherwise be contained in the unexplained residual of the multiple regression, the effect on the dependent variable, industrial production, of net, monotonically operating changes in one or more of several other unspecified variables.

The four independent variables were arranged in such fashion as to produce the seven sets of independent variables listed in Table A-10. It should be emphasized that other changes of an economic or social order which could affect the supply or demand schedule were not considered irrelevant. But it was simply not possible to account for these in a statistically defensible manner which could meet the requirements of the least-squares or other possible techniques. It was assumed that a sufficiently high linear relationship exists between those variables selected and Chilean industrial output to be able to forecast changes in the latter before the last observation point in 1914. Operationally, this restricted the selection of functions with which to test the assumption to the following:

(1) $Y = a_1 + b_1X_1$, which relates changes in the volume of Y to changes in the volume of X_1;

(2) $Y = a_2X_1^b$, which, when transformed to logarithms to the Naperian base $e = 2.718 \ldots$, yields

(3) $\log_e Y = \log_e a_3 + b_3 (\log X_1)$, which relates the rate of change in Y to the rate of change in X_1.

In addition, anticipating the problem of autocorrelation especially due to the use of the time trend variable and the total exports with total exports lagged variables, two other related functions were employed to test the relationship between changes in Y vis-à-vis changes in X_1. These other two functions employ the first differences of functions (1) and (3):

(4) $Y_{(t)-(t-1)} = a_4 + b_4 (X_1)_{(t)-(t-1)}$, and
(5) $(\log_e Y)_t - (\log_e Y)_{t-1} = \text{Log}_e a_5 + b_5 (\log_e X_1)_t - (\log_e X_1)_{t-1}$.

The regression exercise was, therefore, executed using four functions—1, 3, 4, and 5. Application of them to each of the seven sets of variables specified in Table A-10 resulted in a total of twenty-eight equations that then had to be screened for statistical acceptability.

TABLE A-10
ALTERNATIVE SPECIFICATION OF VARIABLES FOR FORECASTING THE GROWTH IN CHILEAN AGGREGATE INDUSTRIAL PRODUCTION, 1880–1913

Specification	Dependent Variable	Independent Variable
1	(IO)	(E)
2	(IO)	(E), (EL)
3	(IO)	(E), (EL), (T)
4	(IO)	(RI)
5	(IO)	(E), (RI)
6	(IO)	(RI), (PT)
7	(IO)	(E), (RI), (PT)

NOTE: (IO), real industrial output; (E), total exports; (EL), total exports lagged by one year; (RI), raw and intermediate material imports; (PT), protectionist tariff legislation; (T), a time trend variable.

The data inputs for all variables are given in Table A-11. It was decided to use the seventeen observations of industrial production expressed in 1950 escudos found in Oscar Muñoz' recent study, inasmuch as this is generally agreed to be the most reliable time series available and has the merit of offering enough observations for the least-squares technique to be validly employed. The export and raw-and-intermediate imports data are those of Tables A-1 and A-2 of this text, presented in index form with 1880–85 = 100.

The acceptability of each of the twenty-eight regression equations was judged with reference to the value and significance of several generally accepted statistics: the coefficients of multiple correlation (R) and determination (R^2), the Durbin-Watson autocorrelation statistic, and the Bartlett (heteroskedasticity) statistic,

TABLE A-11

DATA INPUTS FOR FORECAST EQUATIONS OF CHILEAN INDUSTRIAL OUTPUT, 1880–1913

Year	Industrial Output (IO)	Total Exports (Index 1880–85=100) (E), (EL)	Raw and Intermediate Material Imports (Index 1880–85=100) (RI)	Protectionist Tariff Legislation (PT)	Time Trend Variable (T)
1879		57			
1880		84	69	0	1
1883		128			
1884		92			5
1885		84	85	0	
1889		108			
1890		113	138	0	11
1894		119			
1895		117	155	0	16
1899		127			
1900		133	142	0	21
1905		194	177	0	
1906		216			27
1909		226			
1910		241	299	0	31
1912		300	300	0	
1913		312	301	0	
1914	6,530	234	220	0	35
1915	7,170	257	135	0	36
1916	8,260	403	229	1	37
1917	9,050	506	364	0	38
1918	9,620	608	449	0	39
1919	9,700	239	414	0	40
1920	9,253	620	455	0	41
1921	9,460	325	319	1	42
1922	9,470	263	228	1	43
1923	10,330	427	332	0	44
1924	11,120	478	370	0	45
1925	11,110	496	337	0	46
1926	10,692	385	384	0	47
1927	10,275	439	346	0	48
1928	11,330	515	364	1	49
1929	13,900	609	508	1	50
1930	13,810	352	403	1	51

as well as F and t values. Significance of all test statistics was set at the 5 per cent level as a minimum standard of acceptance.[11]

Of the twenty-eight equations, all but two were eliminated by these rigorous statistical screening criteria and only these could be

11. For a complete discussion of these statistical criteria see the chapters indicated in Kane, *Economic Statistics*, and Blalock, *Social Statistics*.

utilized to forecast aggregate Chilean industrial production, 1880–1913. The equations are those which resulted from function 3 given above (t values shown in parentheses):

(1) Δ ($\log_e$ Real Industrial Output) = 6.669 + .428 Δ ($\log_e$ Raw-and-Intermediate Materials Import Index) + .143 (Protective Tariff Dummy Variable)

$$\Delta(\log_e \text{Real Industrial Output}) = \underset{(12.5)}{6.669} + \underset{(4.6)}{.428}\,\Delta(\log_e \text{Raw-and-Intermediate Materials Import Index}) + \underset{(2.3)}{.143}\,(\text{Protective Tariff Dummy Variable})$$

the test statistics for which are

R: .81; R^2: .66; F: 13.4; Durbin-Watson statistic: 1.00; Bartlett's statistic for heteroskedasticity: .24; and

(2)

$$\Delta(\log_e \text{Real Industrial Output}) = \underset{(6.8)}{5.735} + \underset{(2.5)}{.260}\,\Delta(\log_e \text{Total Export Index}) + \underset{(3.1)}{.318}\,(\text{Time Trend Variable})$$

which gave the following test statistics:

R: .74; R^2: .55; F: 8.4; Durbin-Watson statistic: .78; Bartlett's statistic for heteroskedasticity: .92.

Equation (1) is the stronger of the two. It is economically meaningful and relates the rates of change in industrial primary material imports (and implicitly also total exports), as well as protectionist-oriented government action to the rates of change in overall industrial output. Equation (2) also yields positive results. It fails only the Durbin-Watson test, since autocorrelation is present in the use of the time trend variable. Although this violates one of the least-squares assumptions (that the error terms of different observations are distributed independently of each other), the equation passed all other tests, and it was considered defensible by me on intuitive grounds with respect to sources from the period which were qualitative in nature. The additional factors forthcoming from this material (e.g. corporate annual reports) which would have helped to explain industrial growth, however, could not be introduced into the equation in lieu of the time trend variable.

Nonetheless, when the pattern of contribution to the coefficient of explanation (R^2) of each of the independent variables is considered, the usefulness of Equation (2) is weakened substantially. By the same token this test, known as Beta analysis, strengthens the case for Equation (1). This is shown in Table A-12.

According to Beta analysis, in an equation with two or more independent variables, the result should indicate that each independent variable makes a significant and positive contribution to R^2. This is true of both equations. Yet it is important to note in the case of Equation (2) that 60 per cent of the explanatory power of the equation is provided by the time trend variable. This weakens the usefulness of this equation since the time trend was introduced for the purpose of extrapolating all of those unspecified factors which could not be explained in the equation. The time trend did indeed serve its purpose of indicating the complexity of the function, and consequently we go to Equation (1), up to now the stronger of the two.

TABLE A-12
THE TOTAL CONTRIBUTION TO R^2 OF THE INDEPENDENT VARIABLES

	Total Contribution to R^2		
	X_1	X_2	R^2
Equation (1)	.53 (Raw-and-intermediate material imports)	.13 (Protectionist tariff dummy variable)	.66
Equation (2)	.22 (Total exports)	.33 (Time trend variable)	.55

The Beta analysis of Equation (1) yields results which induce us to accept it and leave the other aside. The variable raw-and-intermediate material imports (which implicitly contains the trend in total exports of other equation) provides 80 per cent of the explanatory power of R^2. This also gives added weight to the importance of the foreign sector, especially the capacity to import industrial inputs, for understanding the evolution of Chilean manufacturing prior to the Great Depression.

It should be pointed out, however, that although the coefficient of determination (R^2) of Equation (1) is high enough to be considered substantially useful for forecast applications, the range of the results produced from the standard error of the forecast at the 95 per cent level is too wide to be considered really useful (see Table 9 of the text). It must be concluded, therefore, that the reconstruction of the absolute output values of Chilean industry at any given date from the War of the Pacific to the outbreak of World War I remains an open issue. Given the lack of other reliable empirical data which may have significantly influenced or been related to early Chilean industrial production, it would appear that the application of the least-squares technique has only limited value.

Although this conclusion is negative in nature, the exercise is positive in that it provides a concrete example of the possible uses and limitations of some widely used tools of quantitative economic analysis in historical research. Furthermore, the results should not be disregarded for they represent the *most probable* pattern of Chilean industrial output before 1914, and provide the only time series which to me may be considered as both economically meaningful and statistically defensible.

Appendix 3. Ownership and Control of Chilean Industry

This appendix is the source of data and material used in chapter 4. The object is to provide a base upon which conclusions may be drawn regarding the evolution and control of major Chilean industrial enterprises during the period which elapsed between the War of the Pacific and the Great Depression. Essentially two kinds of information are sought; the structure of ownership and the identity of those who controlled the firms. Since most of the firms under review were corporate entities, the two are not always the same. Although most companies were found to be "closed corporations," owned and controlled by a small group of investors and their families, this was not always the case.

It was not uncommon to find that a firm was controlled by an individual, another firm, or an investment group which held only a minority portion of the total voting stock. Studies on the separation of ownership and control of corporations in the United States have revealed that in some cases less than 10 per cent of the total voting stock in the hands of one party is adequate for effective working control of the firm if that party has attained a significant representative block on the board of directors.[1] Strong representa-

1. See Adolf Berle and Gardiner Means, *The Modern Corporation and*

tion on the directorate and ownership of 10 to 30 per cent or more of the stock was the most common form of minority control found in the Chilean firms.

The forty-two companies surveyed were selected on the basis of their size and importance in different industrial sectors. The identification of these firms was made on the basis of data from the Santiago Stock Exchange and contemporary publications.[2] Although other firms of equal size existed in some areas, such as wine-making and metal-working, these companies were not included due to the lack of reliable information on date of establishment or ownership at certain points of time. However, from what was known about these enterprises, there was no reason to believe that their pattern of ownership would have altered the conclusions reached in chapter 4.

The source material used for almost all of the companies was drawn from the statutes of incorporation and shareholder lists of the respective corporations. The former were found principally in the *Diario Oficial.* The latter are filed in the Archive of the Santiago Stock Exchange. Letters, memoranda, and other unpublished material on the history of firms are also to be found in the five volumes of manuscripts entitled "Estudios sobre sociedades anónimas, con motivo de los setenta años de la Bolsa de Comercio" and in the one volume of "Estudios sobre empresas," both of which are in the Santiago Stock Exchange. Some nineteenth-century material was also forthcoming from the Ministerio de Hacienda, Archivo Nacional, volumes 2,839, 4,227, and 2,658. Short company histories published in the *Boletín de la Sociedad de Fomento Fabril* and other publications far too numerous to detail were also useful.

Since limitations of time and resources did not permit calculations to be made for every year, and yet a dynamic analysis was sought, I decided to analyze stockholder information at six-year intervals from 1914 on, even though all years were reviewed. Stock-

---

Private Property, pp. 70–92; R. Joseph Monsen et al., "Effect of Separation of Ownership and Control on the Performance of the Large Firm"; U.S., Temporary National Economic Committee, *Bureaucracy and Trusteeship in Large Corporations*, p. 103.

2. Apart from information in the *BSFF*, the following were most useful: Enrique Espinoza, *Geografía descriptiva de la República de Chile*; González, ed., *El esfuerzo nacional, estudios de política industrial*, passim; Alvarez, *Historia*, pp. 194–204; Bolsa de Comercio de Santiago, *La riqueza*, passim; Jorge Ramírez Barahona, *Anuario guía de sociedades anónimas*, passim.

holder lists were analyzed more regularly, however, if any significant changes in ownership occurred. Since the data were available on a very irregular basis before 1914, I studied the statutes of incorporation (which often provided information on previous ownership) and company histories.

The material in the tables is ordered according to six major categories of ownership. If the enterprise was not a corporation, only the "proprietor" category is applicable. For the appropriate dates to which this category corresponds, a "C" or an "I" is entered depending upon whether the owner was Chilean or an immigrant. If an unincorporated industry was owned by foreign interests, the letter "F" was used. The five remaining categories are employed for corporations. The category "Directorate and family holdings" refers to all members of the board of directors and their respective families. Family holdings occasionally include the stock held by an enterprise which was almost completely owned by the director or principal stockholder and members of his family. "Foreign participation" is defined as that stock held by a foreign-owned business entity or nonresident foreigner. The figures are percentages of total voting stock to be found in each of these divisions. It should be stressed that the groupings are not mutually exclusive and do not, therefore, add up to 100.0 per cent. Thus, trading houses may also be entered together with Chilean firms or represent foreign participation. In like fashion, the principal stockholder and his family is usually but not always included in the category "Directorate and family holdings."

Finally, a "summary" text is included for each firm in order to complete and interpret the skeletal structure of the quantitative ownership data above. It identifies the party which exercised effective control over the firm and where possible identifies this party's links with other economic sectors. The firms are listed according to industrial grouping.

Food

Compañía de Refinería de Azúcar de Viña del Mar

	1887	1914	1920	1926	1932
(1) Proprietor					
(2) Directorate and family holdings	90.4	11.3	6.0	6.9	10.7
(3) Principal stockholder and family	67.6	5.4	5.0	4.0	4.4
(4) Chilean firms and banks		3.2	1.5	15.3	17.7
(5) Trading houses	12.0	5.9	2.5	2.1	5.3
(6) Foreign participation	12.0	5.0	11.8	14.3	14.2

Summary: Founded in 1873 by a German immigrant, Julio Bernstein, this firm, the largest sugar refinery in Chile, remained under his control until his death in 1891. Foreign trading houses were quite influential in the affairs of the company through the extensive credit which they extended it and, at the time of its incorporation, through direct investment. The trading houses together with the Edwards group (involved before World War I) maintained minority control over the firm until 1920. At that time the Edwards group in league with its British banking affiliate, the Banco Anglo Sud-Americano, exercised undisputed control through 13 per cent of the total voting stock and representation on the board of directors. This was increased to about 20 per cent by 1926, giving the Edwardses a much firmer hold over the company which they maintained until at least 1932.

Compañía Molinos y Fideos Carozzi

	1907	1913	1927
(1) Proprietor	C		
(2) Directorate and family holdings			30.66
(3) Principal stockholder and family		27.37	12.95
(4) Chilean firms and banks			
(5) Trading houses			
(6) Foreign participation			

Summary: The firm was founded by seven partners, all of Italian origin, among whom the principal figure was Augusto Carozzi Passani. In 1913 the enterprise was incorporated, and Carozzi, the president, was the principal shareholder. His share in the ownership declined by 1927, representing then only 12.95 per cent of the total shares outstanding although he remained as the major active force in the management of the company working with his original partners and their sons. It should be noted that the firm was a closely held corporation in the hands of a small group of people and no outside corporate activity, trading house, or foreign participation was evident in the period.

Molinera Pérez Cotapos y Cía. S.A.

	1894	1948	1966
(1) Proprietor	C		
(2) Directorate and family holdings			
(3) Principal stockholder and family		68.75	85.45
(4) Chilean firms and banks			
(5) Trading houses			
(6) Foreign participation			

SUMMARY: From 1894 this firm was in the hands of the Pérez Cotapos family. Available evidence indicates that at no moment (even up to 1966, at which time Julio Pérez Cotapos Arteaga held 85.45 per cent of all stock) were any other interests represented in significant amounts.

Compañía Molinera San Cristóbal

	1916	1920	1926	1932
(1) Proprietor				
(2) Directorate and family holdings	29.60	24.40	31.02	19.49
(3) Principal stockholder and family	16.00	16.33	16.33	11.52
(4) Chilean firms and banks				1.55
(5) Trading houses	68.40	65.21	64.77	62.42
(6) Foreign participation	68.40	59.21	59.43	58.19

SUMMARY: Williamson Balfour y Cía., a trading house of English origin, had majority share of the stock and exercised active control of the firm by placing several of its members on the board of directors throughout the period. The gradual decline in foreign participation reflects the "Chileanization" of Williamson Balfour & Co. as its partners, residents in Chile, die and their shares are left to their families who, although maintaining close ties with the trading house, are Anglo-Chileans.

Compañía Molinera "El Globo"

	1905	1920	1926	1932
(1) Proprietor				
(2) Directorate and family holdings	49.2	7.4	8.6	5.2
(3) Principal stockholder and family	40.0	3.0	4.6	4.6
(4) Chilean firms and banks	8.0	1.0	10.0	7.1
(5) Trading houses	28.4	25.5	23.3	32.5
(6) Foreign participation	26.6	29.8	15.7	50.2

SUMMARY: In 1905, the English trading house, Duncan Fox y Cía., acquired the flour mill from the Bunster family. Duncan Fox maintained minority control throughout the period. Its stock participation did not go below 20 per cent and it usually held three out of seven directorates.

Galletas McKay

	1892	1930	1940
(1) Proprietor	C	C	
(2) Directorate and family holdings			51.0+
(3) Principal stockholder and family			
(4) Chilean firms and banks			
(5) Trading houses			
(6) Foreign participation			

SUMMARY: This firm was under the complete ownership of the McKay family until 1930 and under majority control from then on.

Hucke Hermanos S.A.C.

	1872	1926	1932
(1) Proprietor	C		
(2) Directorate and family holdings		69.2	58.4
(3) Principal stockholder and family		30.8	29.6
(4) Chilean firms and banks		8.7	2.8
(5) Trading houses			
(6) Foreign participation		19.9	26.3

SUMMARY: From its founding in 1872 until at least 1924 the firm was owned and controlled by the Hucke family. After its incorporation in 1924, they maintained minority control with 28 to 30 per cent of the total stock and by holding positions on the board of directors. Most of the foreign participation (16.3 per cent in 1926 and 14.3 per cent in 1932) was on the basis of individuals who were residents of Germany.

Fábrica de Conservas de Fruta y Conservas Juan Nieto

	1892	1906
(1) Proprietor	C	C
(2) Directorate and family holdings		
(3) Principal stockholder and family		
(4) Chilean firms and banks		
(5) Trading houses		
(6) Foreign participation		

SUMMARY: This important food-processing plant was founded and owned by a well-known agriculturalist, Juan Nieto.

Fábrica Nacional de Conservas Alimenticias

	1896	1909
(1) Proprietor	C	C
(2) Directorate and family holdings		
(3) Principal stockholder and family		
(4) Chilean firms and banks		
(5) Trading houses		
(6) Foreign participation		

SUMMARY: The sole owner of the enterprise was Juan Nicolás Rubio, a large landowner.

Fábrica de Leche Condensada de Weir Scott y Cía.

	1907	1924	1945
(1) Proprietor			
(2) Directorate and family holdings			
(3) Principal stockholder and family			
(4) Chilean firms and banks			
(5) Trading houses	100.0	100.0	100.0
(6) Foreign participation	100.0	100.0	100.0

SUMMARY: The factory was established and owned throughout the period by the commercial house of Weir Scott y Cía. This trading house was an English-owned enterprise. The condensed milk plant was never incorporated but rather maintained as a limited liability company under Weir Scott's ownership until about the time of the Great Depression. It was then driven out of business by the establishment of a branch plant of the Swiss-owned Nestlé corporation.

BEVERAGES

Compañía Cervecerías Unidas

	1902	1914	1920	1926	1932
(1) Proprietor					
(2) Directorate and family holdings	2.8	19.6	18.7	11.1	9.2
(3) Principal stockholder and family	40.3	10.2	7.5	3.0	3.3
(4) Chilean firms and banks	56.9	6.1	8.0	5.1	15.2
(5) Trading houses		1.1	0.7	0.6	0.3
(6) Foreign participation		5.0	9.0	26.1	19.5

SUMMARY: The company was founded in 1902 by the fusion of the Fábrica Nacional de Cerveza located in Limache and the Cervecería Cousiño, controlled by Carlos Cousiño. He was the largest single shareholder with 40.3 per cent of the stock in 1902 and exercised control on the management of the firm through his representative on the board of directors, Thompson Matthews. The rest of the stock was distributed among the shareholders of the Fábrica Nacional de Cerveza. Although it is known that Chilean firms and foreign trading houses had interests in the enterprise, their participation in 1902 is not specified. The

Cousiño group maintained undisputed control of the enterprise through two representatives on the board of directors and stockholdings which averaged between 14 and 19 per cent of the outstanding shares. From 1914 the Edwards group maintained one directorship, but it was not until around 1926, when, in league with the Banco Anglo Sud-Americano, they obtained 27 per cent of the stock and two directorships. At this time the Cousiño interests had fallen to around 8 per cent, although they were still able to hold three places on the board of directors. The situation was much the same by 1932, at which time the Edwards group in league with the English banking interests held 22 per cent of the stock and two directorships; the Cousiños still maintained two representatives in the management of the firm although their stock had dwindled to 4.65 per cent. Nevertheless, there is no indication throughout the company history of a dispute between these two major investment groups which controlled the firm through minority stockholdings.

Cervecería Anwandter

	1850	1905	1916
(1) Proprietor	I		
(2) Directorate and family holdings		100.0	
(3) Principal stockholder and family		100.0	
(4) Chilean firms and banks			100.0
(5) Trading houses			100.0
(6) Foreign participation			

Summary: The brewery was founded as a modest enterprise in 1850 by the German immigrant Carlos Anwandter and controlled by him and his partner and brother-in-law, Teodoro Korner, until Anwandter's death in 1889. From then, past its incorporation in 1905 as Compañía Cervecera Valdivia, and until 1916, it was owned and controlled by the Anwandter family. In 1916 the enterprise was purchased by the Compañía Cervecerías Unidas.

Fábrica de Cerveza de Limache

	1883	1891	1902
(1) Proprietor	I	I	
(2) Directorate and family holdings			
(3) Principal stockholder and family			51.6
(4) Chilean firms and banks			24.6
(5) Trading houses			1.7
(6) Foreign participation			1.7

Summary: Established in 1883 by the German immigrant Carlos Hoffmann, this firm remained under his and a partner's ownership until its incorporation shortly after 1891. By the time the brewery was fused with Carlos Cousiño's brewery in Santiago to form the Compañía Cervecerías Unidas, the Edwards group owned the majority of the Limache stock, either personally or through the family bank, Agustín Edwards y Cía.

Fábrica de Cerveza Gubler y Cousiño

	1883	1894	1902
(1) Proprietor	I, C	C	
(2) Directorate and family holdings			
(3) Principal stockholder and family			
(4) Chilean firms and banks			100.0
(5) Trading houses			
(6) Foreign participation			

Summary: This brewery was founded in 1883 by Augusto Gubler, a Swiss immigrant, who had considerable experience in the import-export business and was skilled in the techniques of the beer industry, and Carlos Cousiño, the head of the Cousiño group. By 1894, Carlos was sole proprietor, and in 1902 the firm was fused with the Fábrica Nacional de Cerveza to form the Compañía Cervecerías Unidas.

Sociedad Fábrica de Cerveza Andrés Ebner

	1880	1890	1900	1906	1914	1916
(1) Proprietor	I	I	I			
(2) Directorate and family holdings						
(3) Principal stockholder and family				[a]	[a]	
(4) Chilean firms and banks						100
(5) Trading houses						
(6) Foreign participation						

Summary: The firm was founded by Andrés Ebner, a German immigrant, in 1872 and completely owned by him until his death in 1905. In 1906, stock was issued as the company expanded operations. Carlos Cousiño then held controlling interest in the firm until 1916, at which time it was acquired by the Compañía Cervecerías Unidas, then a Cousiño-controlled enterprise.

a. See summary section.

Viña Concha y Toro

	1883	1922	1931
(1) Proprietor	C		
(2) Directorate and family holdings		100.0	72.0
(3) Principal stockholder and family		96.2	71.2
(4) Chilean firms and banks			9.8
(5) Trading houses			
(6) Foreign participation			

Summary: The vineyard was incorporated in 1922 but throughout the period 1883–1931, it was either completely owned or controlled through majority ownership by the Concha y Toro and Subercaseaux families, who were related through multiple marriages. Mining and railroad ventures formed the basis of the Subercaseaux fortune in the nineteenth century.

Tobacco

Compañía Chilena de Tabacos

	1897	1914	1920	1926	1932
(1) Proprietor					
(2) Directorate and family holdings	11.2	9.0	3.5	2.2	5.4
(3) Principal stockholder and family	3.3	5.7	2.1	20.8	1.6
(4) Chilean firms and banks		9.8	13.8	4.0	12.6
(5) Trading houses	83.3	6.2	2.3		
(6) Foreign participation		32.3	18.0	27.7	24.5

SUMMARY: The trading house of Fernando Rioja y Cía., owned by the Spanish immigrant Fernando Rioja Medel, was the major element in the founding of this company, and its owner was president for many years (at least until 1920). The ownership structure of the firm varied considerably, however. Spanish interests, particularly those of the Banco Hispano Americano of Barcelona and Madrid, accounted for the largest block of shares from just before the First World War to the 1920s (21.7 per cent in 1914 and 13.8 per cent in 1920). In 1926, foreign participation was quite heavy, but by this time the principal foreign investor was the Banco Anglo Sud-Americano Ltd. (with 9.7 per cent of the total stock). The real power in the enterprise, however, was that of the Edwards clan, which controlled 22.6 per cent of the stock and a directorate in that year. The Compañía Chilena de Tabacos remained under their control until the end of the period under study.

Textiles

Sociedad Fábrica Nacional de Paños de Bellavista

(Sucesora de Carlos Werner, Tomé)

	1904	1923	1930	1932
(1) Proprietor	C			
(2) Directorate and family holdings		95.6	4.1	4.7
(3) Principal stockholder and family		93.6	73.7	55.1
(4) Chilean firms and banks			3.1	3.1
(5) Trading houses				20.1
(6) Foreign participation				21.4

SUMMARY: Originally founded in 1865 by Eduardo Délano, this textile enterprise languished and passed through the hands of numerous owners until Carlos Werner, a prominent figure in mining and agriculture, acquired it in 1904. He remained as its sole proprietor until its incorporation in 1923. From then until his death in 1927, he controlled the firm with over 90 per cent of its stock in his possession. His widow and sons maintained majority ownership of the stock and delegated the management of it to a friend of the family, the German chemist Dr. Konrad Behn. In 1932, the American trading house W. R. Grace and Company and the English firm Duncan Fox and Company began to invest heavily in the industry.

Compañía Nacional de Tejidos "El Salto"

	1870–99	1905	1910	1920	1926	1932
(1) Proprietor						
(2) Directorate and family holdings		25.9	34.6	14.8	19.8	5.0
(3) Principal stockholder and family		15.0	15.2	12.9	12.6	5.0
(4) Chilean firms and banks		12.5	16.4		5.9	6.9
(5) Trading houses						
(6) Foreign participation	a				5.7	2.0

SUMMARY: Originally founded in 1830, this was the oldest textile factory in Chile. It languished until the 1870s, when it was taken over by Belgian interests which held the company until the end of the century. In 1900, El Salto was incorporated and brought under the minority control of the Cousiño family. It remained under their influence until at least 1926. By 1932 other investors had displaced the Cousiño representatives in the directorate. Nevertheless, the stock had become so widely dispersed that the holdings of the Cousiño family and their lifelong associate Ricardo Lyon, which amounted to over 9 per cent of the total voting stock, represented potential control of the firm.

a. See summary section.

Sociedad Nacional de Paños de Tomé

	1893	1904	1920	1926	1932
(1) Proprietor	C	C			
(2) Directorate and family holdings			88.9	43.5	28.1
(3) Principal stockholder and family			42.2	16.1	20.1
(4) Chilean firms and banks				6.3	5.3
(5) Trading houses				6.3	
(6) Foreign participation					2.6

SUMMARY: From 1893 to 1913, the enterprise passed through the hands of several individuals. In 1918 it became a limited liability company owned by a small group of investors. This group, principally Carlos Aguirre Luco and Marcos Serrano, maintained minority control of the firm until 1932. By then the Edwards group had taken an interest in the company and had acquired 20 per cent of the stock and one directorate, giving them an edge in the control of the firm.

Establecimientos Americanos Gratry (CHILE) S.A.

	1906	1932
(1) Proprietor		
(2) Directorate and family holdings		
(3) Principal stockholder and family		
(4) Chilean firms and banks		
(5) Trading houses		
(6) Foreign participation	100.0	100.0

SUMMARY: This cotton textile mill was founded in 1906 in Viña del Mar as a subsidiary of the Belgian textile corporation Etablissements Américains Gratry.

It remained under the complete control of the Belgian company throughout the entire period.

Compañía Chilena de Tejidos

	1904	1917	1920
(1) Proprietor	I	I	
(2) Directorate and family holdings			80.0
(3) Principal stockholder and family			17.4
(4) Chilean firms and banks			69.0
(5) Trading houses			57.3
(6) Foreign participation			

Summary: The enterprise was owned from 1904 to 1916 by the Milanese textile and exporting interests of Enrico Dell'Aqua. In 1917 it was acquired by Ercole Perreau, a French immigrant who owned the commercial house Perreau y Cía. Upon its incorporation in 1920, the firm was still controlled by Perreau y Cía. whose share of the total stock was over 60 per cent. To obtain additional capital for expansion, however, Perreau had sold 17.4 per cent of the stock to the nitrate trading firm Buchanan Jones y Cía.

Fábrica Italo-Americana de Paños Tomé

	1933
(1) Proprietor	
(2) Directorate and family holdings	6.7
(3) Principal stockholder and family	7.9
(4) Chilean firms and banks	4.7
(5) Trading houses	13.1
(6) Foreign participation	4.0

Summary: This firm was founded by a group of Italian immigrants prior to 1930 (the exact date is uncertain). In 1932, it was incorporated and controlled by the importing concern Días Hermanos, which maintained minority control consisting of 9.7 per cent of the stock and two directorates held by its major partners. The Moukarzel family (Levantine merchants resident in Chile) held the next largest block of voting stock, 7.9 per cent.

The Chilean Mills Co. Ltd.

	1900	1922
(1) Proprietor	F	F
(2) Directorate and family holdings		
(3) Principal stockholder and family		
(4) Chilean firms and banks		
(5) Trading houses		
(6) Foreign participants		

Summary: This cotton textile factory was founded in 1900 and began operations in 1902. It was owned by the English trading house Allardice and Co. Ltd., under whose control it remained until passing into receivership in 1922.

Fábrica Victoria de Puente Alto

	1894	1905	1939
(1) Proprietor	C		
(2) Directorate and family holdings		99.9	40.0
(3) Principal stockholder and family		99.0	37.4
(4) Chilean firms and banks			
(5) Trading houses		99.0	
(6) Foreign participation		99.0	

SUMMARY: Founded in 1894 by a Chilean commercial house, this textile plant was acquired in 1904 by the German trading house Vorwerk y Cía. Its two partners, Juan Fischer and Juan Eduardo Pini, maintained active control over the factory until at least 1939.

Sociedad Industrial de Los Andes

	1902	1935
(1) Proprietor		
(2) Directorate and family holdings	3.3	
(3) Principal stockholder and family	50.0	
(4) Chilean firms and banks		
(5) Trading houses	50.0	a
(6) Foreign participation		

SUMMARY: Founded in 1902, this firm was controlled by the trading house Noguera Vives y Cía. Later on, this commercial establishment came to be known as Casa Martínez, Velasco y Cía. and continued to exert majority control over the Sociedad Industrial de Los Andes until at least 1935 (exact participation is not known).
a. See summary section.

CLOTHING

Camiserías Matas y Cía.

	1882	1889	1920
(1) Proprietor	I	C	
(2) Directorate and family holdings			
(3) Principal stockholder and family			75.8
(4) Chilean firms and banks			
(5) Trading houses			
(6) Foreign participation			

SUMMARY: This clothing factory was organized in 1882 by Juan Matas, a Spanish immigrant with previous industrial experience in Barcelona. In 1889, his son, Godofredo, and son-in-law, Arturo Battlé, became the proprietors. The firm was incorporated in 1920 but was still controlled by the majority participation of the Matas family.

Chemical Products

Compañía Chilena de Fósforos

	1913	1920	1926	1932
(1) Proprietor				
(2) Directorate and family holdings		29.3	27.3	9.9
(3) Principal stockholder and family		10.0	9.6	3.1
(4) Chilean firms and banks	100.0	3.6		
(5) Trading houses		6.2	5.0	1.7
(6) Foreign participation		13.0	9.0	53.2

Summary: The largest match company in Chile was incorporated through the fusion of three firms of which the most important was Schleyer, Rivera y Cía. A partner in the latter, Luis Rivera, is reported to have been the dominant figure in the daily management of the firm in the early years. He was also manager of the Banco de Talca and occupied the position of director and general manager of the match company, until the second half of the decade of 1920. The major participants in the management of the firm during this period have diverse backgrounds and are identified as agriculturalists, merchants, industrialists, and bankers, with one being a surgeon. This small group, about ten in number, which controlled the company decided to sell out controlling interest in 1927 to the Swedish match consortium, Svenska Tändsticks A.B. From then on this firm exercised majority control over the Chilean match factory.

Compañía Industrial

	1901	1915	1920	1926	1932
(1) Proprietor					
(2) Directorate and family holdings	64.7	24.0	22.4	9.1	7.5
(3) Principal stockholder and family	29.7	9.7	7.5	2.6	1.7
(4) Chilean firms and banks		1.1	5.8	2.0	4.6
(5) Trading houses	13.3		1.8	0.5	0.5
(6) Foreign participation	13.3	19.2	10.4	4.2	8.6

Summary: From its founding in 1901 until 1920, this firm was largely under the control of Dr. Ernesto Anwandter, a chemist, who managed the daily activities of the firm and maintained an important minority block of stock (ranging from 28 per cent in 1901 to 5.8 per cent in 1920). From that point on, control passed to Juan Fischer, senior partner in the German trading house of Vorwerk y Cía. Fischer was president of the firm from the early 1920s until 1932. The large proportion of foreign participation in the early period of the company's history was for the most part in the hands of individuals who resided in Germany. Between 1926 and 1932 the Edwards-controlled Fundación Santa María held between 46 and 28 per cent of the company's stock, but exercised no active control over its affairs.

Compañía Sud-Americana de Explosivos

	1920	1923	1932
(1) Proprietor			
(2) Directorate and family holdings	0.9	0.9	1.5
(3) Principal stockholder and family			
(4) Chilean firms and banks			
(5) Trading houses			
(6) Foreign participants	99.1	99.1	98.5

SUMMARY: One of the largest high-explosive plants in Latin America, this firm was founded in 1920 by Explosive Trades Ltd., of England, a subsidiary of Nobel Industries Ltd. In 1923, E. I. Du Pont de Nemours & Co., of Wilmington, Delaware, entered into participation, and the enterprise was controlled by these two until 1943. At that time Du Pont bought out the small minority interest of Atlas Powder Company, an American firm, and exercised control over the Compañía Sud-Americana de Explosivos.

PAPER AND PRINTING

Compañía Manufacturera de Papeles y Cartones

	1920	1926	1932
(1) Proprietor			
(2) Directorate and family holdings	45.3	27.4	26.3
(3) Principal stockholder and family	26.4	14.8	16.2
(4) Chilean firms and banks	3.3	8.7	6.1
(5) Trading houses			2.6
(6) Foreign participation		1.2	4.9

SUMMARY: This enterprise was technically formed in 1920, when the Compañía Fábrica de Cartón Maipú (founded 1918) took over control of Ebbinghaus, Haensel y Cía. (established in Puente Alto by the German paper technician Germán Ebbinghaus, in 1914). The company which resulted from this fusion was under the control of Luis Matte Larraín until at least 1932. He and his family maintained a very strong minority stock participation and also held chairs on the board of directors.

Imprenta y Litografía Universo

	1895	1906	1914	1920	1926	1929
(1) Proprietor	I					
(2) Directorate and family holdings		30.4	55.9	25.5	36.2	36.1
(3) Principal stockholder and family		16.4	48.9	13.3	35.9	35.8
(4) Chilean firms and banks		20.1	14.9	2.5		
(5) Trading houses		0.8	1.9	1.0		
(6) Foreign participation		1.8	12.9	53.6	20.4	24.4

SUMMARY: Founded in 1875 by the German import agent and publisher Guillermo Helfmann, the company remained under his family's control until the end of World War I. The Helfmann family's influence appears to have declined about 1920 when majority interest in the firm was acquired by the Banco Anglo Sud-Americano (52.6 per cent) and the Helfmann holdings were at a low of 13.3 per cent. It was at this time that the Edwards group obtained a position on the board of directors. In 1926, the Edwards held majority interest in the stock (55.6 per cent) through the Fundación Santa María, which Agustín Edwards administered, and the Banco Anglo Sud-Americano (20.4 per cent), an affiliate of the Banco A. Edwards since 1920. From then on, the Edwards group appear to have been the principal force in the company.

Nonmetallic Mineral Products

Compañía de Cemento El Melón

	1906	1914	1920	1926	1932
(1) Proprietor					
(2) Directorate and family holdings	48.0	33.5	39.9	3.7	3.2
(3) Principal stockholder and family	40.0	29.6	38.4	31.8	26.2
(4) Chilean firms and banks			4.5	3.2	2.1
(5) Trading houses			0.9	2.3	0.7
(6) Foreign participation			0.5	5.1	5.1

Summary: Founded in 1906, El Melón was controlled by Alfredo Cox and Juan Brown until the former's death just before World War I. Both were outstanding members of the Chilean oligarchy. In the statutes, Cox is identified as a rentier. Brown, who controlled the enterprise thereafter, was reported by Virgilio Figueroa to be the wealthiest resident in Valparaíso, with innumerable assets in all areas of the economy.

Compañía Industrial El Volcán

	1908	1916	1920	1925	1932
(1) Proprietor	C				
(2) Directorate and family holdings		70.8	46.7	28.9	38.9
(3) Principal stockholder and family		45.0	21.1	11.9	13.0
(4) Chilean firms and banks		5.0	2.7	2.3	0.1
(5) Trading houses		5.0			
(6) Foreign participation				4.0	0.1

Summary: Founded in 1908 by the trading house Besa y Cía., the enterprise was incorporated in 1916, at which time it passed into the hands of another closely knit group of investors, all of prominent families, who controlled the firm throughout the rest of the period. The most important families of this group were Zamudio Flores, Johnson Gana, Huneeus Gana, and Vidal Garcés.

Compañía Cristalerías de Chile

	1904	1914	1920	1926	1932
(1) Proprietor					
(2) Directorate and family holdings	50.0	13.2	17.5	8.3	6.6
(3) Principal stockholder and family	13.8	4.6	3.8	4.6	7.6
(4) Chilean firms and banks	7.5	34.8	25.0	35.0	39.6
(5) Trading houses					
(6) Foreign participation				2.0	11.3

SUMMARY: Founded in 1902 by Nemorino Cotapos and Jesué Benaglia, an Italian immigrant, the firm was purchased two years later by a corporation headed by Carlos Cousiño and Juan Enrique Concha Subercaseaux. Cousiño exercised minority control over the firm, principally through the stcck held by the Compañía Cervecerías Unidas, and as the Edwards group became more predominant in the latter, they were to appear as a major controlling faction in the 1920s. From then, both groups controlled the firm throughout their corporate and family holdings and representatives on the board of directors. As in the case of the Compañía Cervecerías Unidas, no rivalry was ever apparent and the two monied groups cannot be clearly separated on that basis.

Fábrica de Vidrios y Cristales "La Yungay"

	1922	1930
(1) Proprietor	F	F
(2) Directorate and family holdings		
(3) Principal stockholder and family		
(4) Chilean firms and banks		
(5) Trading houses		
(6) Foreign participation		

SUMMARY: La Yungay was founded by the English trading house Weir Scott y Cía., which maintained complete ownership until at least 1930.

Fábrica Nacional de Loza de Penco

	1887	1927	1930
(1) Proprietor	C		
(2) Directorate and family holdings			74.3
(3) Principal stockholder and family			74.3
(4) Chilean firms and banks			
(5) Trading houses		a	74.3
(6) Foreign participation			

SUMMARY: Founded in 1887 by Agustín and Arturo Edwards, the factory was destroyed in 1891 by President Balmaceda's troops. It went through a succession of owners until the importing house owned by the Spanish immigrant Pablo Díaz Boneu purchased it in 1927. The firm became a very successful enterprise and remained under the control of Díaz Hermanos.

a. See summary section.

Metallic Products

Compañía Electro Metalúrgica

	1918	1920	1926	1932
(1) Proprietor				
(2) Directorate and family holdings	25.6	15.3	24.1	38.9
(3) Principal stockholder and family	8.2	8.3	10.0	10.0
(4) Chilean firms and banks			3.3	3.1
(5) Trading houses				
(6) Foreign participation			0.2	5.8

Summary: Founded in 1918, this metallurgical firm was always controlled by a small group of investors, the most important of whom was the Belgian immigrant Amadeo Heiremans. He was president of the corporation for most of the period under study. His business interests were quite varied and first included import-export ventures, mining, and agriculture, as well as other industrial pursuits.

Compañía de Maestranzas y Galvanización

	1880	1922	1923
(1) Proprietor	I		
(2) Directorate and family holdings		8.2	
(3) Principal stockholder and family		5.1	
(4) Chilean firms and banks		10.4	
(5) Trading houses		10.4	
(6) Foreign participation		27.3	100.0

Summary: Originally founded in 1860 by the Irish immigrants Richard Lever and William Murphy, it remained under the control of their families until around 1903, when the firm was incorporated as Fundición de Chile. In 1906, it was sold to J. H. Sandiford. Ownership of this, the largest foundry in Chile at the time, is unclear until 1922 when it was reorganized under the name Compañía de Maestranzas y Galvanización. At this time, it was in financial difficulty and was controlled by several importing firms, principally Williamson Balfour y Cía., and the Sociedad Baburizza, Lubinovic y Cía., and the Banco Anglo Sud-Americano, who received stock in payment of a loan outstanding on the predecessor corporation. Very shortly thereafter, the foundry was acquired by United States Steel, which after fourteen years (1937) liquidated the factory as uneconomical.

Fundición y Fábrica de "La Unión"

	1890	1905
(1) Proprietor	I	
(2) Directorate and family holdings		12.9
(3) Principal stockholder and family		9.5
(4) Chilean firms and banks		33.3
(5) Trading houses		
(6) Foreign participation		

SUMMARY: The foundry was established in 1890 by a small group of English immigrants who formed the firm Hardie y Cía. They were proprietors until 1905, when the foundry was incorporated. At that time Hardie y Cía. maintained minority control with a third of the stock and one directorate.

Fábrica Nacional de Envases y Enlozados, S.A.

	1906	1914	1920	1926	1932
(1) Proprietor					
(2) Directorate and family holdings	52.5	51.5	31.3	18.7	16.2
(3) Principal stockholder and family	37.9	38.2	17.8	11.5	15.2
(4) Chilean firms and banks	9.7	19.4	4.8	10.6	5.1
(5) Trading houses	0.5	0.9	10.0		
(6) Foreign participation	2.0	1.4	7.3	6.7	13.0

SUMMARY: Incorporated in 1905, the factory was controlled by Georges Breynat, who held over one-third of the stock and was manager until shortly after World War I. From then until the late 1920s, a small group of investors ran the firm. At that time, control passed to Luis Mitrovich, a Yugoslav immigrant with trading interests and other industrial participations.

Compañía Industrial de Catres

	1914	1920	1926	1932
(1) Proprietor				
(2) Directorate and family holdings	52.8	46.0	63.9	19.0
(3) Principal stockholder and family	38.0	23.5	23.1	12.9
(4) Chilean firms and banks	14.6	2.3	5.2	2.3
(5) Trading houses	3.1	1.4	5.2	0.7
(6) Foreign participation			2.4	3.6

SUMMARY: Incorporated in 1913 through the consolidation of four factories, the firm was under the control of the Smits family, who owned the largest of the four, Smits y Assler, in Talca. They maintained minority control throughout the entire period.

Bibliography

ARCHIVAL SOURCES

Archivo de la Bolsa de Comercio de Santiago (ABCS):

"Estudios sobre empresas." One-volume collection of typewritten and mimeographed sheets with background information and financial analysis of corporations until 1967.

"Estudio sobre sociedades anónimas con motivo de los setenta años de la Bolsa de Comercio." 5 vols. A useful collection of documents and letters from corporations with information on their origin and on their evolution until the 1960s.

The annual reports, balance sheets, and stockholders' lists for the following firms and respective years were also located in the archives of the Santiago Stock Exchange:

Banco de A. Edwards y Cía., 1920–23.
Compañía Cervecerías Unidas, 1914–32.
Compañía Chilena de Fósforos, 1914–32.
Compañía Chilena de Tabacos, 1914–32.
Compañía Cristalerías de Chile, 1914–40.
Compañía de Cemento El Melón, 1911–32.
Compañía Electro Metalúrgica, 1918–32.
Compañía Industrial, 1915–32.
Compañía Industrial de Catres, 1913–32.
Compañía Industrial El Volcán, 1916–32.
Compañía Manufacturera de Papeles y Cartones, 1920–32.
Compañía Minera e Industrial, 1926.
Compañía Nacional de Tejidos "El Salto," 1921–32.

Compañía Refinería de Azúcar de Viña del Mar, 1914–32.
Compañía Molinera "El Globo," 1920–32.
Compañía Molinera San Cristóbal, 1920–32.
Fábrica Italo-Americana de Paños Tomé, 1933.
Fábrica Nacional de Envases y Enlozados, 1906–32.
Fábrica Nacional de Loza de Penco, 1932.
Fábrica Victoria de Puente Alto, 1939.
Galletas McKay, 1940.
Establecimientos Americanos Gratry (CHILE) S.A., 1968.
Hucke Hermanos S.A.C., 1924–32.
Imprenta y Litografía Universo, 1906–38.
Molinera Pérez Cotapos y Cía. S.A., 1948–66.
Sociedad Fábrica Nacional de Paños de Bellavista, 1923–32.
Sociedad Nacional de Paños de Tomé, 1918–32.

Archivo de la Sociedad de Fomento Fabril (ASFF):
Consejo Directivo de la Sociedad de Fomento Fabril. "Libro de Actas del Consejo Directivo," 1883–1932.

Archivo Nacional:
Ministerio de Hacienda (ANMH). Vols. 2,556, 2,658, 2,839, 2,972, 3,152, 3,209, 3,331, 3,593, 3,596, 4,225, 4,227, 4,346, 4,584, and 4,803.
Ministerio de Industrias y Obras Públicas (MIOPAN). Vols. 1,356, 1,357, 2,394.

Government and Official Publications

"Antecedentes y decreto que aprueba los estatutos de la Compañía General de Tabacos." *Diario Oficial*, July 17, 1897, pp. 1714–16.
Congreso Nacional, Cámara de Diputados. *Boletín de las sesiones extraordinarias*, 1895–1928.
———. *Boletín de las sesiones ordinarias*, 1896–1928.
Congreso Nacional, Senado. *Boletín de las sesiones extraordinarias*, 1896–1928.
———. *Boletín de las sesiones ordinarias*, 1896–1928.
Chile. Dirección de Estadística y Censos. *Sinopsis estadística año 1928*. Santiago: Imprenta y Litografía Universo, 1930.
Chile. Dirección General de Estadística. *Censo industrial y comercial, 1937*.
Chile. Instituto de Crédito Industrial. *Memoria*, 1929.
Chile. Ministere des Relations Exterieures. *Les Capitaux au Chili*. Santiago, 1927.
Chile. Ministerio de Fomento. *Monografía industrial de Chile*. Santiago, 1929.
Chile. Ministerio de Industrias y Obras Públicas. *Boletín*, 1888–1900.
———. *Memoria*, 1898.
———. *Registro general de patentes de invención, 1840–1912*. Santiago: Imprenta y Encuadernación El Globo, 1913.
Chile. Oficina Central de Estadística. *Anuario de comercio exterior*, 1870–1930.
———. *Anuario estadístico*, 1909. Vol. 3.
———. *Anuario estadístico, industrias*, 1910–30.
———. *Censo de la industria manufacturera y del comercio de 1928*. Santiago: Imprenta Universo, 1928.
———. *Sinopsis estadística y geográfica de Chile en 1883*. Santiago: Imprenta Nacional, 1884.
Chile. Servicio Nacional de Estadística y Censos. *XII Censo General de Población*, 1952. Vol. 1. Santiago, 1956.
"Decreto y antecedentes de la disolución y liquidación de la sociedad anónima

denominada Fábrica Nacional de Cerveza." *Diario Oficial*, March 26, 1902, pp. 1067–69.

"Estatutos de la Compañía Industrial." *Diario Oficial*, January 29, 1901, pp. 260–63.

"Estatutos de la Compañía de Cemento El Melón." *Diario Oficial*, August 14, 1906, p. 2857.

"Estatutos de la Compañía Cervecerías Unidas." *Diario Oficial*, March 19, 1902, pp. 1049–54.

"Estatutos de la Compañía Chilena de Fósforos." *Diario Oficial*, July 10, 1913, pp. 2238–42.

"Estatutos de la Compañía Chilena de Tejidos." *Diario Oficial*, October 23, 1920, pp. 2646–50.

"Estatutos de la Compañía de Explosivos de Chile." *Diario Oficial*, November 9, 1920, pp. 2789–94.

"Estatutos de la Compañía de Maestranzas y Galvanización." *Diario Oficial*, December 18, 1922, pp. 2653–58.

"Estatutos de la Compañía Manufacturera de Papeles y Cartones y decreto N°589 que los aprueba y la declara legalmente instalada." *Diario Oficial*, March 16, 1920, pp. 721–25.

"Estatutos de la Compañía Molinos y Fideos Carozzi." *Diario Oficial*, October 6, 1913, p. 3134, February 25, 1927, pp. 797–806.

"Estatutos de la Sociedad Anónima Camiserías Matas y Cía." *Diario Oficial*, May 28, 1920, p. 2852.

"Estatutos de la Sociedad Anónima Fábrica Nacional de Loza de Penco." *Diario Oficial*, December 12, 1930, pp. 6568–73.

"Estatutos de la Sociedad Anónima Fábrica Victoria de Puente Alto." *Diario Oficial*, October 11, 1905, p. 3306.

"Estatutos de la Sociedad Anónima Viña Concha y Toro." *Diario Oficial*, November 6, 1922, pp. 2250–52.

"Estatutos de la Sociedad Compañía Molinera 'El Globo.' " *Diario Oficial*, May 11, 1905, p. 1957.

"Estatutos de la Sociedad Fábrica Nacional de Vidrios." *Diario Oficial*, August 13, 1904, p. 2595.

"Estatutos de la Sociedad Fábrica de Paños de Bellavista, Sucesora de Carlos Werner, Tomé." *Diario Oficial*, July 10, 1923, pp. 1419–22.

"Estatutos de la Sociedad Fábrica de Uniformes." *Diario Oficial*, October 29, 1926, pp. 2699–706.

"Estatutos de la Sociedad Industrial de los Andes." *Diario Oficial*, November 29, 1902, p. 4227.

"Legalización de las reformas de los estatutos sociales de la sociedad anónima denominada Compañía Sud-Americana de Explosivos." *Diario Oficial*, October 24, 1932, pp. 2989–91.

"Ley 4110." *Diario Oficial*, December 12, 1926, pp. 3574–76.

Naciones Unidas. Comisión Económica para América Latina. *América Latina, el pensamiento de la CEPAL*. Santiago: Editorial Universitaria, 1969.

Presidencia de la República. *Mensaje Presidencial*, 1880–1934.

"Reforma de los estatutos de la Compañía de Explosivos de Chile." *Diario Oficial*, June 27, 1923, pp. 1355–56.

United States. Department of Commerce. *Investment in Chile*. Washington: Government Printing Office, 1960.

United States. The Temporary National Economic Committee. *Bureaucracy and Trusteeship in Large Corporations*. Washington: Government Printing Office, 1940.

NEWSPAPERS AND JOURNALS

Boletín de la Sociedad de Fomento Fabril, 1883–1934.
Boletín de la Sociedad Nacional de Agricultura, 1910–25.
Chile industrial y comercial. Valparaíso, 1908–11.
El Ferrocarril. Santiago, 1906–8.
El Heraldo. Valparaíso, 1892–1902.
La industria chilena. Santiago, 1875–77.
El Mercurio. Antofagasta, 1912.
El Mercurio. Valparaíso, 1875–1914.
La Revista Comercial. Valparaíso, 1897–1929.
La Unión. Valparaíso, 1911.

BOOKS, PAMPHLETS, ARTICLES, AND THESES

Acevedo, E., and Vergara, H. "Algunos antecedentes sobre concentración, participación extranjera y transferencia tecnológica en la industria manufacturera chilena." Memoria de grado, Universidad de Chile, Facultad de Ciencias Físicas y Matemáticas, 1970.

"Acta de la 39ª junta general de socios en 10 de enero de 1923." *Boletín de la Sociedad de Fomento Fabril (BSFF)* 41 (January 1923):59–60.

Alexander, Alec. "The Supply of Industrial Entrepreneurship." *Explorations in Entrepreneurial History*, 2d ser. 4 (Fall 1967).

Alvarez Andrews, Oscar. *Historia del desarrollo industrial de Chile*. Santiago: Imprenta y Litografía La Ilustración, 1936.

Amador Fuenzalida, Enrique. *Galería contemporánea de hombres notables de Chile, 1850–1901*. 2 vols. Valparaíso: Imprenta del Universo, 1901.

Anguita, Ricardo. *Leyes promulgadas en Chile desde 1810 hasta 1 de junio de 1913*. 5 vols. Santiago: Imprenta Barcelona, 1913.

Astorquiza, Octavio. *Lota: antecedentes históricos con una monografía de la Compañía Carbonífera e Industrial de Lota*. Valparaíso: Imprenta y Litografía Universo, 1942.

Astorquiza, Octavio, and Galleguillos, Oscar. *Cien años de Lota*. Santiago: Editora Zig-Zag, 1952.

Ballesteros, Mario, and Davis, Tom E. "The Growth of Output and Employment in Basic Sectors of the Chilean Economy, 1908–1957." *Economic Development and Cultural Change* 11 (January 1963):152–76.

Banco de Chile. *Banco de Chile, 1894–1944, reseña histórica*. Santiago, 1944.

Bauer, Arnold. *Chilean Rural Society from the Spanish Conquest to 1930*. Cambridge: Cambridge University Press, 1975.

———. "Chilean Rural Society in the Nineteenth Century." Ph.D. dissertation, University of California, Berkeley, 1969.

———. "Expansión económica en una sociedad tradicional: Chile central en el siglo XIX." *Historia* 9 (1970):137–235.

Benavides, Ricardo, ed. *Anuario general de Chile, 1919–1924*. N.p., n.d.

Bennett, Juan. "La fundición de acero en el país." *BSFF* 44 (January 1927): 41–43.

Berle, Adolf, and Means, Gardiner. *The Modern Corporation and Private Property*. New York: The Macmillan Co., 1932.

Bianchi, Andrés, ed. *América Latina, ensayos de interpretación económica*. Santiago: Editorial Universitaria, 1969.

Blakemore, Harold. *British Nitrates and Chilean Politics 1886–1896: Balmaceda and North*. London: The Athlone Press of the University of London, 1974.

———. "The Chilean Revolution of 1891 and Its Historiography." *Hispanic American Historical Review* 45 (August 1965):393–421.

Blalock, Hubert M. *Social Statistics.* New York: McGraw-Hill Book Company, 1960.

Bolsa de Comercio de Santiago. *La riqueza mobiliaria de Chile.* Santiago: Sociedad Imprenta y Litografía Universo, 1923.

Bonder, León. "La industria de curtiduría en Chile y sus derivados." *BSFF* 31 (October 1914):829–32.

Carmagnani, Marcello. *Sviluppo Industriale e Sottosviluppo Economico, Il Caso Chileno (1860–1920).* Torino: Fondazione Luigi Einaudi, 1971.

Chile en Sevilla. Santiago: Empresa Editorial "Cronos," 1929.

"Chile puede y debe ser industrial." *BSFF* 1 (January 1884):3–4.

"La Compañía Cervecera Valdivia." *BSFF* 31 (March 1914):232–35.

Compañía Electro Metalúrgica S.A. *Estatutos.* Santiago: Sociedad Imprenta y Litografía Universo, 1918.

———. *Memorias,* 1918–32.

Compañía Industrial, 1900–1964. Santiago: Imprenta Lord Cochrane, 1964.

Compañía de Refinería de Azúcar de Viña del Mar (CRAV). *50 años.* Santiago, 1937.

Compañía Molinos y Fideos Carozzi. *Bodas de oro, 1907–1957.* Santiago, 1957.

"La construcción naval en Chile." *BSFF* 18 (July 1901):223–25.

"Crónica de Don Carlos Anwandter." *BSFF* 6 (August 1889):381–82.

Davies, Eric. "A History of Duncan, Fox & Co." Manuscript, Instituto de Economia, Universidad de Chile, Santiago.

Dean, Warren. *The Industrialization of São Paulo, 1880–1945.* Austin: University of Texas Press, 1969.

"Debentures." *BSFF* 47 (October 1929):660–61.

de la Cuadra Gormaz, Guillermo. *Familias chilenas.* 2 vols. Santiago: Editorial Zamorano y Caperan, 1948–49.

Diccionario biográfico de Chile, 1936. Santiago: Sociedad Imprenta y Litografía Universo, 1936.

Diccionario personal de Chile. Santiago: Imprenta Claret, 1921.

"Don Carlos E. Justiniano." *BSFF* 46 (October 1929):659–60.

"Don Carlos Klein." *BSFF* 9 (June 1892):247.

"Don José Rabinovitch." *BSFF* 46 (September 1929):594–95.

Dooley, Peter C. "The Interlocking Directorate." *The American Economic Review* 59 (June 1969):314–23.

Dorfman, Robert. *Prices and Markets.* Englewood Cliffs, N.J.: Prentice Hall Inc., 1967.

Dorte, Louis. *El porvenir en Chile de los emigrantes europeos.* Translated by A. Labin. Santiago: Imprenta de la República, 1884.

"Efectos de la ley de impuestos del 23 de diciembre de 1897: el progreso de la industria nacional." *El Mercurio,* Valparaíso, August 30, 1901, p. 4.

Ellsworth, P. T. *Chile, An Economy in Transition.* New York: Macmillan Co., 1945.

"Emisión de obligaciones industriales o debentures." *BSFF* 46 (January 1928): 35–36.

Encina, Francisco. *Historia de Chile.* Vol. 16. Santiago: Editorial Nacimiento, 1949.

———. *Nuestra inferioridad económica.* Santiago: Editorial Universitaria, 1955.

Espinoza, Enrique. *Geografía descriptiva de la República de Chile.* 4th and 5th eds. Santiago: Imprenta Barcelona, 1897 and 1903.

Espinoza, Roberto. *Cuestiones financieras de Chile.* Santiago: Imprenta Cervantes, 1909.

"Estadística comercial." *BSFF* 14 (November 1897):348.
"Estadística industrial del país I." *La Revista Comercial*, March 17, 1900, pp. 34–71.
Estatutos de la Compañía Chilena de Tabacos. Valparaíso: Sociedad Imprenta y Litografía Universo, 1917.
Estatutos de la Compañía Industrial "El Volcán." Santiago, 1916.
Estatutos de la Compañía Molinera San Cristóbal. Santiago: Imprenta Nacional, 1947.
Estatutos de la Compañía Nacional de Tejidos "El Salto." Santiago: Imprenta Nacional, 1922.
"La exposición nacional I." *BSFF* 1 (October–November 1884):379–430.
Eyzaguirre, Jaime. *Chile durante el gobierno de Errázuriz Echaurren, 1896–1901*. Santiago: Empresa Editora Zig-Zag, 1957.
"La fábrica de los señores Hardie y Cía." *BSFF* 13 (August 1896):128–29.
"Fábrica de Tejidos de Lana 'El Salto.'" *BSFF* 22 (November 1905):691–93.
"Fábrica de Vidrios y Cristales 'La Yungay.'" *BSFF* 47 (October 1930):744–48.
Fábrica Nacional de Cementos de la Cruz. *Tercera memoria correspondiente al 2° semestre de 1903*, December 1903.
"Fábrica Nacional de Clavos y Puntas de Alambre." *BSFF* 36 (May 1919): 271–73.
"Fábrica Nacional de Conservas Alimenticias." *BSFF* 8 (August 1909):387–91.
Fábrica Nacional de Envases y Enlozados. *Memoria, Balance y Estatutos*. Valparaíso: Establecimientos Gráficos Excelsior, 1905.
"Fábricas de tejidos de algodón." *BSFF* 41 (February 1924):97–107.
"Las fábricas en Concepción." *BSFF* 22 (January 1905):42–46.
"Fábricas en Penco." *BSFF* 22 (February 1905):97–99.
"El fallo de los jurados." *BSFF* 1 (December 1884):23–24.
Fetter, Frank. *Monetary Inflation in Chile*. Princeton: Princeton University Press, 1931.
Figueroa, Pedro Pablo. *Diccionario biográfico de extranjeros en Chile*. Santiago: Imprenta Moderna, 1900.
Figueroa, Virgilio. *Diccionario histórico y biográfico de Chile*. 5 vols. Santiago: Establecimientos Gráficos Balcells & Co., 1931.
"Fundición Libertad de Strickler y Küpfer." *BSFF* 20 (June 1903):181–87.
"Fundición y fábrica de Orchard Hnos." *El Mercurio*, Antofagasta, August 9, 1912, pp. 972–73.
Galdames, Luis. *Geografía económica de Chile*. Santiago: Imprenta Universitaria, 1911.
"Galletas McKay." *BSFF* 47 (June 1930):384–88.
Gandarillas, Guillermo. *Legislación sobre fomento de las industrias minero, agrícola y fabril*. Santiago: Imprenta Nacimiento, 1929.
———. *Recopilación de leyes y reglamentos sobre fomento de las industrias minera, agrícola y fabril*. Santiago: Imprenta Nacimiento, 1930.
Garretón, Oscar, and Cisterna, Jaime. "Algunas características del proceso de toma de decisiones en la gran empresa; la dinámica de concentración." Santiago: ODEPLAN, 1970. Mimeographed.
Gasic, Gabriel. "Concentración, entrelazamiento y desnacionalización en la industria manufacturera." Santiago: Universidad de Chile, Centro de Estudios Socio-Económicos, 1971. Mimeographed.
Gerschenkron, Alexander. *Economic Backwardness in Historical Perspective, A Book of Essays*. New York: Frederick A. Praeger, 1965.
González, Pedro Luis. *Albúm gráfico de la Sociedad de Fomento Fabril*. Santiago: Imprenta Cervantes, 1926.
———. *Chile industrial, 1918*. Santiago: Imprenta y Litografía Universo, 1918.

———. *Chile industrial, 1920.* Santiago: Imprenta y Litografía Universo, 1920.
———. "Derechos de aduana: el recargo de cincuenta por ciento." *BSFF* 38 (April 1921):181–82.
———. "Las fábricas de tejidos de punto." *BSFF* 35 (January 1918):28–29.
———. "Las industrias fiscales." *BSFF* 38 (August 1921):405–6.
———. "La labor parlamentaria." *BSFF* 36 (May 1919):269–71.
———. "Las nuevas empresas industriales." *BSFF* 22 (February 1905):91.
———. *La Sociedad de Fomento Fabril, su labor durante veinticinco años.* Santiago, 1908.
———. "Protección y libre cambio." *BSFF* 23 (December 1906):820–23.
———, ed. *El esfuerzo nacional, estudios de política industrial.* Santiago: Sociedad Imprenta y Litografía Universo, 1916.
Heise González, Julio. *Historia de Chile, el período parlamentario 1861–1925.* Santiago: Editorial Andres Bello, 1974.
Hirschman, Albert. *Journeys toward Progress.* Garden City, N.Y.: Doubleday & Company, Inc., 1965.
———. "The Political Economy of Import-Substituting Industrialization in Latin America." *The Quarterly Journal of Economics* 82 (February 1968):1–32.
History and Description of Casa Grace in the Republic of Chile, 1881–1953. Santiago, 1955.
Hoerhl, Alberto. *Los alemanes en Chile.* Santiago, 1910.
Hormann, Jorge. *Chile industrial y económico, 1897–1917.* Santiago: Imprenta Cervantes, 1918.
———. "Efectos de la ley de impuestos del 23 de diciembre de 1897." *El Mercurio*, Santiago, November 11, 1902, p. 99.
———. "Efectos de la ley de impuesto del 23 de diciembre de 1897; el progreso de la industria nacional." *El Mercurio*, Valparaíso, August 30, 1901, p. 4.
———. "El impuesto adicional de diez por ciento." *La Unión*, Valparaíso, June 14, 1911, p. 4.
———. "Las refinerías de azúcar." *El Heraldo*, Valparaíso, November 6, 1902, p. 3.
———. "La reforma del arancel aduanero." *BSFF* 35 (July 1918):75–83.
Hurtado, Carlos. *Concentración de población y desarrollo económico—el caso chileno.* Santiago: Universidad de Chile, Instituto de Economía, 1966.
"La imprenta y encuadernación Barcelona." *BSFF* 15 (September 1898):239–44.
"La industria siderúrgica de Chile." *La Revista Comercial*, October 13, 1928, p. 57,170.
Jaffray, Robert, and Duval, George. *Revista del centenario del negocio fundado por Augustus Hemenway de Boston en 1825 y conducido actualmente por Wessel Duval & Co.* New York: Wessel Duval & Co., 1925.
Joslin, David. *A Century of Banking in Latin America.* London: Oxford University Press, 1963.
"Junta general de socios en 6 de enero de 1912." *BSFF* 29 (February 1912): 143–46.
"Junta general extraordinaria de socios en 8 de septiembre de 1911." *BSFF* 28 (October 1911):860–61.
Kane, Edward J. *Economic Statistics and Econometrics, An Introduction to Quantitative Economics.* New York: Harper & Row, 1968.
Keller, Carols. *La eterna crisis chilena.* Santiago: Editorial Nacimiento, 1931.
Lagos, Ricardo. *La industria en Chile: antecedentes estructurales.* Santiago: Universidad de Chile, Instituto de Economía, 1966.
Laso, J. Tadeo. *Catálogo de la exposición permanente y museo industrial de la Sociedad de Fomento Fabril.* Santiago, 1904.
"Liberación de derechos de internación." *BSFF* 6 (August 1889):383–84.
"La litografía y la imprenta Gillet." *BSFF* 17 (March 1900):80–85.

"La Sociedad de Fomento Fabril, su labor durante cincuenta años." *BSFF* 50 (October 1933):460–83.

"La Sociedad Fábrica de Cemento El Melón." *BSFF* 47 (April 1930):224–26.

"Locomotoras para los ferrocarriles del estado." *BSFF* 10 (October 1893):461.

Macchiavello Varas, Santiago. *Política económica nacional.* Vol. 1. Santiago: Establecimientos Gráficos, Balcells & Co., 1931.

———. *El problema de la industria del cobre y sus proyecciones económicas y sociales.* Santiago: Imprenta Fiscal de la Penitenciaría, 1923.

Mamalakis, Markos, and Reynolds, Clark. *Essays on the Chilean Economy.* Homewood, Ill.: Richard D. Irwin, Inc., 1965.

Marín Vicuña, Santiago. *Los ferrocarriles en Chile.* Santiago: Imprenta Barcelona, 1912.

Márquez, Alberto. *Libro internacional sudamericano: sección comercial chilena.* 2 vols. Santiago: Sociedad Imprenta y Litografía Universo, n.d.

Martínez, Mariano. *Industrias santiaguinas.* Santiago: Imprenta y Encuadernación Barcelona, 1896.

Martner, Daniel. *Estudio de política comercial chilena e historia económica nacional.* Vol. 2. Santiago: Imprenta Universitaria, 1923.

"Medidas de protección a la curtiduría nacional." *Chile Industrial y Comercial* 3 (May 1911):3.

Memorandum de la revolución. Santiago, 1892.

"Memoria de la Sociedad de Fomento Fabril que corresponde a 1891." *BSFF* 8 (March 1891):129–36.

Monsen, R. Joseph et al. "Effect of Separation of Ownership and Control on the Performance of the Large Firm." *Quarterly Journal of Economics* 82 (August 1968):435–511.

Morris, James O. *Elites, Intellectuals and Consensus: A Study of the Social Question and the Industrial Relations System in Chile.* Ithaca: Cornell University, 1966.

Mullen, Joseph. "Energy in the Japanese Economy, 1878–1965." Ph.D. dissertation, New York University, 1972.

Muñoz, Oscar. *Crecimiento industrial de Chile, 1914–1965.* Santiago: Universidad de Chile, Instituto de Economía y Planificación, 1968.

Myrdal, Gunnar. *Asian Drama: An Inquiry into the Poverty of Nations.* 3 vols. New York: The Twentieth Century Fund, 1968.

———. "What Is Development?" *Journal of Economic Issues* 3 (December 1974): 729–36.

Nolff, Max. "Industria manufacturera." In *Geografía económica de Chile, texto refundido,* by Corporación de Fomento de la Producción. Santiago: Editorial Universitaria, 1967.

"No se concede la garantía del estado a la Compañía Electro Siderúrgica de Valdivia." *La Revista Comercial,* September 22, 1928, pp. 57,106–7.

"Nuestra situación económica." *BSFF* 30 (September 1914):739–42.

"Nueva refinería de azúcar La Internacional." *BSFF* 21 (December 1904):632.

Ortúzar, Adolfo. *Chile of Today: Its Commerce, Its Production and Its Resources.* New York: The Tribune Association, 1907.

Parada, Teodorindo. "Algunas consideraciones sobre inmigración." Santiago, 1913. Memoria de prueba, Universidad de Chile, Facultad de Leyes y Ciencias Políticas.

Pelegrini, Amadeo, and Ciro Aprile, Jorge. *El censo comercial-industrial de la colonia italiana en Chile.* Santiago: Imprenta La Ilustración, 1926.

———. *El progreso alemán en América, Chile: resumen general de las actividades que ha desarrollado en Chile la colonia alemana.* Santiago: Editorial Río de la Plata, 1934.

Pérez Canto, Julio. *La industria nacional: estudios y descripciones de algunas fábricas de Chile*. Santiago, 1893.

———, ed. *La industria nacional, estudios y descripciones de algunas fábricas de Chile*. Santiago: La Imprenta Nacional, 1896.

Pfeiffer, Jack. "The Development of Manufacturing Industry in Chile, 1820–1940." Ph.D. dissertation, University of Chicago, 1947.

Phelps, Dudley Maynard, *Migration of Industry to South America*. New York: McGraw-Hill, 1936.

Pike, Frederick. *Chile and the United States, 1880–1962*. Notre Dame: University of Notre Dame Press, 1963.

Pinochet Le-Brun, Tancredo. *La conquista de Chile en el siglo XX*. Santiago: Imprenta, Litografía y Encuadernación "La ilustración," 1909.

Pinto, Aníbal. *Chile, un caso de desarrollo frustrado*. Santiago: Editorial Universitaria, 1962.

Prado Martínez, Alberto. *Anuario Prado Martínez: Chile, 1902*. Santiago, 1902.

"Progreso industrial." *El Mercurio*, Valparaíso, August 28, 1895, p. 2.

"Protección a la industria de refineración de azúcar." *BSFF* 9 (November 1892):495–99.

Ramírez Barahona, Jorge. *Anuario guía de sociedades anónimas*. Santiago: Talleres Gráficos La Nación, 1939.

Ramírez Necochea, Hernán. *Balmaceda y la contrarrevolución de 1891*. 2d ed. Santiago: Editorial Universitaria, 1969.

———. *La guerra civil de 1891: antecedentes económicos*. Santiago: Editorial Universitaria, 1953.

"La reforma del arancel aduanero." *BSFF* 35 (July 1918):81–83.

"Registro de hipotecas de Valparaíso." *La Revista Comercial*, 1921–27.

"Reunión del Consejo Ejecutivo de la Cámara Industrial de Valparaíso." *La Revista Comercial*, Valparaíso, September 24, 1921, p. 48,931.

Rivera, Arnoldo. "La industria del tabaco en Chile." Memoria de Grado, Universidad de Chile, Facultad de Ciencias Económicas, 1963.

"Rol de industrias." *BSFF* 47 (June 1930):238–40.

Sánchez Hurtado, Carlos. *Evolución histórica de la industria siderúrgica chilena e ibero-americana*. Santiago: Editorial Nacimiento, 1952.

Segall, Marcelo. *Desarrollo del capitalismo en Chile*. Santiago: Editorial del Pacífico, 1953.

Sociedad de Fomento Fabril. *Boletín de la estadística industrial* 1–20 (June 1895–February 1897).

———. *Boletín de la estadística industrial, Valparaíso*, 6 (August 1896).

———. *Estadística industrial*. Santiago, 1907.

———. *Estadística industrial de la República de Chile*, 1910.

———. *Exhibición de productos industriales, informe de los jurados, 1904*. Santiago, 1904.

———. *Informe sobre el impuesto de internación y proyecto de reforma del mismo*. Santiago: Imprenta Nacional, 1887.

———. *Memoria que la Sociedad de Fomento Fabril presenta sobre el concurso de molinería*. Santiago, 1892.

———. "Memorias." *BSFF* 2–54 (1884–1936).

———. "Monografía sobre la industria textil." In *Estadística industrial de la República de Chile correspondiente al año 1910*, pp. 145–58.

Sociedad de Maestranzas y Galvanización. *Album de Caleta Abarca*. N.p., n.d.

Sociedad Nacional de Agricultura. *Boletín*. 1910–25.

"Sociedad Nacional de Paños de Tomé." *BSFF* 31 (February 1914):112–13.

Solberg, Carl. *Immigration and Nationalism: Argentina and Chile, 1880–1914*. Austin: University of Texas Press, 1970.

Soto Rojas, Salvador. *Crónicas chilenas*. Santiago: Imprenta, Litografía y Encuadernación Barcelona, 1913.

Subercaseaux, Antonio. "La administración de los ferrocarriles del estado." *El ferrocarril*, Santiago, February 26, 1908, p. 1.

Sunkel, Osvaldo, and Paz, Pedro. *El subdesarrollo latinoamericano y la teoría del desarrollo*. Santiago: Siglo XXI, 1970.

Tocornal, Juan. *Exposición leída por el presidente de la Sociedad Fábrica Nacional de Vidrios en la Junta General del 6 de septiembre de 1921*. Santiago: Sociedad Imprenta y Litografía Universo, 1921.

Tornero, Recaredo. *Chile ilustrado*. Valparaíso: El Mercurio, 1872.

"Los trabajos de la Sociedad." *BSFF* 8 (September 2, 1891):5–7.

"Una neuva industria." *BSFF* 10 (March 1893):135.

"Una visita a Caleta Abarca." *BSFF* 10 (January 1893):6–7.

Urzúa Valenzuela, Germán, and García Barzelatto, Anamaría. *Diagnóstico de la burocracia chilena (1818–1969)*. Santiago: Editorial Jurídica de Chile, 1971.

Vaella, Jacinto. *Estructura y evolución de la economía colonial*. Santiago: Universidad de Chile, Instituto de Economía, 1971.

Valdivieso, José. *El Instituto de Crédito Industrial y su labor desarrollada en beneficio de la economía nacional*. Santiago: Imprenta "El Esfuerzo," 1947.

Valga, E. *Album de la colonie française au Chili*. Santiago, 1904.

Vattier, Charles. *L'Avenir de la metallurgie du fer au Chili*. Paris: A. Roger et F. Chernoviz, 1890.

Véliz, Claudio. "La mesa de tres patas." *Desarrollo económico* 3 (April–September 1963):231–47. (Also published in *Estructura social de Chile*, ed. Hernan Godoy, pp. 232–40. Santiago: Editorial Universitaria, 1971.)

———, ed. *Obstacles to Change in Latin America*. London: Oxford University Press, 1965.

Vicuña Pérez, Angel. *Proteccionismo aplicado a la industria chilena*. Santiago: Imprenta Universitaria, 1905.

Wright, Thomas C. "Agriculture and Protectionism in Chile, 1880–1930." *Journal of Latin American Studies* 7 (May 1975):45–58.

Wythe, George. *Industry in Latin America*. 2d ed. New York: Columbia University Press, 1949.

Yrarrázaval, José Miguel. *El Presidente Balmaceda*. 2 vols. Santiago: Editorial Nascimiento, 1940.

Zegers, Julio. *Estudios económicos, 1907–1908*. Santiago: Imprenta Nacional, 1908.

Zeitlin, Maurice, et al. " 'New Princes' for Old? The Large Corporation and the Capitalist Class in Chile." *American Journal of Sociology* 80 (July 1974): 87–123.

LATIN AMERICAN MONOGRAPHS–SECOND SERIES

NUMBER 1 (1965): *Fidel Castro's Political Programs from Reformism to "Marxism-Leninism"*
by Loree Wilkerson

NUMBER 2 (1966): *Highways into the Upper Amazon Basin*
by Edmund Eduard Hegen

NUMBER 3 (1967): *The Government Executive of Modern Peru*
by Jack W. Hopkins

NUMBER 4 (1967): *Eduardo Santos and the Good Neighbor, 1938–1942*
by David Bushnell

NUMBER 5 (1968): *Dictatorship and Development: The Methods of Control in Trujillo's Dominican Republic*
by Howard J. Wiarda

NUMBER 6 (1969): *New Lands and Old Traditions: Kekchi Cultivators in the Guatemalan Lowlands*
by William E. Carter

NUMBER 7 (1969): *The Mechanization of Agriculture in Brazil: A Sociological Study of Minas Gerais*
by Harold M. Clements, Sr.

NUMBER 8 (1971): *Liberación Nacional of Costa Rica: The Development of a Political Party in a Transitional Society*
by Burt H. English

NUMBER 9 (1971): *Colombia's Foreign Trade and Economic Integration in Latin America*
by J. Kamal Dow

NUMBER 10 (1972): *The Feitosas and the Sertão dos Inhamuns: The History of a Family and a Community in Northeast Brazil, 1700–1930*
by Billy Jaynes Chandler

NUMBER 11 (1973): *The Moving Frontier: Social and Economic Change in a Southern Brazilian Community*
by Maxine L. Margolis

NUMBER 12 (1973): *San Rafael—Camba Town*
by Allyn MacLean Stearman

NUMBER 13 (1974): *The Afro-Asian Dimension of Brazilian Foreign Policy, 1956–1972*
by Wayne A. Selcher

NUMBER 14 (1975): *Population and Energy: A Systems Analysis of Resource Utilization in the Dominican Republic*
by Gustavo A. Antonini, Katherine Carter Ewel, and Howard M. Tupper

NUMBER 15 (1975): *Rubén Darío and the Pythagorean Tradition*
by Raymond Skyrme

NUMBER 16 (1975): *The Embattled Colossus: Economic Nationalism and United States Investors in Latin America*
by Robert H. Swansbrough

NUMBER 17 (1976): *Blacks in Colonial Cuba, 1774–1899*
by Kenneth F. Kiple

NUMBER 18 (1976): *Family Size and Family Size Determination: The Evidence from Seven Latin American Countries*
by M. J. Carvajal and David T. Geithman

NUMBER 19 (1976): *Land Tenure and the Rural Exodus in Chile, Colombia, Costa Rica, and Peru*
by Paul R. Shaw

NUMBER 20 (1976): *The Forgotten Ones: Colombian Countrymen in an Urban Setting*
by Michael B. Whiteford

NUMBER 21 (1977): *Industrial Development in a Traditional Society: The Conflict of Entrepreneurship and Modernization in Chile*
by Henry W. Kirsch